AGEING, AUTONOMY AND RESOURCES

To Margaret.

Ageing, Autonomy and Resources

Edited by
A. HARRY LESSER
University of Manchester

Ashgate

Aldershot • Brookfield USA • Singapore • Sydney

Published by
Ashgate Publishing Ltd
Gower House
Croft Road
Aldershot
Hants GU11 3HR
England

Ashgate Publishing Company
Old Post Road
Brookfield
Vermont 05036
USA

British Library Cataloguing in Publication Data
Ageing, autonomy and resources. - (Avebury series in
    philosophy)
    1. Autonomy (Psychology) in old age 2. Aged - Care - Moral
    and ethical aspects 3. Aged - Government policy 4. Autonomy
    (Philosophy)
    I. Lesser, Harry, 1943-
    362.6'01

Library of Congress Catalog Card Number: 99-72599

ISBN 1 84014 971 X

Printed and bound by Athenaeum Press, Ltd.,
Gateshead, Tyne & Wear.

Contents

List of Contributors   *vii*
Acknowledgements   *x*

Introduction   1

1   The effect of ageing on autonomy
    Caroline Dunn   7

2   Personal development in old age
    John Hostler   23

3   Ageing and autonomy: the case for genetic enhancement
    Ruth Chadwick   35

4   Practical problems with the discharge of old people
    from hospital - a physician's perspective
    Simon Winner   51

5   A mental health perspective on ageing
    Joe Herzberg   67

6   Ending lives: age, autonomy and the quality of life
    Gavin Fairbairn   88

7   Therapy abatement
    David Lamb   116

8   The global distribution of health care resources
    Robin Attfield   133

9   Population ageing, social security, and the distribution
    of economic resources
    Paul Johnson   142

10 'Last time buyers'; markets and marketing in services
for the elderly
Rod Sheaff   161

11 Justifying ageism
Oliver Leaman   180

12 The felicific calculus strikes back
Alan Cribb   188

13 Justice and the principle of triage
Harry Lesser   201

14 Health care access, population ageing, and intergenerational
justice
Clark Wolf   212

List of Contributors

Caroline Dunn

is a part-time lecturer in Philosophy at Manchester University, and the author of *Ethical Issues in Mental Illness* (Ashgate, 1998).

John Hostler

is Director of the Centre for the Development of Continuing Education at Manchester University, and has spent most of his professional life in the field of adult education. He is the author of several articles on adult education and personal development.

Ruth Chadwick

is head of the Centre for Professional Ethics and Professor of Moral Philosophy at the University of Central Lancashire. Her research activities include co-ordinating a number of multinational and multi-disciplinary research projects funded by the European Union, acting as editor-in-chief for the *Encyclopaedia of Applied Ethics* (1998), and the authorship of *Ethics, Reproduction and Genetic Control* (1992), as well as other books and a large number of papers in learned journals.

Simon Winner

is a Consultant Physician in the Department of Clinical Geratology, The Radcliffe Infirmary, Oxford, and honorary Senior Clinical Lecturer, University of Oxford.

Joe Herzberg

is a Consultant Old Age Psychiatrist for Tower Hamlets Healthcare Trust and Associate Dean of Postgraduate Medicine (Mental Health) for the University of London, being currently responsible for ensuring high training standards for over 500 doctors who are training to be psychiatrists. He has published in particular in the fields of medical education, social psychiatry, neuro-psychiatry and psychology, and extensively in Old Age Psychiatry, where his main research interests are centred on service provision and multi-disciplinary working.

Gavin Fairbairn
is Reader in Education at the North East Wales Institute of Higher Education, having spent the earlier part of his professional life in social work and special education. He is the author of *Contemplating Suicide* (Routledge, 1995), and of numerous articles on applied ethics.

David Lamb
is Reader in Philosophy in the Department of Biomedical Science at Birmingham University, and the author of numerous books in the field of medical ethics.

Robin Attfield
is Professor of Philosophy at Cardiff University and the author of *Value, obligation and metaethics* (Value Inquiry Book Series, 1995) and *The ethics of global environment* (Edinburgh UP, 1999), as well as numerous other books and articles in the field of ethics.

Paul Johnson
is Reader in Economic History at LSE, and editor of *Old age from antiquity to post-modernity* (Routledge, 1998) and has written widely on the history and economics of old age and ageing.

Rod Sheaff
is a Senior Researcher at the National Primary Care Research and Development Centre at Manchester University. His background is that of a political theorist, specialising in the study of quasi-markets in health care. His most recent book is *The need of health care* (Routledge, 1996).

Oliver Leaman
is Professor of Philosophy at Liverpool John Moores University, and the author of many books on Jewish philosophy, Islamic philosophy, and social philosophy.

His recent books include *Evil and Suffering in Jewish philosophy* (Cambridge UP, 1995) and *Death and loss* (Cassell, 1996), and he has edited *The future of philosophy* (Routledge, 1998).

Alan Cribb
is Senior Lecturer in Ethics and Education at the Centre for Public Policy Research, King's College, London. He is the editor of *Health Care Analysis*, and the author of numerous articles in applied ethics and health care ethics.

Harry Lesser
is Senior Lecturer in Philosophy at Manchester University, and the co-editor of *Ethics, technology and medicine* (Ashgate, 1988) and author of a number of articles on social philosophy and medical ethics.

Clark Wolf
is Associate Professor in the Department of Philosophy at the University of Georgia. He has published a number of articles, primarily in political and legal philosophy and ethical theory; his recent papers can be found in *Ethics, Philosophical Studies* and *Ethics and the Environment*, among other places. He is currently writing a book on intergenerational justice.

Acknowledgements

My warmest thanks to all the contributors, not least for their patience with this book's gestation, and their readiness to update and strengthen their contributions; to Kim Bevington for her preparation of the manuscript with such speed and accuracy: and to the members of the Centre for Social Ethics and Policy at Manchester University, who sponsored the conference in 1992 at which early versions of many of these papers were read.

Introduction

The fourteen papers in this volume deal with two questions of growing practical importance in a society where the proportion of elderly people is increasing. The first is the question of how the autonomy of the elderly can be best preserved and increased. This question, or set of interrelated questions, has a conceptual element: what is autonomy and how should it be defined? It has an ethical element: when is it right to preserve a person's autonomy and when, in contrast, should autonomy take second place to the need to prevent people harming others or themselves? And it has a practical element: how is autonomy to be preserved and how are the obstacles to the elderly remaining autonomous for as long as possible to be removed?

All three of these questions are discussed in Caroline Dunn's *The effect of ageing on autonomy*, which in many ways sets the scene for the book. Having suggested that the essence of autonomy is to be self-governing, to be able to take one's own decisions, and that therefore autonomy admits of degree, and is not all-or-nothing, and having pointed out that the process of ageing always has a tendency (though not an invariable one) to threaten a person's autonomy because of the increased likelihood of illness or weakness, she goes on to consider two socially generated threats to the autonomy of the elderly, which could be reduced. One is the widespread set of negative assumptions about, and perceptions of, old age; the other is the growth of consumerism, which, while it enhances the autonomy of the wealthy elderly, further weakens that of the less well off. The paper explores both how these threats could be reduced, and also the question of when and why the autonomy of the elderly becomes less important than their general welfare, ie. when a person becomes no longer able to act competently and autonomously. A crucial conclusion is that while this does happen not infrequently, it never happens as a result of age alone.

This key theme, that we need to rid ourselves of the negative perception of old age, and of the notion that decline and loss of autonomy are inevitable, is taken up and elaborated in John Hostler's *Personal development in old age*, which argues in effect that a positive conception of old age requires us to see it as a time not merely of putting up a resistance to impairments of one's physical and mental functioning, but of positive personal development. Much of the paper is concerned with defining personal development and with considering

1

different models of it. The main conclusions are that such development has both an individual and a human aspect, that to be a genuine development it must involve changes and adaptations that are seen as desirable by the people themselves, and that disseminating a notion of such growth and development may itself contribute to encouraging and enhancing it.

Ruth Chadwick's *Ageing and autonomy, the case for genetic enhancement* turns our attention to the physical, rather than social, conditions for autonomy. Since the process of biological ageing, ie. the physical weakening over time which takes place eventually in everyone, through at very varying chronological rates, is genetically based, it could in principle be counteracted by genetic intervention. Given this possibility, whether or not it will ever be practically feasible, the paper considers the ethical arguments for and against it. In favour of such intervention are arguments from the increase in autonomy, reduction of suffering and social benefits this could bring, and also an argument from social justice. Against it are arguments from the possible physical and social benefits of ageing, and the argument that there are more important uses for scarce resources. The paper concludes by suggesting that what needs to be combated, by all means available, is not biological ageing as such, but the consequent loss of autonomy, and this requires both challenging negative social images and where possible trying to maintain a person's physical independence by whatever means are available.

Dr. Joe Herzberg's *A mental health perspective on ageing* moves to the threat to autonomy produced by mental illness in old age. The paper surveys the changes that have taken place this century in the provision of care for the mentally ill elderly, and the range of services now available, and explains the main types of mental illness to which the elderly are subject. A number of case histories are given, which illustrate both the range of problems and the range of ways of dealing with them. Particular points which emerge are the need for multi-disciplinary teamwork; the need to consider the families of the elderly and their carers; the need for a considerable range of options to deal with a variety of very different cases; and - something which perhaps the government is at last tackling - the need to increase substantially the provision of local mental health community services.

Dr. Simon Winner's *Practical problems with the discharge of old people from hospital - a physician's perspective* again deals with a practical medical issue; this time a more specific one, though one that nevertheless covers many different types of case. Once again, case histories are used to illustrate the range of problems. Also, there is once again a basic commitment to preserving the autonomy of the elderly whenever possible. As a result, the ethical issue that particularly emerges is that of competence: how one decides which patients are able, with assistance, to maintain their autonomy and to look after themselves and which, having lost the competence to do this, have to be treated paternalistically. It is argued that the presumption should be against paternalism and in favour of maintaining autonomy, unless the patient's incompetence is obvious. Dr. Winner also points out the need to use a person's behaviour as well as what they say in assessing what they actually want; the need, in order to promote autonomy, for the natural professional instinct for caution to be replaced sometimes by a willingness to take risks; and the need to improve community care resources.

The next two papers switch to a different issue, whether respecting a person's autonomy requires one to help them to die, if that is what they wish. Gavin Fairbairn's *Ending lives: age, autonomy and the quality of life* argues that it does. The paper attacks the 'death-making' elements of our culture, and argues strongly against non-voluntary euthanasia at either end of life, but argues also that to keep people alive against their will and when their quality of life is zero (as when they are in unrelievable and terminal pain) is in itself 'death-making'. The paper acknowledges that there is a problem in determining when an expressed wish to die is the product of a rational decision, but argues that it certainly sometimes is. However, it also argues against the legalization of euthanasia, on the ground that, though euthanasia is sometimes morally right, to make it lawful would lead inevitably to morally wrong and 'death-making' euthanasia.

David Lamb's *Therapy abatement*, while similarly apposed to what is 'death-making', though he does not use this term, deals mainly with passive euthanasia and the right to refuse treatment, whether at the time or by an advance directive or living will. The paper discusses various case histories, and argues that a right to refuse therapy, if not backed up by appropriate safeguards and set in an appropriate context, fails to protect the patient's autonomy. Advance directives need to be framed so that they do not create any general right to kill; and in general the right to refuse therapy only preserves autonomy if the patient is made properly aware of the various alternatives. This all brings out another element in autonomy: the need for proper communication, and proper understanding by the patient of what the options are and what they are committing themselves to.

Indeed, what emerges, among many other things, from these seven papers is that the increasing of autonomy (defined roughly as the ability to maintain some control over one's life and one's decisions) for the elderly requires at least four different kinds of conditions. Mentally, it requires the replacement of the negative attitude to old age, and the assumption that the elderly are all alike and all decaying, with an attitude that is both positive and capable of understanding the great variations in the situation of individuals. Verbally, it requires a vast improvement in communication, both in skilled interpretation of what the words and behaviour of the elderly convey and in willingness to make sure they understand (if they can) their situation and their options. Socially, it requires the provision of many kinds of services which can enable many of the elderly to continue largely looking after themselves. Medically, it requires the treatment of those physical and mental conditions which interfere with autonomy but are capable of being cured and alleviated. Now the first two of these require only time, intelligence and goodwill; but the last two require an input of social and medical resources. And this brings us to the second question with which this book is concerned. Granted that we need to improve the autonomy (and the general welfare) of the elderly, if resources, social and medical, are finite, as they clearly are (they could certainly be increased - many people would say they should be increased - but they are not infinite), can the claim of the elderly to these resources be justified? It is this that the next seven papers consider.

The first two of these are concerned with the general background. Robin Attfield's *The global distribution of health care resources* is essentially concerned with the ethical background and with making the point that any plausible moral theory, once its consequences are taken seriously, will lead to the conclusion that in the rich countries of the world there is an obligation to help to meet the basic health care needs of people in the poor countries, as well as those of people in their own. As applied to the situation of the elderly in our own country, this raises the question of what is a need, which there is an obligation to meet, and what is simply desirable. It also reinforces the point already suggested, that health care resources perhaps should be increased: indeed if the argument is correct, they clearly should be increased substantially.

However, even the provision of adequate resources for the elderly in the UK (and in the other major industrialized countries) is set to run into a problem which is explored in Paul Johnson's *Population ageing, social security and the distribution of economic resources*. This is the problem of an ageing society, in which the proportion of those requiring support from the social security system is steadily increasing relative to the working population, with the result that the level of benefit may come to be seen as too high for society to maintain. This in its turn could lead to a particular injustice suffered by the generation 'on the change', which will be taxed during their working lives to provide benefits at the higher rate, but then receive benefits when retired at the lower rate. Paul Johnson's paper considers some proposed solutions to this problem, put forward by economists and social philosophers, and argues, first, that none of these is entirely satisfactory as it stands, and secondly, that any adequate solution must take account not simply of economics and moral ideals but also of political realities and of what is generally perceived to be just.

Rod Sheaff's *'Last time buyers': markets and marketing in services for the elderly* is similarly concerned with political realities, in this case the increasing reliance on the market and the private economic sector to meet the needs of the elderly. The paper gives practical and theoretical arguments against either adopting a pure 'free market' provision of services or regarding services for the elderly as a special case to be dealt with purely by the application of welfare principles. But the conclusion goes beyond the mere analysis of a 'mixed' economic system to argue that we should recognize the fact that in effect new, 'hybrid', forms of economic organization are being developed, and not only in the elderly welfare section. We then need to consider which features of the two systems must be retained, such as the guaranteeing of access to services, characteristic of a welfare state, together with the flexibility made possible by the free market. But we also must recognise that what is emerging is not a conflation of two existing systems, but a new and different system, requiring both new theoretical concepts and new organisational solutions.

The remaining four articles turn our attention from ways of meeting the needs of the elderly to the question of to what they are justly entitled: the two questions are, as several papers have already indicated, not independent of each other, since different kinds of provision are appropriate to different levels of obligation to provide. Three of the four articles attack specific arguments for discriminating against the elderly. Oliver Leaman's *Justifying ageism* argues that the so-called 'fair innings' argument, that if resources are scarce it is right to favour those who have not yet reached a reasonable life-span at the expense of those who have, is attractive, because it provides a way of deciding what to do in hard cases, but invalid, because it regards the lives of different people as commensurable, whereas each person is unique, and while a person may choose to sacrifice themselves for others no one else has the right to force them to make the sacrifice. Alan Cribb's *The felicific calculus strikes back* attacks the use of QALYs to determine the allocation of resources, and argues that the attempt to do this results either in incoherence, because impartiality is maintained but at the cost of leaving every issue open, so that no one allocation can be said to be better than any other, or in unfairness, because a result can be obtained, but only as a consequence of building some arbitrary discrimination, eg. discrimination against the elderly, into the system from the start. The paper goes on to generalise this point, that while hard decisions have to be made in the distribution of medical resources, it cannot be right to build forms of discrimination, such as ageism, into the decision-making system itself. Harry Lesser's *Justice and the principle of triage* argues that triage is a principle of justice, rather than, as it is sometimes take to be, a utilitarian principle, and though, it is the appropriate principle to use for the distribution of resources in an emergency, it is not an appropriate principle for use in considering the general distribution of medical resources in non-emergency conditions, and in any case provides no justification for discrimination on the ground of age alone. Triage provides a ground for withholding treatment that can do no good: this occurs more often in the old than the young, but it does occur in both, and it occurs because a person is, for example, terminally ill, never simply because they are old.

Finally, Clark Wolf's *Health care access, population ageing and intergenerational justice* makes an extended investigation into the question of what constitutes distributive justice between the young and the old. It proceeds by considering in some detail Norman Daniels' theory of intergenerational distributive justice, possible objections to it, and comparisons between it and two alternative theories. The conclusion is that both practical politics and moral considerations require us to prioritise meeting the basic needs of the elderly (and of everyone else), and to see need as what creates a claim to resources. It is further pointed out that even to meet this limited goal of satisfying basic needs would involve a considerable improvement over the status quo (Clark Wolf is speaking of the United States, but the same is true of the United Kingdom). Indeed, this sums up points on which all the contributions to this book are agreed - that even in advanced industrial countries the elderly are needlessly denied autonomy, and even their basic needs are all too often not met, if they are elderly and poor; and that this situation could be appreciably improved without requiring 'Utopian' social engineering, if there were a change in attitudes and an increased commitment of resources.

1 The effect of ageing on autonomy

CAROLINE DUNN

The issues raised by the question of the relationship between ageing and autonomy are considerable, but this chapter will be limited to considering the fundamental issue of the consequences of ageing on autonomy. In order to do this, of course, it is first necessary to have a definition of autonomy, and this is not as straightforward as might be imagined. Although autonomy is a central issue in the Western conception of a person and features prominently in ethical theories of post-Enlightenment Western culture, it is an ill-defined notion, often equated with liberty, self-rule, dignity, integrity, individuality, independence, freedom of will, responsibility, freedom from obligation and the absence of external constraints, amongst other things; it therefore simultaneously encompasses political, moral and social ideals. Gerald Dworkin (1988) has concluded that

> About the only features held constant from one author to another are that autonomy is a feature of persons and that it is a desirable quality to have (Dworkin, 1998, p.6).

Despite the difficulties in reaching a definitive definition of autonomy (arguably, an impossible task), the essence of autonomy would appear to be that a person is autonomous if and only if he or she is self-governing. Dworkin's own definition of autonomy defines it as

> ...a second-order capacity to reflect critically upon one's first-order preferences and desires, and the ability either to identify with these or to change them in the light of higher-order preferences and values. By exercising such a capacity we define our nature, give meaning and coherence to our lives, and take responsibility for the kind of person we are (*Ibid.*, p.108).

The relationship between the definition of a person and the ascription of autonomy is a somewhat circular one. To be a person is a necessary, though not sufficient, condition for the ascription of autonomy; no-one seriously suggests that animals possess autonomy. But equally, the non-autonomous are likely to be regarded as to some degree less than fully human, for if autonomy is perceived as a fundamental feature of persons, one's humanity is likely to be perceived as diminished to some extent if autonomy is diminished. The equation of autonomy with personhood and self-identity raises problems, however. Babies and young children are not autonomous; neither are patients in a comatose state nor those under an anaesthetic; nor indeed is a sleeping person. Yet none of these groups would be considered to be less than fully human - Joe does not cease to be Joe to those who know and love or hate him simply because he is comatose or asleep or undergoing an anaesthetic while his appendix is removed. In the case of the comatose patient, it might be argued that, after a certain period of time, when all hope of recovery has been abandoned and brain death has been established, his or her essential humanity exists no longer; this is the justification for switching off life support systems. But one does not necessarily lose one's humanity simply by virtue or being in a coma, for many coma patients recover consciousness and their autonomy.

It therefore follows from this that autonomy must be recognised as a matter of degree, not an absolute, for an individual's autonomy may - and does - very in degree and over time. And it also follows that autonomy may be restricted in many ways and to varying degrees, although there are essentially only two basic ways in which autonomy may be restricted; these are by external constraints - the actions of others - or internal constraints - what might be called limitations in oneself. The process of ageing has a direct bearing on both these forms of constraint upon autonomy.

If autonomy is a feature of persons, then it follows that autonomy is intimately connected with notions of what it is to be human, and, by extension, what constitutes human needs. Certain needs are fundamental to human beings, the needs for food and shelter being the obvious ones; for if these needs are not met the question of autonomy becomes largely irrelevant, since the individual will die. But needs on this basic level are no more than needs that any animal, human or otherwise, possesses. These needs must be met if the animal is to survive, but if only these needs are met for the human animal, it very soon ceases to be fully human, for the essence of what it is to be human lies in the more complex needs that the species has, and these needs are intimately related to values; all the concepts equated with autonomy have value judgements embedded in them.

Meeting the basic human needs of food and shelter can be done in many ways; in contemporary Britain, it is left to what remains of the Welfare State to meet these very basic needs for those unable to do so for themselves. Similarly, the law enshrines basic rights which govern the relationship between individual rights and needs and the needs and rights of the social group, in an attempt to ensure that all are treated equally.

But the human animal also has other, very specific, needs which differentiate it from the rest of the animal kingdom and define it as a human being; these needs are for things such as love, respect and dignity, which are every bit as important as the basic need for food and shelter. These needs cannot be met by the welfare state or enshrined as rights because their provision depends upon the compassion and respect for others that can only come from the feeling of one person for another. In other words, the needs which define us as human can only be met by other humans; and meeting these needs depends upon an acknowledgement of a shared, common humanity between individuals, a feature of which is respect for the autonomy of others. Respecting the autonomy of others not only entails acknowledging their right to be self-governing, but also treating their views and wishes with respect, accepting them as individuals and being aware that their needs are not limited to the bare necessities required for survival. But acknowledging a shared humanity and respecting the autonomy of others does not mean demanding identical values from other individuals; autonomy also means having one's individual differences respected, having a voice which is listened to and taken seriously. Having these uniquely human needs met makes the difference between surviving as little more than an animal and thriving as a human being.

In these respects the elderly are no different from any other persons. Ageing need not necessarily be detrimental to autonomy; indeed, at some stages in life, it is a prerequisite for it. The law prohibits an individual gaining full legal autonomy until the age of eighteen; young children are not considered to be fully autonomous by virtue of their immaturity rendering them incapable of making fully rational or fully informed decisions. But in the context of the consideration of ageing and autonomy, it is taken as read that we are dealing with old age, and that old age carries with it certain factors that may affect autonomy; in Western culture, it is invariably taken for granted that the effects of old age on autonomy must be detrimental. Given the attitudes to ageing that are current in contemporary Western society, this is hardly surprising.

Ageing is not simply a matter of chronology; there is also an element of social construction involved in the concept. One may be considered old at forty in the job-market, but a man of fifty who is head of state of a powerful nation may be considered to be young. The socially constructed aspects of ageing may be reflected in the meanings attributed to old age, which in contemporary Western culture are invariably pejorative; Shakespeare summed up the situation when he wrote:

> ...Youth is full of pleasance, age is full of care;
> Youth like summer morn, age like winter weather;
> Youth like summer brave, age like winter bare.
> Youth is full of sport, age's breath is short;
> Youth is nimble, age is lame;
> Youth is hot and bold, age is weak and cold;
> Youth is wild and age is tame.
> Age I do abhor thee; youth I do adore thee.

The prospect was obviously such a gloomy one for Shakespeare that it adversely affected the quality of his verse! And certainly his sentiments do not appear out of place four centuries later.

Certainly the physiological deterioration that generally accompanies ageing in various degrees is very real and it may result in the elderly becoming less able to care for themselves and consequently more dependent on others. But family structures in the West no longer assume a responsibility to care for elderly members; this, coupled with medical advances in the treatment of the elderly which have resulted in greater numbers of people living to become elderly or, as is more and more the case nowadays, very elderly, means that the old are increasingly the responsibility of the state, with the concomitant financial burdens this places on a population seemingly ever more reluctant to pay taxes for the provision of social services. The elderly may therefore be seen to be consuming continually increasing resources in terms of pensions, medical and social services, and contributing nothing to the provision of these services. And another consequence of medical technology means that not only are far more people enabled to live for much longer, but increasingly, conditions which were regarded as an unpleasant but inevitable consequence of old age may now be alleviated, giving a much better quality of life, but making yet more demands on scarce resources. As a result, the old are increasingly seen as a problem at best and a nuisance at worst, rather than being valued for their wisdom and experience.

This situation may be exacerbated if the elderly are ill (and by virtue of their age they are more likely to be ill than younger people) for illnesses also have meanings ascribed to them. All illness carries with it ethical implications, for it alters our moral status; if this were not the case, then concepts such as malingering, hypochondria and psychosomatic illness would not be necessary; there is a certain comfort to be derived from a definition of illness as a physiological state that can be objectively defined by science, but such a view ignores the human element involved in our view of illness. It is this human element in illness that complicates it, for, as Sacks has pointed out: '...animals get diseases, but only man falls radically into sickness' (Sacks, 1986, p. ix). The distinction implied by Sacks' differentiation between human sickness and animal disease lies in the meaning that humans attribute to sickness.

Becoming sick involves a form of metamorphosis for the sufferer, a metamorphosis that is not limited to her bodily state, for in subtle ways it will affect her moral status; as Sontag has pointed out, '(sickness suggests) judgements of a deeper kind, both moral and psychological, about the ill' (Sontag, 1990, p.43). Sickness causes a paradoxical moral state, for the sick are likely to lose certain rights, but at the same time acquire others, and will be excused certain moral obligations whilst acquiring others. Such changes in moral status will depend upon the meaning that is ascribed to an individual's sickness.

Those involved with the sick have a responsibility not to upset them or do anything that might be perceived as exacerbating their situation. This opens the door to a variety of tactics on the part of the sick person which can be considered as emotional blackmail. Those nearest and dearest to the sufferer can experience considerable guilt, in which case sickness can be used to manipulate. The rights which the sick acquire are bought at a cost; the sick person must forgo pleasures as well as responsibilities, must obey the orders of medical experts and generally do as she is told; the loss of autonomy can, in extreme cases, result in her being treated like a child. Thus the moral overtones associated with illness do not remove moral conditions from the sick, but they do shift the boundaries of the moral conditions that apply to a well person.

Just as the meanings ascribed to illness generally affect the moral status of the sick, so the meanings ascribed to old age may affect the treatment - both in the specific sense of therapeutic treatment and the general sense of the way society reacts - received by the elderly. To begin with, the elderly are more likely to suffer from a wider range of illnesses than the young; so all the meanings and altered moral status that accrues to illness will affect them. The illnesses associated with old age often have pejorative meanings associated with them; they are seen as demeaning, indicative of decay, loss of control, loss of reason, and dependency. And the 'rights' that sickness grants to the old may be bought at the expense of autonomy. Having to behave in certain ways, be grateful for help and treatment, not complain and generally do as one is told may mean that one is not able to exercise one's autonomy if to do so conflicts with the prescribed behaviour. The old therefore may suffer from the negative perception of old age that permeates our culture (and also illnesses they may suffer from have pejorative meanings associated with them) and may have the burden of gratitude imposed upon them as the cost of care which should be theirs as of right. Such attitudes to old age cannot help but diminish the autonomy of the elderly, for they may result in a perception of the elderly as somehow less than fully human; and to be regarded as less than fully human means that one will be denied a voice, or at the very least, that one's voice will in all probability not be listened to or taken seriously. In this respect, the elderly may experience a similar diminution of their autonomy as is experienced by the mentally ill. They may be ignored, regarded with contempt, be perceived as worthless and in extreme cases may suffer neglect, abuse and even death.

It may be argued that such gross denial of autonomy that would result in such appalling treatment of the elderly is extremely rare (though that is arguable), but it remains a fact that the granting or withholding of autonomy is at least to some degree dependent upon the socially constructed meanings that individuals attribute to ageing. No matter what rights may be enshrined in legislation, they cannot guarantee that the autonomy of the elderly will be respected because laws cannot enforce those aspects of autonomy that are outside the scope of the law. Thus laws may protect people from physical maltreatment but cannot protect them from contempt - carrying out the letter of law is possible whilst disregarding its spirit.

There is another aspect of old age that has significant repercussions for the elderly. In a society obsessed with youth and beauty, the manifestations of old age may be feared and found repulsive, for they remind every young, beautiful person that this will be their lot too one day. In Kafka's *Metamorphosis*, Gregor's transformation into a giant beetle is used as a metaphor for disease and its hidden meaning; but it might equally be a metaphor for some of Western society's meanings attributed to ageing and the elderly. Gregor's transformation renders him repulsive, frightening and shameful to his family; it strips him of his humanity and denies him the moral consideration which we take to be a right. Gregor retains his human feelings but his metamorphosis leads his family to begin a slow process of dehumanising him, and they ultimately reject him entirely, feeling only relief when he is dead. This sometimes happens to the old; they may be characterised as smelly, useless, senile wrecks, with a disregarded past and no future.

This may seem to be exaggerating the case, and it is certainly an extreme, but can we really deny that such attitudes exist and are far from uncommon? Thus the meaning of old age goes far beyond that of a person who has lived for a specified number of years; it has a subtext, frequently hidden and denied, but one that is very real nonetheless, and if the social construction of old age is such that old age is perceived to be a problem, associated with negative conditions such as loss of control and dependency, the elderly may undergo a form of metamorphosis similar to that experienced by Gregor which renders them as less than fully human in the eyes of the rest of society.

All the above may be regarded as the malign consequences of diminished autonomy which result from the hidden meanings of old age being pejorative. But the autonomy of the elderly may also be unwarrantedly diminished as a result of the best of intentions - the result of benign but misplaced paternalism. The right of the elderly to be cared for may be given freely and with great compassion; but if the elderly are nonetheless characterised by illness and dependence they may be seen as childlike and helpless, deserving of care and consideration but largely non-autonomous. They may then experience the 'does he take sugar?' syndrome which is often the lot of the disabled. Decisions may be made for them, or their wishes ignored on the grounds that they are not competent to decide for themselves. And they may simply not be seen as individuals at all, but simply as a member of a group - the elderly - which somehow obliterates individuality. Calling old people 'granny' or 'granddad' is a classic example of this, denying them the dignity of being an individual, Mrs X or Mr Y.

It must surely be obvious that the pejorative meanings of old age must be challenged and replaced with an attitude that sees the old as persons just as much as any other members of the human race. If this were done, then the moral imperative that requires us to respect the autonomy of persons would require us to treat the elderly as self-governing agents, and the elderly should be as free as any other autonomous beings to do whatever they choose insofar as the exercise of their autonomy does not infringe the autonomy of others. This would include things that might be considered to be dangerous or stupid, just as the autonomy of younger people is respected when they choose to do dangerous or stupid things, such as motor racing or steeplechasing. Equally, the elderly would be subject to the same considerations regarding conflicts between the respect for autonomy and other values that apply to anyone else; thus, for example, age alone would not be sufficient justification for preserving one individual's autonomy at the expense of another's; in all issues relating to autonomy, age as such would be irrelevant.

At this point attention must be drawn to another aspect of autonomy generally and ageing and autonomy specifically, which is increasingly becoming a feature of contemporary Western society. This is the apparently inexorable growth of consumerism. I have argued that autonomy is not absolute, but a matter of degree, and increasingly autonomy seems to be related to one's power as a consumer - a case of 'to those who can consume shall be given'. In this respect, we are increasingly being made aware of 'grey power' - those elderly people who by virtue of their increased numbers and their spending power are set to become a force to be reckoned with in the years ahead. Of course, the wealthy have always been able to enjoy more autonomy than the poor, for wealth brings with it power. Since autonomy necessarily requires the juggling of individual autonomy with the needs of the social group, which must result in compromises being made, and generally speaking the powerful are more likely to juggle things to their advantage, there is nothing surprising about this. But increasingly things such as autonomy, dignity, respect and the provision of basic social and medical services, which should be taken as a right in a civilised society, appear to be becoming the prerogative of those with money - or to use the term that is becoming increasingly popular, with consumer power. Thus the elderly poor are increasingly seen as a problem; they are not just relatively worse off, but may well lack decent living conditions and an adequate income to enable them to eat well and keep warm enough. They may have to wait for a very long time for medical treatments, such as hip replacements, that will greatly improve the quality of their lives; their social life may be limited or non-existent as a result of poverty and lack of mobility. Those fortunate enough to possess 'grey power', however, are portrayed as having choices - the choice of living in specially designed retirement apartments, for example, where any degree of dependency can be catered for with dignity and designer decor; or the choice to enter a private hospital to have quality-of-life-improving medical treatment. The elderly poor are increasingly condemned to a life of being grateful for seemingly reluctantly given charity, while the elderly wealthy have the right to have their needs met by virtue of their consumer spending power. They are not portrayed as a problem, a drain on resources, but instead as important members of the economic community. Autonomy may be in the process of being redefined as a function of consumer spending power - what price then human needs and the autonomy of the elderly poor?

If it is accepted that respect for autonomy should be considered to be one

14

of the primary values of a civilised society, it should nevertheless not be assumed that this value overrides all others in any circumstances. There will always be cases where an individual cannot be regarded as autonomous by virtue of some form of incapacity. Dworkin's definition of autonomy as being the 'second-order capacity to reflect critically upon one's first order preferences and desires, and the ability to either identify with these or to change them in the light of higher-order preferences and values' requires as a necessary condition that one be free from internal constraints - what can be called limitations in oneself. Ageing may certainly result in limitations in oneself, for physiological performance declines with age. The physical manifestations of ageing may leave the elderly with little choice in some areas - thus, for example, one may have to relinquish one's hopes of exercising one's autonomy to decide to become an Olympic athlete by virtue of one's physical limitations (not a situation exclusively related to ageing, of course!) Arguably more significant in relation to autonomy, however, are the results of ageing which may affect mental functioning.

Returning to Dworkin's definition of autonomy, which seems to be as good as any, being able to reflect critically on one's preferences requires as a necessary condition that one be rational, and this condition has significant consequences for the elderly. If being free of internal constraints is a necessary condition of autonomy, then any limitation in one's mental capacity must limit one's autonomy. It is this necessary component of autonomy that is reflected in Dworkin's definition of autonomy. Undoubtedly the internal constraints on autonomy which may have the greatest consequences for the elderly are those which result from mental deterioration, because such deterioration results in degrees of irrationality, and rationality must be considered to be a necessary, though not invariably sufficient, condition for autonomy.

Rationality is the fundamental premise by virtue of which we understand ourselves as human beings; that is, as creatures capable of adjusting their actions as reasonably efficient means to intelligible ends (Moore, 1980, p.60).

Loss of rationality may therefore affect the autonomy of the elderly in two ways: firstly, as discussed above, by rendering them in the eyes of some as semi-human, and consequently to be denied partial or even any autonomy. But irrationality also diminishes an individual's autonomy by limiting his or her competence to make informed decisions. Notwithstanding the fact that the simplistic and inaccurate perception of the elderly as necessarily irrational is

15

both morally wrong and empirically unjustifiable, it remains the case that serious irrationality must have profound consequences for autonomy.

There are a number of conditions which affect the elderly that may result in varying degrees of irrationality and consequent incompetence. Such incompetence may be total or limited, chronic or intermittent, and may result from any one of a diverse group of conditions which include degenerative neurological disorders (eg. Alzheimer's disease or Parkinson's disease); cerebrovascular accidents and mental disorders that impair cognitive function. In addition, certain drugs may impair mental functions which may in turn impair the recipient's competence.

As a result of incompetence, decisions may have to be made on behalf of the incompetent person which affect not only medical treatment but issues of a broader nature, such as whether or not s/he needs caring for in an institution and who should manage his or her finances if s/he has any money. None of these issues relate solely to the elderly, for incompetence may be suffered by anyone as a result of injury or disease, but it is also true to say that the elderly are more susceptible by virtue of the incidence of chronic illness being higher amongst the elderly, and in the later stages of chronic illness many people become incompetent, particularly nowadays, where the very success of medicine has resulted in many more elderly people surviving for a considerable time after their cognitive functions have declined.

Making decisions for someone considered to be incompetent raises the problem of the conflicting values of autonomy, freedom, paternalism and protection. The problems are exacerbated by the fact that there is no clear test to establish competence; and the fundamental question of how incompetence is determined, and by whom, must also be addressed. Taking the latter question first, let us consider the hypothetical case of Mrs X, a lady in her late seventies who is in reasonably good health. She is fortunate enough to have savings, and decides that she will use some of this money to explore Australia, something she has always wanted to do, but never had the opportunity to do before. Her relatives are horrified, feeling that at her age this is a totally irrational decision and must therefore be evidence of some form and degree of senile dementia, and are arguing that she should be prevented from heading down under. But consider the situation from Mrs X's perspective. She knows that it is highly likely that she will die in the next ten to fifteen years, and possibly much sooner that this. She also knows that her money will be of no use whatsoever to her when she is dead. It seems entirely rational to her to decide to realise a lifelong ambition now, while she still has the chance. The very worst that can happen to her is that she might die whilst on her travels - but she is old, she might die anyway, so why not risk dying while she is enjoying herself? And she probably will not die - she is not proposing to walk to Australia - so why not enjoy her last years? By whose criteria shall we judge her rationality? I do not think that there is any contest here. We should all be wishing Mrs X 'G'day and happy travelling'.And indeed, were she forty years younger that would probably not be disputed. But what if Mrs X was proposing to canoe down the Amazon, rather than taking a jumbo jet to Australia? This must be a much riskier undertaking. But why should Mrs X's age be the deciding factor? People do life-threatening things which others consider utterly ridiculous and irrational - consider the climbers who scale vertical rock faces with no ropes or other equipment to help them. If Mrs X were to die exploring the Amazon it could be argued that she had nothing to lose, having lived most of her life, whereas a 'twenty-something' climber has the rest of her life before her - but nobody argues that she is irrational to pursue her sport.

I have used this example to illustrate the problems of deciding whether an elderly person's rationality is impaired; what may seem to be a rational course of action from one person's perspective may not be so from another's. And these examples also illustrate the importance of examining who is making the claim when an elderly person is declared to be acting irrationally. In the examples given, could it be relatives, more concerned that Mrs X will be spending all the money that they hoped would have been left to them in the next few years? Or perhaps it is simply a case of a loving, but overprotective child who has succumbed to the notion that the elderly by definition must be significantly diminished in terms of mental and physical functioning.

The concept of competence always relates to a particular action. I am not competent to direct a NASA space mission, ride in the Grand National or perform a Mozart piano concerto. I am perfectly competent, however, to direct a motorist from Manchester to London, ride a horse or play a reasonably simple cello continuo part. And, as these examples illustrate, competence is also a matter of degree. If I say I am competent enough to ride a horse it does not follow that I am competent to ride a horse in the Grand National; nor does my level of musical ability mean that I can claim to be a competent musician. I am competent, however, to make the decision that, having weighed up the risks and the costs and the benefits, I wish to try and gain the expertise to enable me to ride in the Grand National or justly claim to be a competent musician: the point is that in all these situations, competence is related to a specific task, it is not a global facility. Thus in deciding whether an elderly person is competent, it is always necessary to be aware of the question, 'Competent to do what?'

And it is also necessary to be aware that the notion of competence also has values embedded in it. To return to the case of Mrs X. Why should anyone be bothered to claim that she is incompetent to explore Australia or canoe down the Amazon? Would they bother whether she was competent to express a preference for tea or coffee? Of course not. The difference relates to the underlying values involved. Preferring tea or coffee does not generally involve serious value judgements (though not bothering to ascertain which is preferred is a diminution of respect for another's autonomy). But in the other examples, the claim that Mrs X was incompetent to decide to set off round the world is justified by virtue of the underlying values that relate to the issue. If an individual is to make a competent decision about the choices open to him or her, then he or she must necessarily have some conception of what is good or bad - both in a personal sense and in a wider sense. Thus my decision not to drink and drive may be based on the belief that it is wrong to risk the safety of others, and that such an action would therefore be bad; it might be a more selfish decision, based on the knowledge that if I am caught, I might lose my licence, which would be bad for me, or that I might injure or kill myself, which would be very bad for me. In the case of Mrs X, her relatives might genuinely believe that it will be bad for her well-being to canoe down the Amazon; her decision that it will greatly enhance her well-being may conflict so greatly with their values that they simply cannot accept it as rational. Or, to be cynical, they may believe that it will be bad for their bank balance if she spends her money this way rather than leaving it to them (although it is likely that they would claim the first reason rather than admit to the second!) All in all, then, competence is a tricky thing to decide, and it is hardly surprising that there are no definitive measurements of it. And indeed, it can be equally difficult to decide what constitutes anyone's well-being. Moral philosophy encompasses a number of theories concerning what constitutes individual well-being, which it is beyond the scope of this chapter to consider. However, each allows that a considerable degree of subjectivity is involved in the definition of well-being, and also that an individual may be mistaken as to what course of action will genuinely promote his or her well-being.

This is an important consideration. Notwithstanding the problems associated with competence and incompetence - where the threshold is to be set, who decides and who should make decisions for those judged incompetent - it is the case that some elderly people are indeed incompetent to make decisions that will enhance their well-being. I suggested earlier that autonomy is only one value, albeit an extremely important one, amongst others, and cannot necessarily override all other values. As such there will be occasions where autonomy may conflict with other values, one of which is beneficence, which can broadly be considered to be a responsibility to care for the welfare of others. There are a number of issues surrounding the notion of beneficence, such as whether it can rightly be considered to be a duty or merely a moral ideal, which I shall not consider here; in the context of ageing and autonomy the most important issue that beneficence raises is that of paternalism. If we take the position that autonomy is one of the prime values and should therefore be preserved and promoted whenever possible, then it is inevitable that paternalism will conflict to some degree with it, because paternalism involves substituting another's judgement of what is good for an individual instead of their own, and overriding their wishes in order to promote their well-being or to prevent harm to them.

Can paternalistic intervention ever be justified in overriding the wishes of the elderly in order to promote their well-being or prevent harm to them? In general terms, the answer must be yes. Consider the situation with young children. No-one would seriously argue that respect for their autonomy must always be the paramount value; indeed, below a certain age, young children may be argued to have very little, if any, autonomy, by virtue of immaturity. But because young children are generally valued, we consider it justified to protect them from themselves where necessary. Now, if we are to value the elderly and respect them as individuals, which I think we are morally bound to do, then we cannot simply ignore those situations when they may be as incompetent to make rational judgements as young children, on the spurious grounds that their autonomy is all important, even if the exercise of it may lead to great harm. Such an argument is spurious because in such situations one cannot be considered to be fully autonomous, by virtue of limitations in oneself.

Paternalistic intervention must be acknowledged to be the lesser of two evils in some cases. I suggest that the conditions for justifying it are met if the benefits of paternalism outweigh the harm that might result from loss of autonomy in cases where an individual can not be considered fully autonomous by virtue of his or her condition - the limitations in oneself that by definition restrict autonomy. Let us translate these concerns into an all too familiar scenario that affects many of the elderly. Mrs Y is eighty years old and lives on her own. She is frail and becoming increasingly confused. Her home is getting very dirty because she is unable to clean it adequately, but she refuses any help on the grounds that 'they' will only use it as an excuse to put her in a home, a course of action she adamantly refuses. She is not eating adequately and is at risk of hypothermia in the winter because her home is so cold. It is very obvious to all who have dealings with Mrs Y that she is no longer competent to care for herself, and that to meet her needs for adequate care would require that she is considerably dependent on others. If her autonomy is respected, she will in all probability die of hypothermia during the next spell of cold weather, if not sooner, as a result of injuring herself. In any case, the quality of her life is rapidly diminishing. On the other hand, to deny her autonomy and remove her into care against her will might also precipitate her death, and result in her being deeply unhappy in the interim, thus diminishing the quality of her life. Which is the lesser of the two evils?

I think there is a more fundamental problem here. Given the shift in the demographic profile of the Western world, with increasing numbers of people expected to live to a very old age, we must surely start to acknowledge that dependency in adult life is going to become much more a fact of life than it has been for previous generations. If we are to respect the elderly as human beings, and this will include respecting their autonomy, we can no longer go on asking questions of the 'which is the lesser of two evils' type - respect for autonomy and possible consequent suffering or denial of autonomy and possible consequent suffering. It is time to acknowledge that although there will always be cases where there is no possibility of a happy outcome, there is every possibility of reducing their occurrence if we have the will to alter things. In a society where even a cursory glance down the aisles of any supermarket shows a bewildering choice of such mundane articles as washing powder, lavatory paper and pet food, it surely is not beyond our power to construct a society where there are feasible and valid choices for the dependent. Such a society would need to be organised to enhance the capabilities of the elderly and promote autonomy in the areas where it will not produce undue harm. In situations where autonomy cannot be fully respected because to do so would result in harm, the alternatives offered should be sensitive and tailored to the needs of the individual, not bureaucratically motivated.

In our culture dependency, except in the case of young children, is seen as somehow shameful; it has connotations of having to be grateful for whatever one is given, and is seen to be virtually concomitant with loss of autonomy. Yet this need not be the case. We are above all else social animals, and as such interdependent. The principle of respect for individual autonomy is a vital one, but in the process of respecting it we seem to be taking autonomy out of the context of what human beings need to thrive rather than merely survive. Perhaps it is not the state of dependency as such that is so abhorrent but rather the way it is interpreted that causes so much misery to the elderly dependent. Being dependent should not mean that one loses one's autonomy, dignity and respect.

Respecting the autonomy of the elderly must mean that age as such is an irrelevant factor - the only relevant consideration is that the elderly are human beings, and the same respect for autonomy that is due to any human being is due to the elderly. Like that of anyone else, an elderly person's autonomy may be restricted in certain situations, because in any society there must always be compromises made between the sometimes conflicting interests of individual members.

If the old are to be granted the same right to autonomy as anyone else, it must also follow that old age by itself cannot be used as an excuse for behaviour that would not be acceptable in younger people. Old age does not necessarily transform one's personality for the better - many people are just as bloody-minded and unpleasant in old age as they were in their youth, and old age must not therefore be seen as an excuse for intolerable behaviour. Irrational behaviour, which is likely to affect considerable numbers of elderly people by virtue of their age, may well manifest itself in behaviour that is unpleasant for others, but such behaviour must be regarded in a different light because it can be argued to be the result of illness and therefore non-volitional. The same considerations that apply to anyone in this situation apply to elderly irrational people -it is not the age factor that is important, but the fact of irrationality.

Old age may diminish our faculties, both mental and physical, but it does not and should not diminish our essential humanity. Shakespeare ended his verse by saying:

O my love, my love is young!
Age, I do defy thee.

We would do well to remember this! Many elderly people are hale and hearty, and have the right to defy old age in the sense of rejecting restrictions imposed upon their autonomy by virtue of their age alone; they have the same right to autonomy as any other human beings. Such autonomy is not immutable and eternally fixed, any more than anyone else's, but fluctuates according to circumstances and is necessarily influenced by the interactions of the many individuals who together make up any society composed of moral agents.

For some, old age may indeed bring with it a diminution of those faculties which are a necessary condition for autonomy, and this may necessitate a justified paternalism on their behalf in order to promote their well-being to the greatest extent possible. If we were to shift the moral emphasis from autonomy being considered the prime value to such an extent that unavoidable dependency is seen as somehow diminishing, and acknowledge our mutual dependency, we might be able to afford the respect to the dependent elderly that any human being deserves, irrespective of age.

References

Dworkin, G. (1988), *The Theory and Practices of Autonomy*, CUP, Cambridge.
Kafka, F. (1961), *Metamorphosis and Other Stories*, Penguin, Harmondsworth.
Moore, M. (1980), 'Legal Conceptions of Mental Illness', in B. Brody and H.T. Englehardt (eds.) *Mental Illness: Law and Public Policy*, Reidel Publishing, Boston.

2 Personal development in old age

JOHN HOSTLER

If you ask people - especially young people - how they envisage old age, most of them will tell you that they see it as a time of enfeeblement and decline. The common picture of the old person is of someone whose eyesight and hearing are failing, who is becoming tottery, forgetful and easily confused. It is not a new picture, of course: one need only think of Shakespeare's 'seven ages of man' speech, with its portrait of the old person 'sans teeth, sans eyes, sans taste, sans everything'[1] to be reminded that this stereotype of old age is largely traditional. What is new, perhaps, is the acknowledgement that it has firm foundations in fact. In recent years the emerging discipline of gerontology has given impetus to scientific investigations of ageing, and there is now plenty of evidence to confirm that many old people suffer various forms of impaired functioning.[2] Decay in short-term memory and in auditory and visual acuity, lengthening reaction times and a tendency to confusion are all well documented, and many studies have mapped the ways in which old age tends to become a time of increasing uselessness and dependency. Indeed some gerontologists identify old age with that very process of decline: 'old age is defined by an individual's diminished ability to cope with the ordinary affairs of everyday life ... without help'.[3] By this definition 'old age' is not so much the name of a chronological period (although many writer agree in thinking that its usual onset is around 70-plus) as of a process of deterioration in personal ability.

Hence it can seem almost a contradiction to assert that personal development occurs in old age. Surely a period of life which is so often marked by decay and decline cannot also be a time of development and growth? Yet many say that it is. Some old people of my own acquaintance testify that they are still developing and maturing, and colleagues who are professionally concerned with the elderly (as educators, medical personnel or counsellors) likewise claim that many old people continue to develop in themselves. Thus the assertion is often made, at least informally, that personal development does indeed occur in old age. The question which concerns me as a philosopher is whether the statement has objective meaning: is it just an expression of feeling of contentment or approval, say, about the changes that occur in some old people, or does it say something significant about what kind of changes they are? If we are told that an elderly man is 'developing as a person' can we infer anything about what is actually happening to him? This paper attempts to answer that question by discussing some common ideas of personal development and by examining the criteria for their application to old people.

It will help to start by reflecting on some general conditions for an adequate concept of personal development in old age. One of these, obviously, is that it must denote personal development: in other words, development (in some sense) of the person 'in themselves', growth of the 'inner self' rather than the outward body. When we use such phrases we usually have in mind the behaviour, attitudes and outlook which characterise someone as an individual and which are referred to (rather loosely) as their 'personality'. This is a vexed and ambiguous term, especially among professional psychologists, for whom it represents a major field of investigation;4 informally, however, it denotes those aspects of a person's character which underlie and which somehow account for his or her 'surface' behaviour. It is a concept with explanatory force: we talk about someone's personality when we are trying to make sense of what they do ('he stormed out of the meeting because he's very short-tempered') or when we are hoping to predict how they might behave ('watch out for her - she's the jealous type'). Therefore it tends to be something of a catch-all term which includes several different elements of the psyche: emotional traits, for instance, as in the two examples just given; other aspects of character, such as foresight or self-control; attitudes, combining factual beliefs about something with a tendency to react towards it in predictable ways; even perhaps a person's 'philosophy of life', their basic values, priorities and faith. These elements are very different in kind, but they all help us to understand and predict daily behaviour, not least because they are relatively stable and unchanging.

But if 'personality' comprises such diverse elements, how does it develop? When we say that someone is 'developing as a person' what sort of characteristics do we have in mind? Again we employ an informal concept, different from that used by psychologists for whom 'personality development' can be quantified by means of tests and questionnaires.[5] For instance Havighurst et al., in an important and often cited paper, describe how different personality types cope with ageing - but these are identified with clusters of TAT (thematic apperception test) scores in their experimental data. That is proper and legitimate in a research report but it is certainly not what the 'ordinary person' means when they talk about personality development in themselves or those they know. So what is meant in that context? Usually, when we talk about a headache developing, say, or the development of a storm, we mean that the item in question is becoming bigger or more intense. However this simple sense of 'development' cannot be applied straightforwardly to a congeries of elements like those in personality. Particular aspects of someone's personality may certainly 'become greater' in the course of his or her development, but equally they may do so without the personality developing as a whole. Thus when Hooker says (of the ageing process) that 'there are usually changes in personality, but only in that previous traits have become more exaggerated',[6] she is acknowledging the development of individual elements, but is effectively denying that personal development (in the ordinary sense) takes place. For that to occur, therefore, there has to be some element of novelty over and above the fact that existing characteristics 'become greater'. Contrary to her claim, there are probably some cases in which new traits do appear; but these are rare, no doubt, and novelty more often consists in the fact that existing characteristics combine and interact in new ways. Tensions within the psyche are resolved, perhaps, or traits which were restrained before come to dominate, giving a whole new complexion to the personality as a whole. As a parallel, think of the way in which a political crisis develops, or a problem in working relationships between colleagues. In these cases too a complex system is developing: a large number of elements and factors are interacting, some becoming greater, some new ones appearing: each stage in the development arises out of the one that goes before, and the final state is often quite different in nature and appearance from the first. As Birren suggests,[7] personality development can be thought of in similar terms as a process of cumulative growth, often leading to the conviction that a person is somehow 'different' from what they were before.

But more than that is needed to describe it adequately, for what has been said so far could equally well denote a process of deterioration. For example, consider a woman who becomes increasingly crabby and cantankerous as she ages: friends and family avoid her, and so she becomes more lonely; thus she comes to feel ill-used and aggrieved, besides becoming something of a recluse. This is surely a comprehensible (and not uncommon?) sequence of changes in personality, and it satisfies the description given above of a cumulative process leading to a discernible difference in the person, but one would hesitate to offer it as an example of 'personal development'. The reason is that - as the phrase is commonly used, at least - it connotes a desirable process. It denotes growth in maturity, wisdom, self-knowledge... all of them 'good' characteristics; someone who is 'developing as a person' is to be admired and perhaps even envied. It is not enough therefore to have a concept of personal development which merely identifies certain patterns of change: there must also be an element of evaluation, a judgement that the changes which occur are 'for the better'.

Thus we have identified three general conditions to be met by an adequate concept of personal development in old age. It must concern the 'personality' as that term is generally (and rather loosely) understood; it must identify a process of cumulative change; and it must represent that process as one of betterment or improvement. The final condition to be mentioned here is that there must also be reasonably definite criteria for its use; in other words, we must know when the concept applies, when we have a genuine case of personal development and when we do not. Without such criteria the concept would be vacuous, for a notion which could apply to any and every case would be a mere cipher, lacking real meaning. We must therefore be able to cite specific features in the life history of an elderly person as evidence that theirs is (or is not) a story of personal development in old age. For that to be possible, of course, these features must be identifiable and thus (in a fairly familiar sense) 'objective'. Which features will count as relevant evidence, however, will depend on the actual concept of personal development we employ, since different conceptions of the process have different criteria. By way of illustration, and to introduce some further general issues, let us consider three concepts or 'models' of personal growth which are most often used in thinking about personal development in old age.

The first, which in some ways is the simplest and most general, is the model of progress or advance. This is often used in forming conceptions of human development: for instance, learning a subject or a skill is called 'making progress', and we talk of a child's growth (psychological as well as physical) as 'progressing' towards adulthood. In the same way an elderly person may speak of their personal development as a sense of movement or advance, a feeling that they have not yet 'come to a stop'. But does this metaphor have any significant content? Such language can be pretty vacuous: talk of 'life's journey', for example, may just be a picturesque way of speaking about change, failing to capture the thought that change needs to be both cumulative and desirable in order to count as personal development. One way in which the metaphor can be made more meaningful is by reference - implicit or explicit - to some 'normal path' of development: a sequence of changes or a series of states though which most individuals pass. A familiar example is the well-known series of 'milestones' in children's growth. Such a pattern would certainly allow us to speak meaningfully of personal development in old age, did it exist; but all studies, together with one's own experience, confirm that in the later years of life there is no common path.[8] The pattern of personal development, insofar as there is one, seems to be one of increasing diversity: in the early years most children pass through roughly the same sequence of stages, but as they grow up and mature into adulthood their life histories become increasingly different. But if that is so, how can one speak meaningfully of 'progress' and 'advance' in old age? Clearly if not by reference to a common norm, then only by appealing to criteria within the life history of an individual. Two such criteria suggest themselves. Prospectively, people have personal goals and aspirations, and may be thought of as making progress insofar as they seem to be getting nearer the desired state. For example a man might want to become more serene and detached as he ages, and might try consciously to be less disturbed by everyday events. His goal is (necessarily) seen by him as desirable and therefore any progress towards it counts as 'improvement' (by his own standards at least). Without doubt some elderly people strive towards personal aims like this, but there is evidence to suggest that many do not; for as they get older and become more aware of the likelihood of death they tend to think less in terms of 'futurity' (as Birren calls it),[9] spending less time thinking (or fantasising) about 'what am I going to do/become' and investing less energy in planning for the future. Instead many develop a more retrospective outlook, sometimes becoming quite preoccupied with the past. This need not be (though it sometimes is) maudlin reminiscence: as Birren also explains, elderly people often undertake an 'life review', actively trying 'to integrate one's life as it has been lived in relation to how it might have been lived'.[10] They recall their past choices and decisions, the events that happened to them and how they reacted, asking (in effect) 'if I could live my life again, would I do it differently?' Clearly, through such a review genuine progress can be discovered. For example a woman might realise how much she has developed by seeing how different she is now from the person she used to be: she no longer makes the same mistakes in relationships or undertakings, or she has overcome traumas and personality traits (such as shyness) which used to hinder her.

Personal development in old age can thus be thought of in rather individual terms as a form of progress, as a movement either towards future goals or away from personality states which lie in the past. A second, closely related way of conceiving it is as a form of learning. Particularly influential here is a model of learning as problem-solving, for this underlies the notion of 'successful ageing' favoured by many gerontologists. The core of this idea is that the process of growing old confronts the individual with a series of 'learning tasks': these are generated by the changing conditions of life, which challenge the individual to adapt to them. For example (to borrow Peck's list[11]), one type of problem arises from the changing relation to work and employment. As age people and the opportunity for work (paid and unpaid) diminishes, they are less able to feel useful to others (eg. as a trusted colleague or as someone with valuable expertise) and they need to find alternative sources of self-esteem. Another type of challenge is presented by physical deterioration and the bodily infirmities of old age. When people can no longer enjoy active pursuits requiring strength or vigour, the sense of purely physical capability and achievement is diminished, and there is a corresponding need to find alternative sources of satisfaction - in social relationships, perhaps, or in cultural and intellectual pursuits. Thirdly, Peck discerns a need for people to transcend their own selves as the focus of interest and concern. As the limitations of self become evident (both temporally and in other respects), people need to find sources of interest in abiding things, larger than themselves. Not all individuals are able to make these adjustments, of course: some cling to work, for example, (even to the pretence of it) in order to 'feel useful'; others act and think as if they were immortal, refusing to make a will, for instance. But these, presumably, are 'failures' in ageing: the 'successful' ones are those who manage to solve the problems and adjust to their new circumstances and conditions of life.

In elaborating this kind of account of personal development in old age it will clearly not be hard to identify potential 'problems' in the ageing process. Philosophically at least the difficulty lies rather in specifying the criteria for 'success' so as to do justice to the notion of personal improvement and change 'for the better'. In some accounts the emphasis is merely on adapting to changed circumstances; but there may be several ways of doing that, not all of them equally desirable. When a woman retires from work, for example, she may 'adapt' by developing leisure interests, but equally she may do so by sitting at home, reminiscing fruitlessly and increasingly bitterly about her past career. Clearly, terms like 'adaptation' and 'adjustment' are not sufficiently evaluative by themselves. That is why Bromley finds it necessary to write about 'good adjustment'[12] (italics added) and why Pfeiffer recommends 'making adaptation to ageing a positive success'[13] (as if success could be negative). But if these adjectives are to be sufficiently meaningful there must be some criterion by which to distinguish the right (= desirable) kind of adaptation from other forms of adjustment. One which is offered by many writers is essentially hedonistic. It consists in the view that people who overcome the problems of ageing can be identified by the fact that they remain happy and content. Thus Pfeiffer says that people who 'age successfully' are those who 'have a good time in later years': 'far from complaining ..., [they] have prepared for this phase of the life cycle and now welcome it'.[14]

Thus elaborated, this model too gives a fairly definite, objective meaning to the notion of personal development in old age. Indeed one could argue that the meaning is too definite, in that hedonistic criteria exclude important forms of personal growth. Consider a man, formerly complacent and self-satisfied, who becomes increasingly dissatisfied with himself and the world: as he ages he becomes ever more conscious of all that is wrong and needs improvement, and also of time running out: he 'rages against the dying of the light', bitter at how little he has accomplished when so much remains to be done. Such a man would scarcely meet Bromley's criteria of 'happiness, confidence,... self esteem and productive activity'[15] but he could well be a remarkable instance of personal development in old age. Nevertheless hedonistic criteria do paint a fairly clear picture, and that is an important feature of this model. For the idea of 'progress', as we have seen, is largely schematic: it does not actually describe the changes that are to account as progress but leaves them to be determined by criteria derived from each individual's life history . In contrast, the 'success' model offers a fairly complete picture of successful ageing, which functions as an ideal (albeit a limited one) of what an old person should be like: individual life histories are to be judged not on their own terms but by their approximation to this standard.

The third model is that of self-realisation. In outline, it conceives personal development as a process in which a person's 'self', which is to some extent latent or concealed, becomes manifest, actual or 'real'. The image is one of blossoming or unfolding, and the language derives ultimately from Aristotle's analysis of natural growth and his view that when development occurs, that which was present in the organism 'potentially' becomes a part of its actual being. Taken literally , this is probably not a very helpful way to conceive of or to understand the processes of human development, for in practice the model is nearly always employed *ex post facto*, which deprives it of literal significance. Suppose, for instance, that someone 'develops as a person' through a new interest or hobby which extends their knowledge and outlook: one can say that potential for this development must have been there previously, but obviously that explains nothing and adds nothing to our understanding of what has taken place. Such judgements only gives us useful information when we can identify potential before it is realised, and indeed use it to predict future developments. But that kind of forecasting is notoriously difficult, and there are relatively few cases in which it can be done with any well-founded confidence. The best-known instance is probably the use of IQ tests which (broadly speaking, and within significant limits) seem to give a reliable indication of children's later academic attainments.[16] As a metaphor, however, the image of self-realisation has more value, directing our attention to aspects of personal development which other models may incline us to overlook. For example it reminds us that the process may well be judged best by the person who is developing and who is aware of it as change 'from the inside'. By contrast, the 'success' model considered above invites us to see growth purely as a response to external circumstances, implying that both the challenges of ageing and the individual's adjustment to them may be seen clearly by an external observer. That model thus supports an understanding of personal development which is perhaps rather detached and clinical - which is fine for researchers who want to investigate it, but which probably does insufficient justice to it as a felt experience. The 'progress' model too can usefully be modified by the concept of self-realisation. As we have seen, it tends to emphasise the change involved in personal development, stressing that the individual becomes somehow 'a different person'. In a sense she does, indeed; but still she remains crucially (and not only numerically) the same, the later self being linked to the earlier not only by a temporal continuity but also by the presence of personality characteristics or other traits which survive in a scarcely altered form. For only thus can the later self be seen as a development of the earlier, a blossoming or fruition of what was latent before.

The idea of self-realisation also helps to underpin and make sense of the evaluative dimension of personal development. We saw earlier that the notion of development entails that of betterment, and that personal growth in old age tends to be seen as excellent and admirable; thus, for example, Brown cites 'some magnificent examples of old people' (such as Schweitzer, Russell and Churchill) to illustrate her thesis that old age can be a time of growth and achievement.[17] But on the basis of the two models discussed earlier it is not wholly clear why these individuals should be seen as 'magnificent'. For instance, if they are envisaged as people who have continued to make progress (rather than coming to a stop) why not just call them 'fortunate'? Or if they are seen as successful in overcoming the problems of old age, why not think of them as 'enviable'? The thought that they are admirable surely derives from the notion that they somehow embody or are approaching an ideal, that in some respects they are how others ought to be. It seems to me that the concept of self-realisation underpins that idea in two ways. One is through a notion of stewardship which is deeply rooted in our culture: the thought that each of us has a certain potential which it is our duty to realise to the full. It is often held that we ought to 'make the most of ourselves' (not just in the sense of worldly success), and those who accomplish this task are therefore liable to be held up as examples for the rest of us to emulate. The other way is through the notion of something being 'good of its kind'. We generally accept that a more developed and mature specimen (of a plant, say, or an animal) is 'better' than an immature one. If two individuals both possess the characteristics of a given species, the one that possesses them in a greater degree is a better or more perfect instance. It is thus that cattle and produce are judged at agricultural shows, for example, where points are given for the shape, colour, etc. characteristic of the variety or breed. By analogy the same sort of evaluation can be applied to human beings. Of course we have to have in mind some characteristic features of human beings which constitute an implicit 'ideal of humanity', as it were; but given that, we will naturally think of those who embody those features in a high degree as 'fine specimens' or (as Brown does) 'magnificent examples'. This kind of evaluation therefore presupposes that everyone possesses these features in some degree. They may be thought of as constituting 'human nature' or 'human potential', which exists as potential in all of us but which blossoms fully only in a few individuals. Thus Jung writes that those who develop their personalities are 'the flower and the fruit, the ever fertile seeds of the tree of humanity':[18] the significant point is that he sees humanity as one tree and implicitly believes that all individuals (despite the many differences between them) share a common nature. In this way an elderly person who continues to develop can be thought of as realising a potential which is latent in us all and as providing a fine example of what human beings can become.

We have now considered three models of personal development and the criteria for applying them in old age. Each is still attended with considerable vagueness, of course, but that is probably inevitable in treating a subject such as this. It is nevertheless clear, I hope, that each model can be applied definitely in some cases at least, and equally definitely not in others; and that is sufficient for us to conclude, despite the remaining uncertainties, that we can give objective meaning to the concept of personal development in old age. It is also clear, however, that clear and exact thinking is required in order to do so. It may help if we conclude by outlining two further difficulties which attend the enterprise.

One, which has been hinted at already, is the fact that people are usually best placed to judge their own development for themselves. This is simply

31

because they have the most information: by the time someone reaches an advanced age, it is difficult for anyone else to know as much about them and their life history as they do. In this matter, then, as in so many others in the field of psychology, the first-person perspective has an element of priority, and the judgement 'I am developing as a person' has a claim to be listened to seriously by others. However there is obviously a danger that such judgements may be merely the subjective expression of contentment or self-esteem. To avoid that, the speaker must be able to explain his or her self-assessment to others in such a way that they too can understand it and find it plausible at least. Thus, for example, a man who becomes increasingly introverted and withdrawn in old age may appear, *prima facie*, not to be developing as a person; but if he can persuade us to see this as symptomatic of inner growth (such as spiritual preparation for the next life, like that of the Hindu *sannyasin*, perhaps) we may well revise our opinion. But this kind of explanation presupposes a number of conditions. For instance, he will need to use some conceptual model like those already discussed, perhaps representing the changes which are taking place in him as self-realisation or progress. In addition we, the hearers, have to listen with a measure of sympathetic imagination: up to a point we have to be able to conceive what it is like to be him and to have his experiences. This is akin to the use of imagination in moral judgement emphasised by Hare, the ability to put ourselves 'in someone else's shoes' and to see the world as it appears to them.[19] But there are real limits to the extent to which this is possible, and these are not merely the contingent limitations of our powers of imagination. To the extent that someone's experience departs from that which is common and widely shared, it necessarily becomes more difficult for others to imagine in this way. In the present context, therefore, we will be more ready to acknowledge someone's sense of inner change as an instance of personal development if it comprises psychological processes and traits which are common or fundamental to our own experience. For example, if a woman tells us how, in old age, she has overcome her fear of dying, we can easily acknowledge that as 'success' since most of us share her original apprehensions; whereas if her account concerns something which few of us experience (the drive to artistic creation, perhaps?) it may well prove less comprehensible to us as a form of personal development. The point that emerges here can be expressed as something of a paradox: that although personal development is felt by most people to be a very individual, 'personal' process, and is often best judged by individuals for themselves, its conceptualisation as personal development depends on its relationship to changes and realities which are largely common to us all. That is simply because it is fundamentally the notion of 'development as a person', where that is interpreted as development as a human being, rather than of an individual personality. At the same time, however, it cannot be fully understood without detailed reference to individuals, for if the concept of 'a human being' is not to be a bloodless abstraction it must be derived from and illustrated by individual personal histories.

That conclusion is important in relation to the second problem, which arises from the fact that judgments about personal development are essentially interpretive. As we have seen, they depend on ways of looking at a person's life history. One cannot take the bald facts of a particular biography and, so to speak, just 'read off' that it is or is not a story of personal development: the facts have to be interpreted and evaluated, they have to be seen in relation to each other and in the light of appropriate models of growth. Judgements of personal development therefore take place at a high level of synthesis and abstraction. Arguably they are second-order: given the (uninterpreted) events and actions in a person's life, the first step may be to see these as forming 'careers' (as Johnson argues[20]), ie. as stories of how the person fulfilled particular roles (eg. was a parent) or behaved in recognisable situations (eg. helped a friend in difficulty). Only when their history is understood in such meaningful patterns can one set about viewing these 'careers' as constituting personal growth.

Now in such a complex process of interpretation intellectual 'models': are indispensable, helping us to connect and make sense of otherwise unrelated facts. The problem is that our models may themselves determine what facts we are able to see. There is no doubt that this kind of determination takes place sometimes in science and psychology:[21] but does it also occur in our more informal judgements of personal development? My own inclination is to say that it does, perhaps indeed very strongly. It may be that possessing a concept of personal development in old age not only enables us to see what happens to people as personal development but even facilitates the occurrence of that which is seen in this way. After all, human endeavour and activity is often bounded by cultural limits of what is supposed to be possible or appropriate, and the common stereotype of ageing as outlined at the beginning of this paper probably acts as a powerful constraint on old people themselves.[22] If that is so, developing and disseminating a clear and workable concept of personal growth in old age may itself be an important means of helping elderly people to develop.

Notes

1.   *As You Like It*, Act 2, Scene 7.
2.   D.B. Bromley, *The psychology of human ageing*, 2nd ed., Harmondsworth, 1978, pp.78ff.
3.   *op. cit.* pp.23-4
4.   D. Peck and D. Whitlow, *Approaches to personality theory*, London, 1975, pp.10ff
5.   R.D. Cattell and F. W. Warburton, *Objective personality and motivation tests*, London, 1967.
6.   S. Hooker, *Caring for elderly people*, 2nd Edition, London, 1981, p.4
7.   J.E. Birren, *The psychology of ageing*, New Jersey, 1964, p.8
8.   Bromley, *op.cit.*, pp.29-30
9.   Birren *op.cit.* p.275
10.   *ibid.* p.274
11.   R.C. Peck, 'Psychological development in the second half of life', pp.85-92 in Neugarten (ed) *op. cit.*
12.   Bromley *op.cit.* p.263.
13.   E. Pfeiffer, 'Successful ageing', pp.13-21 in L.E. Brown and E.O. Ellis (eds), *Quality of life - the later years*, Massachusetts, 1975, p.13
14.   *ibid.* p.14.
15.   Bromley, *loc. cit.*.
16.   B. Evans and B. Waites, *IQ and mental testing*, London, 1981, p.137.
17.   P. Brown, *The other side of growing older*, London, 1982, p.176.
18.   C.G. Jung, 'The development of personality', pp.191-210 in A. Storr (ed), *Jung - selected writings*, London, 1983, p.198.
19.   R.M. Hare, *Freedom and reason*, Oxford, 1963, pp.126-7.
20.   M. Johnson, 'That was your life...', pp.99-113 in V. Carver and P. Liddiard (eds), *An ageing population*, Milton Keynes, 1978, pp.108ff.
21.   M. Jahoda, 'One model of man or many?', pp.277-287 in A.J. Chapman and D.M Jones (eds), *Models of man*, Leicester, 1980, p.279.
22.   cf. Brown *op. cit.*

3 Ageing and autonomy: the case for genetic enhancement

RUTH CHADWICK

When I am an old woman I shall wear purple
....
You can wear terrible shirts and grow more fat
And eat three pounds of sausages at a go
Or only bread and pickle for a week
And hoard pens and pencils and beermats and things in boxes

But now we must have clothes that keep us dry
And pay our rent and not swear in the street
And set a good example for the children
We must have friends to dinner and read the papers

(From Jenny Joseph, *Warning*).

Introduction

The extent to which the ageing process is subject to human control is a topic of enduring interest; the idea of a fountain of youth has long been appealing. This has only been increased by developments in human genome analysis, with the possibility that genetic controls over ageing may be discovered. This article will examine the issues that arise in relation to attempts to delay or prevent ageing with special reference to the use of genetic intervention as a means to this goal. I shall begin by examining what ageing is, outline different potential methods of controlling ageing, and then proceed to discuss arguments for and against the use of genetic modification to prevent ageing. The issue is intimately connected with two others, that of extending the human life span and that of devoting resources to curing what are commonly known as the diseases *of* old age, such as atherosclerosis. To avoid confusion, however, I want to discuss the question

35

of preventing ageing *per se*, whether or not it increases life expectancy, and irrespective of the alleviation of any particular disease or set of diseases. We are to imagine the hypothetical situation in which any biological 'clock' controlling the length of life remains unaltered, but in which the manifestations of ageing with which we are currently familiar are subject to control.

What is ageing?

Ageing must be distinguished from chronological age. As Caplan says, 'given the existence of a chronological device, all bodies that exist can be said to age relative to the measurements provided by that device' (Caplan, 1992, 198). This is not our present concern. While ageing and chronological age are closely related, individuals may age at very different rates. There are enormous differences between people who share the same age in terms of number of years. Whereas some enjoy life, others do not; whereas some are healthy, others are not; whereas some have definite plans for the future, others do not and so on. Nor is it the concern of this article to determine when a person counts as 'old' or 'elderly', although there may be questions about the age at which any preventative treatment for ageing should be applied. Ageing may be defined as 'the accumulation of chronological events that render an organism more susceptible to the stresses of life and thereby increase the probability of death' (Martin and Baker, 1995, 85). Martin and Baker note, however, that there are also changes which improve with age, eg. integrative skills. They continue:

> Ageing occurs as the result of events that damage molecules, cells, and tissues, thereby exhausting reparative processes and ultimately resulting in decreased physiological performance...

Neither the type of events nor their cause is explained here, but this will be seen to be an important aspect of the debate concerning our attitudes towards and response to ageing.

Methods of intervention

Martin and Baker outline a variety of interventions that could delay the onset of age-related declines or improve matters for those undergoing the ageing process.

These include:
- lifestyle interventions
- pharmacological interventions
- biological interventions
- molecular-genetic interventions, eg., gene therapy

Some of these are familiar in that they have been practised for a long time, others are still fairly speculative. The divisions between the categories may not always be clear-cut, but it is a useful classification for present purposes.

Lifestyle interventions

It is already common for individuals to try to delay the onset of ageing by adopting certain ways of living, eg., with regard to diet and exercise, care of the skin, reduction of stress, learning new things. Research is ongoing into the effects of low calorie diets. Such means can make a significant difference to the speed of the ageing process and they have led to a substantial industry in anti-ageing products and in manuals of advice from personalities such as Joan Collins.

Pharmacological interventions

Pharmacological interventions fall into two types: therapeutic and preventive. Where therapeutic interventions are in question, what has to be borne in mind is that the physiological changes that take place during ageing themselves affect the body's response to drugs, so that responses to drug therapy for disease, for example, may be atypical (Chadwick and Levitt, 1995). Martin and Baker suggest pharmacological interventions that would reduce the progression of disease, but this is arguably more concerned with counteracting age-related diseases, such as Alzheimer's, than with ageing itself. Of more interest for present purposes would be the possibility of anti-ageing drug interventions taking place prior to the onset of ageing. Drugs might be able to delay ageing insofar as they have, for example, antioxidant properties, where oxidants are considered to be responsible for cell damage.

For example, considerable interest has surrounded the development of Renova, approved as a prescription wrinkle treatment in 1994 (Mestel, 1996).

Biological interventions

In this category we might place hormone replacement therapy, which is now increasingly prescribed (though not uncontroversially) and also possibly interventions to enable post-menopausal women to become pregnant.

Molecular-genetic interventions

Gene therapy is now with us: experimental protocols are now in operation in various centres for genetic disorders such as cystic fibrosis. How might this be relevant to ageing? A preliminary point is that in order for the techniques of gene therapy to be applicable to the ageing process, there would have to be at least a genetic component in the ageing process which would be susceptible to treatment. There is considerable interest in finding the genetic basis of longevity, regarding which there are two aspects: one is negative, namely the lack of a predisposition to the diseases of old age. The second concerns the clock which positively determines the lifespan and ageing of the individual. The latter is related to the fact that even in the absence of any such diseases, ageing itself would lead to death. It is in relation to the latter, a specific clock mechanism, that the possibility of genetic intervention seems most plausible.

It is clearly important, then, to examine theories about the cause of the ageing process, with special reference to the extent to which it has a genetic basis.

Why do we age?

There are several different views concerning why we age (based on the account given by Rusting (1992)).

(1) The human species has evolved with specific genes that control ageing

One possibility is that there is a specific genetic basis for the ageing process. Why might this be the product of evolution? One theory is that it has evolutionary benefits because it brings about the death of the organism and makes room for younger individuals who still have a reproductive capacity. There are two problems with this as a possible explanation. The first is that throughout much of its evolutionary history the lifespan was much shorter than

38

it is now, so that ageing has only relatively recently been construed as a problem. It was more of a challenge to survive long enough to worry about ageing. The second difficulty with this explanation is the type of evolutionary theory on which it rests. As Caplan notes, it is dependent upon the view that selection operates at species level to promote the reproductive success of the species (Caplan, 1992, 202), rather than at the gene level. It is difficult to understand why a *gene* predisposing an organism to age should confer a selective advantage, and be more likely to be passed on to future generations, than a gene which did not have that effect; why a gene predisposing an organism to age should be more likely to ensure the reproductive success of the individual whose gene it was.

(2) *Ageing is a side effect of evolution*

An alternative view, and one favoured by Caplan, is that ageing is a side effect of evolution. On this theory there may be genes that control ageing but they have not been specifically selected for. There is no reason, however, why selection should have operated *against* them, for the following reason. Ageing is analogous to those genetic disorders of a 'late-onset' variety, such as Huntington's chorea, which may not make their presence felt until after reproduction has taken place. In other words, to have genes predisposing to ageing would not be a disadvantage to an individual in attempting to achieve reproductive success. There would thus be no evolutionary pressure acting against such genes.

(3) *Ageing is a result of environmental stress*

A third possible explanation of the ageing process is that it is the result of environmental stress. One element in such damage would be cellular damage caused by molecules produced in the normal course of living, eg. oxygen free radicals. This explanation however need not dispense with a genetic component altogether, but the genetic explanation would be negative - on this theory there is no specific genetic programme directing the ageing process; it is simply that we have not been endowed with an ability to repair wear and tear. There would be an explanation of the absence of evolutionary pressure in favour of such an ability. Since it would be required only after reproduction, typically, had taken place, it would not be conducive to reproductive success.

(4) *Programmed cell death*

As an alternative to the theory of cellular damage caused by external environmental damage, there is evidence for internal limitations which bring about programmed cell death. Leonard Hayflick and Paul S. Moorhead (cited in Rusting) reported in 1961 research that suggested that there is a limit to the number of times human cells can proliferate. It might be argued that this is connected with some genetic basis for ageing itself, but it may have evolved as a natural defence against cancer, rather than to promote ageing *per se* (Rusting, 1992). In that case, this appears to be a version of the side-effect of evolution theory, but with the difference that it is a side-effect of a positive benefit, rather than simply the 'inadvertent subversion of organic function' (Caplan, 1992, 202).

Of these possible explanations of ageing, some support for the view that specific genetic mechanisms might be involved has come from research into the genetic basis of Werner's syndrome (Concar, 1996). Werner's syndrome, which causes premature ageing, occurs when individuals have two defective copies of a gene that codes for an enzyme known as a helicase. One line of thought might be that if lack of helicase causes ageing, would extra helicase delay or prevent it? Critics of this approach suggest that the mechanisms underlying ageing are likely to be very complex and that an interpretation in terms of the expense, in evolutionary terms, of maintenance mechanisms is much more plausible (Kirkwood, 1996).

Genetic intervention: for and against

In so far as ageing has a genetic basis, genetic intervention to counteract it would be in principle possible, although its practical feasibility would of course be affected by the *type* of genetic basis. We now need to consider the arguments for and against this possibility. First, however there is a question of when intervention should occur: when is (undesirable) ageing supposed to begin? Rusting writes that:

> the investment humans have made in protecting the soma provides enough defensive capacity to assure zest for perhaps 40 years - the period we might have expected to survive during much of our evolution. That investment would include some backup capacity, in case of accidental damage. Presumably, we muddle through mid-life and late life by taking advantage of our reserves. As these

backups gradually give out on us, we lose the ability to respond to environmental stress, and, eventually, we die (Rusting, 1992, 89).

If we take our cue from this, then we might aim to prevent people deteriorating beyond the point they have reached at 40. Given the point about differential rates of ageing, to which we have already alluded, this will be better for some than for others, but it does give us a recognisable dividing line.

The case for prevention

The arguments for prevention of ageing can be discussed under the following headings: individual autonomy; prevention of suffering; social benefits; social justice; and the view that ageing is a disease.

The argument from autonomy

The principle of autonomy might have application in a number of different ways in this context, according to how it is interpreted. I shall consider three possibilities here: autonomy understood as self-determination; autonomy as a second order capacity to reflect on first order wants; autonomy as the capacity to live an independent life.

There is abundant evidence to suggest that large numbers of people want to postpone ageing as long as possible. Considerable amounts of money are spent on cosmetics and treatments to achieve this. There may be doubts about the benefits of immortality, but as long as life persists, the benefits of prevention of ageing seem less in dispute. The fact that people want to prevent or delay ageing would be an argument for saying they should be free to do so, where resources are available. It is not sufficient by itself to supply an argument for making the resources available, but does provide *a* reason for doing so, other things being equal.

Gerald Dworkin gives a second-order account of autonomy as follows:

autonomy is conceived of as a second-order capacity of persons to reflect critically upon their first-order preferences, desires, wishes and so forth and the capacity to accept or attempt to change these in light of higher-order preferences and values (Dworkin, 1988, 20).

This capacity of human beings is not only of considerable value to those who have it, but is also of moral importance as the basis of respect for people's choices. It is under threat from the aspect of ageing which affects mental capacities and introduces memory loss and symptoms of senility. On this version of the autonomy argument the case would not be for intervention on the grounds that it is what individuals want, but on the grounds that it is a necessary requirement for the preservation of the second-order capacity.

On a different level the autonomy argument has a third aspect to it, which might be called the capacity to live an independent life, where 'independence' is interpreted in terms of physical independence. Individuals fear ageing because it reduces their chance of being able to care for themselves. It is related to the argument from self-determination but has a specific practical focus. Ordinary tasks, like taking a bath, become increasingly difficult. People dread being a burden to others. A survey by Age Concern found that of 1000 people over 16, 33 per cent expressed concern about loss of independence (Holden, 1992, 8).

Under all three of these interpretations, autonomy provides reasons for the prevention of ageing.

Prevention of suffering

A second form of argument is a consequentialist one, to the effect that genetic intervention in the ageing process could prevent avoidable suffering. There is no doubt that for some individuals ageing may bring real suffering, both physical and mental. People speak of feeling young inside while seeing their bodies deteriorate, and this causes frustration and stress. The 'invisibility' of age causes sadness, as expressed by Kathleen Eileen in *A Sunset of the City*:

> Already I am no longer looked at with lechery or love
> My daughters and sons have put me away with marbles and dolls,
> Are gone from the house.
> ....
> It is a real chill out,
> The genuine thing.
> I am not deceived, I do not think it is still summer
> Because sun stays and birds continue to sing.

It is not clear that the supposed compensations, or consolations, as in the Jenny Joseph poem quoted above, of feeling free from certain social constraints, of withdrawal and disengagement, are sufficient to make up for these

42

disadvantages. The aim of prevention of suffering could therefore also provide a reason, other things being equal, for intervention in the ageing process.

Social benefits

In addition to benefits to individuals there are, arguably, potential social benefits in ageing prevention. There is some evidence that present day Western societies cannot cope with ageing and its effects. In the last ten years or so there has been an increasing amount of concern about demographic changes and the burden this will put on the health care system, social services, and informal carers. If ageing were prevented the need for care would be greatly reduced. This would reduce not only individual stress but also social expenditure on this item (not taking into account for the present the cost of the preventative treatment).

Ageism and positive discrimination

Ageism, treating people differently simply on the grounds of their age, in the absence of any other relevant difference or further argument, is as unjustifiable as sexism or racism, but it is a phenomenon of contemporary life. On some housing estates old people are terrorised and abused; it is more difficult for older people to find work; old people become invisible. In some contexts there are attempts to find arguments to justify treating elderly people less favourably: for example giving the young priority over the old in the context of the allocation of health care resources; and these arguments are the subject of considerable debate.

In so far as it is accepted that ageing is undesirable, however, intervention to prevent it might be welcomed as a way of redressing the balance. It is arguable that the direction of resources to preventing ageing beyond 40, would be justified positive discrimination in favour of older people. Youth, it is said, is wasted on the young - why not give some of it to those who would know how to take advantage of it? An objection to this way of looking at things is that it would be preferable to change attitudes towards ageing, rather than trying to prevent it.

Ageing as a disease

If ageing were classified as a disease it might be argued that such a classification counted as a reason for trying to 'cure' it. Ageing itself is not generally considered to be a disease (Reznek, 1987; Martin and Baker, 1995), but a complex set of biological alterations as outlined above. Art Caplan, however, has argued that ageing has five key properties associated with the category of disease:

> it involves discomfort or suffering
> it is traceable to a cause
> it has a set of clear-cut structural changes
> there is a set of clinical symptoms commonly associated with the structural changes
> it involves functional impairment

In the light of the above discussion about why we age, it is perhaps not entirely fair to say that ageing is traceable to *a* cause. Against this, Caplan argues that there is, 'if we are willing to grant the same tolerance to current theories of ageing as we grant to theories in other domains of medicine, an explicit set of precipitating factors' (Caplan, 1992, 205).

A more serious problem for the view that ageing is a disease, however, may be that the concept of disease itself is in dispute. 'Disease' is defined sometimes biologically, sometimes normatively. The above list is linked with the biological category of definition. Caplan considers an argument against allowing ageing to count as a biological disease, namely that ageing is perceived as natural or normal. There are two versions of this: the first that it is universal and inevitable; and the other that it is fulfilling a function, which might be of a theological or a biological variety. Universality and inevitability he dismisses as insufficient on which to base decisions of moral importance. A theological explanation of function would be unscientific; the possibility that ageing might have a biological function is bad science. Here, Caplan allies himself with theories of ageing which do not think that it fulfils an evolutionary purpose *per se*, seeing it simply as a by-product of evolutionary forces as explained in (2) above.

On a normative type of definition of disease, the classification of a condition as a disease includes an element of negative evaluation. A disease prevents people from engaging in socially valued activities. Ageing arguably does indeed reduce the chances of engaging in useful work, and developing new relationships, for example. There have been similar debates about whether infertility is or is not a disease, on the grounds that infertility prevents people from engaging in a socially valued activity, namely, having children. In fact it is interesting the extent to which the two issues, ageing and infertility, have become bound up with one another in the last few years, with the advent of techniques for facilitating reproduction in the post-menopausal years. It might be argued, however, again as in the infertility debate, that rather than focussing on the negative evaluation of ageing, to the extent that it is considered pathological, social attitudes could be changed.

Caplan considers an argument against counting ageing as a disease based on the social consequences of doing so. He rightly argues that the question of definition cannot be resolved by the social consequences. The converse of this is that the question of definition cannot in itself solve the problem of whether we should try to prevent ageing. In the infertility debate, there has sometimes been an implication that if infertility counted as a disease, then it would be a legitimate target for the expenditure of health care resources. But the definition question and the allocation question are logically separate. Similarly here, the question of whether ageing is or is not a disease is not particularly helpful. The decision as to whether or not to intervene has to be taken on other grounds.

There are arguments, then, on the basis of autonomy, prevention of suffering, social benefits and social justice, in support of genetic intervention to prevent ageing. Let us now turn to the counter-arguments. To some extent these are rejoinders to the arguments set out above; but there are also some positive arguments against intervention.

The case against prevention

The need argument

It might be argued that while individuals might like to avoid ageing, this wish cannot be described as a need which would justify the use of genetic technology. The thinking behind this might be of different types: concerned, for example, with the type of interest that would justify allocation of scarce resources, or the notion of some limit to the applications of genetic technology itself.

Dan Callahan uses the concept in the context of medical goals in an ageing society:

Need will not be a manageable idea, however, unless we forthrightly recognise that it is only in part an empirical concept. It can make use of physical indicators, but it will also be a reflection of our values, what we think people require for an acceptable life. In the case of the aged, I have proposed that our ideal of old age should be achieving a life span that enables each of us to accomplish the ordinary scope of possibilities that life affords, recognising that this may encompass a range of time rather than pointing to a precise age (Callahan, 1987).

This is an argument about life-span, but how might it be applied to ageing? Despite the difficulties noted above of classifying conditions as diseases or not, why is it that we consider Werner's syndrome to be a disorder, whereas we do not normally consider ageing itself to be one? The time at which the symptoms occur cannot in itself be relevant. It is because it is statistically abnormal that they occur at so early a stage in someone's life and that this makes a person less likely to enjoy the ordinary scope of possibilities that life affords. But even in the absence of such a disorder, might there be circumstances in which prevention of ageing itself would be necessary to enable each of us to accomplish the ordinary scope of possibilities? It seems to me that reproduction in older women is a possible example of this. Reproduction is generally considered to be among the ordinary scope of possibilities that life affords, and one that many people think is required for an acceptable life. This particular example would (currently) apply only to a small section of the population, but does provide one counter-example to the need argument, when need is interpreted in the above way.

Gains and losses

It was noted above that ageing causes suffering, and so there is a consequentialist argument for prevention of the suffering so caused. A difficulty with this is that it overlooks the potential benefits of ageing that would be thereby lost. For example, if it is true that programmed cell death is part of the body's natural defence against cancer, then any anti-ageing intervention that interfered with this might actually be counter-productive.

Further, just as knowledge of our own mortality concentrates the mind and drives us to fulfil our goals before it is too late, knowledge of our own ageing fulfils the same function, as Arthur Hugh Clough says:

And almost everyone when age
Disease, or sorrows strike him
Inclines to think there is a god
Or something very like him.

Ageing is a good precaution against *hubris*. In the light of the occasional unedifying and unsuccessful spectacle of people paying large amounts for plastic surgery in the attempts to retain a youthful appearance, the argument that it would be better to accept, and to grow old gracefully, has at least prudential force.

The social function of ageing

Against the view that prevention of ageing would produce social benefits, there are arguments to the effect that ageing performs important social functions. Even if it is not directly selected for, it is true that from the social point of view it is desirable that the old make way for the young, not in this case by dying but by moving on to a different stage of life.

The effect of having everyone still looking and feeling young is hard to imagine. People in their 40s today are young relative to those of, say, 60 and above. But if no one ever aged beyond the stage they had reached at 40, they would lose that advantage. Our concept of what counts as 'old' would change. We at least partly construct out identity by comparing ourselves with others. Those stuck at this stage of development would vastly outnumber those below it. What would be the social effects of this? Large scale social changes would presumably be required in patterns of work, leisure and home. An article in *Newsweek* (Beck et al., 1994) suggested that in the future reproduction might be something that could be postponed for retirement. But would people be willing to retire? There would presumably be more competition for social benefits such as sexual partners, attractive jobs and so on. And people would not feel ready to die. It may be felt that there are certain 'natural' stages in life, through which we progress, and that to undermine this may have undesirable results. This concern may be overstated however. This century has seen substantial changes in our expectations in Western societies about life stages, brought about, for example, both by women having children later and by longer life expectancy.

The intangible benefits of ageing, however, might be lost to society. There may be no reason to think we should lose the wisdom of age, in so far as this comes from having lived a long time and had experience, but in so far as it is a product of undergoing the process of ageing itself, this is less obvious.

Resource implications

An essential question is that of resources. The relevance of age to allocation of resources is a matter of considerable current controversy. The prevention of ageing on a large scale would require a massive investment of resources, and the claims of this application of genetic technology would have to compete with others. What is more likely is that if available genetic forms of ageing prevention would be a privilege of the rich, as other forms of prevention already are to some extent.

Enhancement versus therapy

The final objection that I want to consider concerns the proposed technology itself. While there is disagreement over the possibilities of and desirability of gene therapy, a considerable degree of consensus exists over two distinctions: between somatic and germ-line therapy; and between therapy and enhancement.

In the context of the present discussion, it is the latter distinction that is important, and it relates to the question of whether or not ageing counts as a disease. There is an argument (supported, for example, by the Clothier Committee (1992)), that gene therapy should not be used for enhancement purposes. Would alteration of the genetic controls of ageing count as *therapy*? It is beyond the scope of this discussion to explore the therapy/enhancement distinction in detail. The words 'prevention' and 'enhancement' have been used, rather than 'cure', but the question of classification seems similarly unhelpful here as the question of disease classification was said to be earlier. To rule out a course of action simply on the grounds that it would count as enhancement is unconvincing. (Preventive genetic immunisation, for example, could prove very beneficial.) More needs to be said about what the enhancement would amount to, what its consequences would be. So if there are arguments to support the prevention of ageing, and such prevention would be possible by using genetic means, it is difficult to understand the reason for ruling it out simply because it would count as enhancement.

Conclusion

Several arguments for and against genetic intervention to prevent ageing have been considered. If individuals want to prevent ageing, and if it were possible to bring this about by genetic intervention, should it be done? The strongest arguments in favour of ageing prevention are those that depend on autonomy, particularly in so far as the aim is to promote independent living. This would have immense benefits both for the individuals concerned and for society, in reducing the extent of the need for care. Serious objections include the resource implications and the point about changing attitudes towards age rather than trying to prevent it. The latter may serve to reinforce ageism.

What I want to suggest, however, is that it may be a mistake to speak of 'ageing' as a whole. Ageing has many aspects. We have noted those aspects that concern how a person looks, and others that are disabling with regard to the tasks of everyday life and cause considerable frustration and possibly physical suffering. We need a twin track approach - opposition to ageism and negative images of ageing, while promoting the autonomy, particularly in terms of physical independence, of the elderly. While facilitating the ordinary scope of possibilities that life affords may not provide an argument for prolongation of life, it should be interpreted to include the ability to engage in such activities as having a bath. In so far as promotion of independence is feasible, resources where available should be targeted on that. If it were possible to use genetic technology to do that, the advantages of the prevention of ageing could be had while retaining some of the physical manifestations of ageing and thus not losing some of the purported advantages of growing old gracefully.

References

Beck, M. et al. (1994), 'How far can we push Mother Nature?' *Newsweek*, vol. 3, no. 123, pp.38-43.

Callahan, D. (1987), *Setting Limits: Medical Goals in an Ageing Society* New York: Simon & Schuster.

Caplan, A.L. (1992), 'Is ageing a disease?' in *If I Were A Rich Man Could I Buy A Pancreas? and other essays in health care.*

Chadwick, R. and Levitt, M. (1995), 'When drug treatment in the elderly is not cost effective: an ethical dilemma in an environment of healthcare rationing', *Drugs and Ageing*, vol. 7, no. 6, pp.416-9.

Clothier, C., Chairman (1992), *Report of the Committee on the Ethics of Gene Therapy* London: HMSO.

Concar, D. (1996), 'Death of old age' *New Scientist*, vol. 150, no. 2035, pp.24-29.

Dworkin, G. (1988), *The Theory and Practice of Autonomy* Cambridge U.P.

Holden, W. (1992), 'Old age "frightens" one in four people', in Craig Donnellan (ed.) *Ageing: Everyone's Future*, Cambridge: Independence Educational Publishers.

Kirkwood, T. (1996), 'How can we live forever?', *British Medical Journal*, vol. 313, No. 7072, p.1571.

Martin, George R. and Baker III, George T. (1995), 'Theories of ageing and life extension', in W.T.Reich (ed.), *Encyclopedia of Bioethics*, Revised edition New York: Macmillan.

Mestel, R (1996), 'Wrinkle wars' *New Scientist*, vol. 150, no. 2031, pp.42-46.

Reznek, L. (1987), *The Nature of Disease*, London: Routledge & Kegan Paul.

Rusting, R.L. (1992), 'Why do we age?', *Scientific American*, pp.87-95.

4 Practical problems with the discharge of old people from hospital - a physician's perspective

SIMON WINNER

Ethicists point up ways in which custom and practice can lead to injustice, but clinicians sometimes complain that ethical discourse is too far removed from the world of patient care, where decisions are shaped and compromise is imposed by competing problems and practical constraints. This chapter deals with aspects of the discharge of elderly patients from hospital, and is an attempt to infuse the issues with the flavour of everyday work on the wards.

It is important when discussing elderly people to avoid giving the fallacious impression that they are an homogeneous group. Individual variability increases with age, and a disabled seventy-year-old may have more in common with an unfit forty-year-old than with an elderly twin who happens to be fit. Most old people admitted to hospital have acute illnesses from which they recover; most are admitted from and discharged to their own homes where they lead independent lives - fewer than 5 per cent of over-65s in the United Kingdom live in institutions such as residential homes, nursing homes and hospitals (Victor 1991). Only a small minority of elderly people resemble the commonly held stereotype of old age characterised by extreme physical disability and mental impairment - though these attributes are commoner amongst those who are admitted to hospital and they frequently cause problems with discharge.

Clinicians (in all professions) attempting to comply with the wish of a frail patient to return home can face dilemmas, distractions and downright barriers. Some problems arise from characteristics of the patient, particularly when there are doubts about her ability to decide for herself. Some are caused by relatives, friends, and neighbours, or other representatives of the community. Sometimes professional carers are themselves the source of problems, both in hospital and in the community. Some problems occur when old people are admitted to clinical settings that are not well-tuned to their needs, and some result from

51

social services departments being separate from health authorities as providers of continuing care. These different challenges will be considered in turn.

Useful guidance on how to plan hospital discharges can be found in a form usually associated with bureaucratic minutiae; a circular from the Department of Health, issued after the Parliamentary Ombudsman drew attention to people sent home without appropriate support or discharged into institutional care without adequate choice (Department of Health 1989). This document emphasized early planning of support services and the importance of placing the patient, the family and carers at the centre of the planning process. Good liaison was stressed, both between different professions within the hospital and between hospital and community, and a booklet that accompanied the circular illustrated the need for coordinated teamwork. Authority over decisions about discharge was placed unequivocally with the hospital consultant responsible for the patient's medical care. Subsequent guidance from the Department has reiterated these priorities and described ways of putting them into practice, stressing the importance of effective communication (Department of Health 1994, 1995).

Translating these principles into action for frail elderly people with multiple problems requires expertise. Geriatricians and psychogeriatricians may be said to specialise in difficult discharges. Specialist care of old people in the UK usually involves a multi-disciplinary team which combines relevant medical skills with expertise in rehabilitation and continuity with community support services. A typical team, comprising ward nurses, consultant and junior medical staff, occupational therapist, social worker, liaison nurse (or other representative from community nursing) and others (eg. physiotherapist on a team in geriatric medicine, or psychologist on a psychogeriatric team) will meet weekly to discuss each patient, to pool assessments, and to set and review objectives. Comprehensive discharge planning is an integral part of the process, and the necessary coordination is enhanced by the team approach.

Frail old people in hospital confront the clinician with a complex web of interacting problems, medical and social, practical and ethical. Many people are involved in decisions about hospital discharge: relatives, friends, other carers, and the multi-disciplinary team. The patient's preferences must be defined and enacted as far as possible, and ethical problems must be perceived clearly despite the surrounding 'noise'.

Mrs A, aged 74 years, was admitted to hospital having 'gone off her legs'. Since her husband's death seven years ago she had lived alone in a bungalow visited by her niece and friendly neighbours, with meals-on-wheels and a home help provided by the local authority Social Services Department. Her mobility had been worsening slowly for years; she no longer went outside the house but spent most of the day sat in a chair, though able to rise unaided and go to the lavatory or prepare a snack. All visitors had noticed a deterioration in her memory and occasional episodes of disorientation over the last 18 months. In the six weeks before admission, she had several falls and was intermittently incontinent of urine. She now required help to dress and wash fully, and often spent all day in bed. At first she refused to consider extra help or medical attention, but with her niece close to exhaustion she finally consented to hospital admission.

Physical examination suggested cerebrovascular disease as the cause of her progressive dementia; a recent mild stroke, heart failure, and urinary infection had contributed to her deterioration. With treatment and rehabilitation she regained precarious mobility, and become able to take a few steps with a walking frame and transfer from chair to lavatory without help. She was continent provided she used the commode regularly, though she sometimes forgot to do this without prompting. She required help to dress and wash, and was able to make a cup of tea. Her short-term memory was poor, and she was often disorientated as to time of day, though she knew she was in hospital. When asked, she expressed a strong desire to return to her bungalow, and vehemently refused to consider moving, particularly 'not to a home'. She seemed to have some understanding of the risks involved, saying that falls had never harmed her before. Her niece was supportive of her wishes. A home visit was arranged, attended by patient, niece, and various professionals. Mrs A was only just able to move from her chair to the kitchen, but insisted she would be better when the house was less 'full of strangers'. She was discharged home with a comprehensive care package, including care assistants alternating with her niece to get her up and put her to bed, strategic visits from the neighbours by day, and a personal alarm for summoning help in the event of an emergency such as a fall.

Mrs A illustrates several everyday aspects of geriatric medicine. The processes that culminated in acute hospital admission had been progressing for months, and were only fully appreciated in retrospect. The crisis took the form of a change in dependency, but behind this were several medical causes amenable to improvement with treatment or appropriate rehabilitation - there is seldom such a thing as a purely 'social admission', and multiple pathology is common in later life. The success of a complex care package depends on the consent and cooperation of many people. From the viewpoint of the elderly patient, hospital admission combines threats to health with losses of privacy, dignity and home comforts, and her independence suddenly becomes subject to the opinions of others.

The patient

Problems with discharge arising in the patient are mainly associated with mental impairment or physical disability or both.

Clinical decisions, such as whether or not to have an investigation or to undergo a particular treatment, involve drawing up a balance for the individual between the likely benefits and the risks, a process in which the physician's ideal role is as advisor to the patient, whose wishes should be paramount. The decision about whether a frail old person should return home is a clinical decision like any other. Difficulties arise when the patient expresses a desire to return home but there are doubts as to whether she will manage, combined with doubts about whether she understands the risks. The clinician faces a situation where a judgement must be made: to deny rights to self-determination may be unjust, but to expose an unwitting patient to risk is negligent.

Several issues are bound up in this judgement. Autonomy and the empowerment of mentally impaired people have received attention in this book and elsewhere. Norman (1980) has focussed discussion on the rights of old people to choose to take risks, both in institutional care (Centre for Policy on Ageing 1996) and in the community (Wynne-Harley 1991). The problems of defining competence and of facilitating the participation of demented people in decisions about their care have been discussed by Oppenheimer (1991). Much of the literature on testamentary capacity and consent to treatment is of questionable relevance to decisions about 'risky' hospital discharge. Competence is relative and should be assessed in connection with specific decisions. An old person who is unable to run her own financial affairs or understand medical interventions may still be judged competent to decide about going home.

Clinicians are essentially practical, and will assess competence by analogy with the process of diagnosing physical illness: an impression formed from the history and examination at the bedside will as far as possible be supplemented by appropriate tests.

There are various standard psychological tests of cognitive function in common use, usually applied in abbreviated forms designed as screening tests. For example, the Mini-Mental State examination (Folstein *et al* 1975) tests standard domains such as orientation, registration, attention, and recall, and has been shown to be valid and reliable in detecting and quantifying cognitive impairment. Abnormal scores can be followed up by more complex tests, carried out in some hospitals by a clinical psychologist. When deciding about discharge from hospital, however, this kind of measurement is of limited use. In the psychology of ageing there is a discrepancy between *cognitive ability* and what might be called cognitive competence. The former describes the intellectual level of an individual as measured by conventional tests of intelligence and cognitive function, while *cognitive competence* may be defined as the degree of success in functioning in a specific environment. The limitations of current psychometric tests in predicting this kind of performance are greater with increasing age, and the development of tests of cognitive competence applicable to elderly people has been recognised as an important challenge (Salthouse 1990). In practice, impairment of cognitive ability can be documented with some precision, but cognitive competence remains an informal judgement. The clinician's impression may be all there is to go on.

The picture is further complicated by two practical accompaniments of hospital admission. Old people who are usually mildly confused will be at their worst when taken out of familiar surroundings and into a noisy crowded hospital ward. The effects of concurrent illness must also be taken into account: the commonest type of confusion seen in elderly patients is delirium caused by a physical illness such as acute infection. At its simplest, this is a temporary and obvious phenomenon which rapidly passes, but it can be subtle and slow to clear. The resulting disorientation can adversely affect all aspects of mental (and also physical) performance, and improvement may take weeks. No patient's competence to decide her own fate should be discounted before time has been allowed for the effects of physical illness to pass; on the other hand, the longer she is kept in hospital, the more disorientated, dependent and depressed she may become as a result of institutionalisation.

The upshot of these difficulties with assessment is that decisions about 'risky' hospital discharges vary widely according to the judgement and policies of individual clinicians. Maintaining an appropriate balance between paternalism and permissiveness requires constant vigilance. Paternalism may be appropriate for patients who are unequivocally incompetent, but perhaps all others should be given the benefit of the doubt. In practical terms, this means that for most patients who want to go home the fairest test is to try it and see, with appropriate support and surveillance in place. The results are sometimes surprising.

Mrs B lived alone in a ground floor flat. She was found on the floor in a coma, with a severe and near-fatal degree of hypothermia (core body temperature 32 degrees Centigrade). She made an uncomplicated recovery, and mild heart failure responded to treatment. It seemed likely that she had fallen and had been unable to get up, since she had severe osteoarthritis of both knees which were deformed and unstable. Her tendency to catastrophic falls was graphically illustrated after two weeks in the ward when she fell onto a chair and injured her eye. Throughout her stay in hospital, Mrs B was disorientated in time and usually in place, with poor short-term memory, scoring at best 5/10 on a brief mental test. She was consistent on only one issue: the frequently expressed desire to return home, and refusal to consider alternative accommodation. She was difficult to draw into conversation. When asked about her difficulty with walking and her tendency to fall, she said she would be alright once she got home. After prolonged rehabilitation on the ward, Mrs B became independent in going to the lavatory and to bed and could prepare a snack. On a visit home, she was observed to be unsafe when pouring a kettle of water and lighting her gas fire with a match. Plans were made to install support rails and alternative heating, but discharge home was considered to carry immense risks: of recurrence of hypothermia, of physical damage from falls, of deterioration through self-neglect, and of fire. Her desire to return home was clear, but there were differing opinions as to Mrs B's understanding of the risks. Meanwhile she again fell catastrophically, wounding her arm, but her resolve was firm and the clinician in charge of her care decided she was competent to decide for herself. She was discharged when her arm had healed, some four months after admission, with daily visits from a home help during the week and from a relative on the weekend, meals-on-wheels four times a week, and a bath assistant for a weekly wash. The liaison nurse visited occasionally to assess progress and maintain contact with everyone involved. Mrs B remained at home for six months, when she was readmitted with recurrence of heart failure and slightly worsened mobility. She improved only slightly after treatment, had frequent falls on the ward, but once again refused to consider anything other than home, to which she was returned after five weeks with a more intensive package of care. She was readmitted next day after another fall with injury to a hand, and on this occasion agreed to a month's trial in a local authority residential home. She found this satisfactory and was readily accepted as a permanent resident.

A practical trial of discharge is the fairest test of whether a patient can manage at home, but also serves another purpose. Oppenheimer (1991) stresses the importance of finding ways of presenting choices to the patient that circumvent as much as possible the obstacles posed by her illness or handicap. This means that information should be presented in a way that takes account of the individual's ability to grasp it. A patient with dementia may have problems with language and memory, and limited ability to form a conceptual view of the future, all of which will make abstract choices difficult. Concrete choices should be offered as far as possible, and a trial at home with appropriate support may be necessary before some who wish to return home can realistically address the possible discomforts and risks. A patient's choice in discussion may be contradicted by her behaviour when her desire becomes reality: for example she may repeatedly summon help that she previously declined, or she may actively seek readmission to hospital, thereby expressing her true preference. A carefully organised discharge, with the community and hospital teams cooperating to form a safety net, may thus serve as a pragmatic test of competence.

When (unlike Mrs B) a patient continues to opt for home with a maximal care package despite frequent accidents, crises and prolonged re-admissions to hospital, problems of equity arise. When resources are finite, one individual's right to an expensive package of care must be set against the rights of others who may receive a less-than-adequate share as a result of that expense. At present, mechanisms for striking an appropriate balance in everyday clinical practice are imperfect. Some local health authorities and social services departments have placed a ceiling on the cost of a domiciliary care package, related to the costs of alternative forms of care (such as a nursing home) and to the total resources available, thereby systematising some aspects of equity but setting limits on individual choice. When resources are inadequate a balance cannot be struck, and broader ethical issues are at stake. Recognition that individual clinical decisions must take account of the equitable use of resources should not detract from the wider responsibility of clinicians to act as advocates for the public in pressing for necessary resources to be made available (Grimley Evans 1992a).

For patients who are physically disabled but without mental impairment, resource constraints are the most important source of problems with hospital discharge, since few other factors limit the help - mechanical, electronic and human - that can be provided to facilitate independence or at least autonomy. If you are quadriplegic and ventilator-dependent but rich, arrangements can be made for you to be nursed with intensive care in your own home; physically disabled patients dependent on the public purse usually have more limited options. The clinician's role with these patients, who can clearly decide for themselves, is as advisor and ally in the struggle for the resources necessary to maximise choice. In patients with mental impairment, accompanying physical disability has special relevance as a factor complicating assessment, and as an added source of risk.

Other members of the community

Relatives, friends and others who may be involved with care are involved in the discharge process when, as is usually the case, this is desired by the patient. There is no substantial evidence for the commonly held view that families in the modern world no longer care for their elderly members: where relatives exist, they generally contribute actively to care (Freer 1988). After long years of neglect, so-called 'informal carers' (6 million in the UK in 1995 (Rowlands and Parker 1998)) are beginning to receive appropriate attention, but shortfalls in public provision for community care often amount to exploitation. Most hospital discharges are crucially dependent on the goodwill and labour of members of the community whose appraisal of the rights and risks involved may differ substantially from those of the patient and her professional attendants.

There are important differences of perspective between those for whom returning a patient home means hard work and sacrifice, and others for whom the options are more academic. However, it is probably true that the public at large tend to be less liberal than professionals in extending choices to disabled people, especially those who are confused. Discussion of these issues with all concerned is an essential part of hospital work, but can be demanding. Occasionally, an exposition of rights, autonomy and the futility of keeping someone 'safe' but miserable in the 'glass case' of an institution is met by assertions that the patient's expressed desire to take on the risks of going home certifies her inability to decide for herself, and that discharge 'should not be allowed'.

Family tensions come into focus on these occasions, and it is important for clinicians to avoid making assumptions about motivation, and to avoid being put in the position of arbitrating between family members. Dependence can engender anxiety, ambivalence and guilt on all sides; the clinician is seldom in a position to do more than observe the changes in relationships between patients, spouses and offspring, and speculate on why some are prepared to carry a burden of care that seems beyond all reason while others turn their backs. It is remarkable how often in case-conferences it is those relatives who make no contribution to day-to-day care that are most vocal and least disposed to give the patient the benefit of the doubt on self-determination. The clinician's role as the patient's advisor and advocate can lead to dilemmas. Many carers are themselves old (Rowlands and Parker 1998), and supporting a patient's dubious preference to return home to the care of a frail spouse may threaten the latter's health and welfare. It is seldom clear whether the clinician should be responsible solely to the patient or whether wider responsibility must be accepted.

A patient's resolve to return home can prove vulnerable: most old people fear 'being a burden' more than they fear dying, and clinicians sometimes observe a patient changing her mind and accepting institutional care following pressure from within the family, a form of abuse that is difficult to counter despite judicious advocacy. Some hospital discharges are complicated by the suspicion of physical abuse by a carer, often enshrouded in secrecy with which the victim complies. As with younger age-groups, these situations can make exacting demands on professional teams and on the law (Bennett and Kingston 1993).

Other members of the community may be involved in decisions about hospital discharge through matters of public health or public nuisance. For example, the memory impairment at an early stage of progressive dementia (such as Alzheimer's disease) commonly manifests as a tendency to leave saucepans burning on the cooker, or to switch on a gas fire and forget to light it. Clearly, the right to risk self-harm must be balanced against the risk to others - concern about the greater good must come into everyday ward decisions, and this may affect the options for someone living in an apartment closely surrounded by neighbours. These particular examples are amenable to a practical approach: the installation of electrical hobs and heaters with time-switches that cut out unless re-primed. When the patient fails to acknowledge the risk to others, some pragmatists favour direct action (despite the ethical risks) to prevent public health considerations from jeopardising continued independence at home.

Mrs C was almost blind, and unsteady on her feet due to damaged nerves (peripheral neuropathy). She was admitted to hospital with acute pneumonia and made a good recovery. On a home visit, she demonstrated precarious but independent mobility around her flat and was able to prepare simple meals on an electric hob. She also had a gas-ring, which she left switched on while she unsuccessfully sought a match. Burn-marks around the kitchen were explained when Mrs C described her preference for deep-fried chips, but showed that she could barely lift the heavy saucepan in which she kept the oil. The warden of the flats gave a story of worsening mobility and confusion over the past year. On one occasion, the electric hob had been left on unattended. Mrs C accepted the offer of a new hob and a smaller saucepan, but refused to give up her gas-ring, denying that she or anyone else was at risk. She was discharged home, and when the hob was installed the gas-ring was simply disconnected. When visited subsequently, Mrs C was clearly pleased with her new hob and its controls designed for the partially-sighted. She had no difficulty with the time-switches, and seemed to have given up deep-frying. The gas-ring was never mentioned again.

In this case, the patient's expressed desire was tested pragmatically by altering her circumstances and observing her reaction, a judicious form of paternalism that allowed her to regain substantial autonomy by eliminating the threat to public safety. Public nuisance is more difficult to judge, and clinicians become involved mainly as targets for criticism and complaints.

Mrs D had slowly progressive dementia attributed to Alzheimer's disease. She lived alone in some squalor in her own apartment and consistently refused offers of help. She sometimes got lost wandering around the local neighbourhood. More frequently she shut herself out without her front-door key, whereupon she would bang on one of the neighbours' doors to summon help. Disorientation in time with day/night reversal meant that these episodes often occurred in the early hours. Her desperate neighbours would call the Social Services department, the police, or her doctor in turn, and she was sometimes admitted to the General Hospital on suspicion that her confusion was acutely worse secondary to an infection or other illness. She always refused to consider any alternative to a return home. Over a period of a couple of years she occasionally let the community psychiatric nurse into the flat, allowing confirmation that no new clinical features had developed since the psychogeriatrician's original diagnosis of early dementia, and specifically that there was no evidence of severe self-neglect or of a functional illness that would justify consideration of further medical intervention.

Professionals

Some problems with discharge paradoxically arise from professionals on the rehabilitation team. The multi-disciplinary approach carries many benefits, including breadth of assessment and inter-professional communication, but *laissez-faire* does not always come easily to a team of specialists highly trained in various forms of therapeutic intervention. In the case of Mrs B, physiotherapists understandably had difficulty recommending discharge home alone for someone whose mobility was so precarious, just as her unsafe conduct in the kitchen particularly alarmed the occupational therapists. Nurses are bound to be uncomfortable in colluding with self-neglect even when this pleases the patient, and few doctors are famous for non-intervention. Superficially, the multi-disciplinary team might seem to be a conveniently available jury, but it is important to recognise that the consensus may be unduly weighted by professional concerns. A noisy ward meeting can resemble the top deck of an omnibus, but it is by no means certain that the destination is Clapham.[1] Citizen advocacy, when one person represents the rights and interests of another in a mutually agreed partnership, aims to balance the weight of professionals in decision-making by providing the vulnerable individual with an ally and an additional voice (Dunning 1995). Controversial aspects of advocacy include recruitment and training, and the tension between 'substituted judgement' and 'best interest' approaches. Whatever the future for citizen advocacy, clinicians should never consider themselves released from a duty to put the patient's best interests as far as possible above their professional loyalties and constraints.

Professional carers based in the community can also affect hospital admissions and discharges, both formally through their input to the rehabilitation team and informally through their reaction to problems or simply their availability.

Mrs E was a diabetic with obesity, osteoarthritis of the knees and hips, and slowly worsening cognitive impairment attributed to multiple small strokes. She was assessed in a Local Authority warden flat, her home for some years since the death of her husband. She had previously been able to walk a little and to transfer unaided from a chair onto a commode. She had managed with twice daily visits from a care assistant to get her up and put her to bed, and support from a neighbour who provided food and company. Worsening arthritis and the development of heart failure progressively reduced her contribution to these manoeuvres, and urinary incontinence supervened, partly attributable to her immobility. Her usual care assistant took sick-leave with back trouble, and a team of two was substituted but complained of increasing difficulty. At first, Mrs E refused hospital admission, making light of sitting in her own urine, which she regarded as a temporary problem, but eventually she gave consent.

Treatment for heart failure produced marginal improvement, but Mrs E remained largely immobile, requiring help in most activities of daily living, and continent only after she accepted urinary catheterisation. She would not consider alternatives to living in her home: any suggestion that practical problems might complicate her discharge produced an angry assertion that she would be able to manage. She was considered to be on the borderline of competence to assess these choices, and preparations for discharge were made. Care assistant posts were advertised by the local Social Services department. During the ensuing weeks, Mrs E increasingly spoke as though she thought she was already at home. She seemed content on the ward, surrounded by photographs of her husband and herself in stage-clothes, telling anecdotes of her career as a dancer. She remained highly immobile and dependent. Eventually, transfer to a nursing-home was suggested again and explained in detail. She accepted without protest, and a successful trial fortnight led to continuing care.

Mrs E demonstrates how multiple factors - in this case the severity of her disability, the unavailability of carers, and the passage of time - can shape decisions about hospital discharge to the point where there is hardly a decision left to take. It is possible that the delay in finding carers led to deterioration in Mrs E's mental state, with a degree of institutionalisation. A more positive interpretation is that her acceptance of the ward as home showed that institutional care was more acceptable in reality than in the abstract, a satisfactory outcome given the immense problems posed by supporting her at home.

The clinical setting

In Britain, 11 per cent of those aged 65 and over are admitted to non-psychiatric hospitals in any one year (Victor 1991). If paediatrics and obstetrics are excluded, patients aged 65 years and over account for 60 per cent of all hospital discharges. Some problems with the discharge of elderly people from hospital arise from care in clinical settings that are not well-tuned to their needs. In general hospitals, patients over 65 form the largest single patient group in most of the major specialities, such as general medicine (44 per cent), general surgery (32 per cent), ophthalmology (49 per cent) and orthopaedics (27 per cent) (Victor 1991). Units vary in the degree to which working practices are orientated towards assessment and management of the problems of frail elderly people. How many patients would benefit from the specialist approach described earlier is a matter of debate, with different opinions reflected in the wide variety of patterns of service provision in geriatric medicine (Grimley Evans 1992b), some of which concentrate elderly patients under specialist teams while others aim to ensure that all clinicians looking after old people develop appropriate expertise in an integrated service. The latter approach is perhaps best able to cope with the demand predicted by demographic changes. Models of care aimed at improving quality (including aspects of discharge) for specific patient groups are exemplified by Orthogeriatric Units, in which the care of people with hip fractures is shared between orthopaedic surgeons and geriatricians (Currie 1989).

Specialists naturally like to think that their attentions benefit patients, and geriatricians would lay claim to 'better' hospital discharges as a result of their methods. Evidence for this is beginning to accumulate. A systematic review of randomised controlled trials has shown that various forms of specialist geriatric intervention significantly improve the chances of a patient living at home rather than in institutional care at the time of follow-up (Stuck *et al* 1993). Similar outcomes have been demonstrated in a systematic review of randomised trials of specialist inpatient care for patients with acute stroke (Stroke Unit Trialists' Collaboration 1997), much of which in the UK is carried out by geriatricians.

Separation of health and social services

The 1990 NHS and Community Care Act brought about major changes in provision of health and social care in the UK, many of which have directly affected the discharge of elderly people from hospital. The act enshrined the principles of assessment and flexible provision of care according to individual needs, with involvement of patients and carers in the process. The range of services which health authorities must commission and fund has been detailed, as have key areas in which health authorities must collaborate with local government (especially social service departments) so as to avoid disputes about responsibility for provision (Department of Health 1995). Formal inspection of these new arrangements for hospital discharge and care management has recently revealed significant improvements, though much remains to be done (Horne 1998).

The establishment of a seamless service remains hampered by the contrast between NHS care, which is free of charge, and social service provision, sometimes including nursing home care, for which fees may be charged according to the individual's means. This results in a perverse incentive, pursued by occasional patients or their families, to continue with hospital care rather than be discharged. The Department of Health has attempted to clarify this situation, stating that when patients have been assessed as not requiring further NHS on-going inpatient care, they do not have the right to occupy indefinitely an NHS bed; they do, however, have the right to refuse to be discharged from NHS care into a nursing home or residential care home (Department of Health 1995). In such cases, the social services department is exhorted to work with all concerned to explore alternative options. If these are rejected, it may be necessary for the hospital, in consultation with the social services department, to implement discharge to the patient's home with a package of health care and social services, for which charges may be payable (by the patient). The consultant in clinical charge of the patient is designated as 'responsible, in consultation with other key staff working with (him), especially nurses, for deciding when a patient no longer needs acute care', and may thus be responsible for triggering awkward confrontations and a sequence that can result in a discharge home that neither doctor nor patient considers appropriate. At such times, an harmonious multi-disciplinary team and an effective working relationship with the local social services department are essential.

As yet, there is little evidence that the new internal market in health care in the UK, with competition between provider units, has resulted in fewer hospitals catering adequately for frail elderly patients who require careful rehabilitation and do not lend themselves to 'profitable' handling with short lengths of stay. In the USA, the introduction of a prospective payment scheme for hospital care led in some locations to decreased quality of care for elderly patients with hip fracture, suggesting that costs were trimmed by cutting rehabilitation. Compared with before the introduction of the scheme, patients were discharged from hospital earlier having received less physiotherapy, and achieved less recovery in terms of mobility; far more were discharged into institutional care and remained so one year later (Fitzgerald *et al* 1988).

Future problems with hospital discharge are likely to arise from the impact of demographic changes on available resources. A Royal Commission on long-term care for the elderly was due to report to ministers in December 1998, and its conclusions are awaited with interest and some trepidation.

This attempt to illustrate the complexity of issues surrounding the discharge from hospital of old people is not intended to provide excuses for clinicians who lose sight of ethical problems in the labyrinth. In this, as in many other enterprises in clinical medicine, skilful navigation is required with the patient's preferences as the guiding light. Empowering frail old people who wish to leave hospital requires clinicians to be liberal and permissive in the best sense of these much-abused words, to find practical ways of loosening constraints and giving vulnerable people the benefit of any doubt. Allowing patients to choose risk often involves risk to the professionals from complaints and scape-goating when things go wrong. The pressures towards defensive practice should be vigorously resisted. A good clinical service is one that has a small but definite incidence of discharges that go wrong: a paternalistic service that never risks sending a doubtful prospect home should only seem desirable to the uninformed.

References

Bennett, G. and Kingston, P. (1993), *Elder abuse: concepts, theories and interventions*, London, Chapman and Hall.

Centre for Policy on Ageing (1996), *A better home life: a code of good practice for residential and nursing home care*, London, Centre for Policy on Ageing.

Currie, C.T. (1989), 'Hip fractures in the elderly: beyond the metalwork', *British Medical Journal* vol. 298, pp.473-4.

Department of Health (1989), 'Discharge of patients from hospital', *HC* 89/5, London, Department of Health.

Department of Health (1994), *Hospital Discharge Workbook*, London, Department of Health.

Department of Health (1995), NHS responsibilities for meeting continuing health care needs, *HSG*(95)8, *LAC*(95)5, London, Department of Health.

Dunning, A. (1995), *Citizen advocacy with older people: a code of good practice*, London, Centre for Policy on Ageing.

Fitzgerald, J., Moore, P., and Dittus, R. (1988), 'The care of elderly patients with hip fracture: changes since implementation of the prospective payment system', *N Engl J Med*, vol. 319, pp.1392-1397.

Folstein, M.F., Folstein, S.E., and McHugh, P.R. (1975), 'Mini-Mental State. A practical method for grading the cognitive state of patients for the clinician', *Journal of Psychiatric Research*, vol. 12, pp.89-198.

Freer, C. (1988), 'Old myths: frequent misconceptions about the elderly', in Wells, N. and Freer, C. (eds.) *The ageing population: burden or challenge?*, Basingstoke, Macmillan.

Grimley Evans, J. (1992a), 'Towards an ethic of service provision', Journal of the Royal College of Physicians of London, vol. 26, pp.90-91.

Grimley Evans, J. (1992b), 'Hospital services for elderly people: the United Kingdom experience', in Grimley Evans, J., Williams, T.F. (eds.) *Oxford Textbook of Geriatric Medicine*, Oxford, Oxford University Press.

Horne, D. (1998), *Getting better? Inspection of hospital discharge (care management) arrangements for older people*, London, Department of Health.

Norman, A.J. (1980), *Rights and risk: a discussion document on civil liberty in old age*, London: Centre for Policy on Ageing.

Oppenheimer, C. (1991), 'Ethics and psychogeriatrics', in Bloch, S. and Chodoff, P. (eds.) Psychiatric Ethics, Oxford, Oxford University Press.

Rowlands, O. and Parker, G. (1998), *Informal Carers*. An independent study carried out by the Office for National Statistics on behalf of the Department of Health as part of the 1995

General Household Survey. London: The Stationery Office.

Salthouse, T.A. (1990), 'Cognitive competence and expertise in ageing', in Birren, J.E. and Schaie, K.W. (eds.) *Handbook of the psychology of ageing*, San Diego, Academic Press.

Stroke Unit Trialists' Collaboration (1997), 'Systematic review of randomised trials of organised inpatient (stroke unit) care after stroke', *British Medical Journal*, vol. 314, pp.1151-9.

Stuck, A.E., Siu, A.L., Wieland, G.D., Adams, J. and Rubinstein, L.Z. (1993), 'Comprehensive geriatric assessment: a meta-analysis of controlled trials', *Lancet*, vol. 342, pp.1032-6.

Victor, C.R. (1991), *Health and health care in later life*, Milton Keynes, Open University Press.

Wynne-Harley, D. (1991), *Living dangerously: risk-taking, safety and older people*, London, Centre for Policy on Ageing.

Note

1. Lord Bowen referred to 'the man on the Clapham omnibus' as an example of a reasonable man. Quoted by Collins (Master of the Rolls) in McQuire v Western Morning News Company (1903) 2 King's Bench Division 100,109.

5 A mental health perspective on ageing

JOE HERZBERG

Introduction

There is widespread acceptance of the principle that working with the elderly requires high quality skills. In recent years there has been a shift away from the traditional 'medical model' of health assessment in which the opinions of doctors predominate, to a model which provides for closer working across and between the various disciplines whose opinions and input are necessary for the formulation of 'care plans' designed for the benefit of any one individual. This concept of 'multi-disciplinary work' has been prevalent within mental health work for many years and is increasingly the norm in general medical and surgical specialties. Within medical specialties, the fields of Geriatric Medicine and Psychiatry have pioneered this approach. Clearly people are prone to increasing levels of physical and mental disability with increasing age, and physical and psychiatric illnesses may and often do coexist in an individual. Most health workers would agree that any elderly person admitted to hospital for treatment of physical or psychiatric illness, should have access to a health care team including doctors, nurses, occupational therapists, physiotherapists and social workers. In addition the skills of other professionals, eg. psychologists, speech therapists, dieticians, chiropodists and many others, may be required for the treatment and rehabilitation of an individual, depending on their particular disability and needs.

Traditionally the most physically or mentally disabled elderly people in society were cared for in National Health Service facilities. Very physically dependent patients would receive care in a 'long stay' geriatric medical ward, and typically, such patients would require high input nursing care geared towards assisting them with most activities of daily living. They would tend to be immobile or require close supervision of walking. They would also need help with the processes of feeding, elimination and all the various activities that most of us take for granted as being problem-free. Detailed discussion of the effects of physical illness in elderly people lies outside the scope of this chapter.

The elderly patients with severe mental illnesses who required long stay care fell into two main groups. There were those who had suffered from longstanding and often lifelong psychiatric illness and who had been considered in need of permanent institutional care. Individuals in this group suffered from schizophrenia, treatment resistant depressive illnesses, or longstanding brain damage. The second group of elderly patients who required care were those who developed devastating mental illnesses in their senium, typically those suffering from dementia. The effects of this group of illnesses on intellectual functioning will be described later, but suffice it to say here that those individuals most handicapped by dementia, and particularly those whose illnesses led to major problems with their behaviour, such as aggression, would generally receive care in a long stay 'psychogeriatric' ward in a large mental hospital. In order that the reader appreciates the setting in which the mental health services operate today, it is necessary to briefly consider the changes in the treatment of mental illness and the provision of health care services which have occurred over the last two hundred years.

Until the nineteenth century the care of the mentally ill in society had been a largely haphazard affair with the provision and quality of care being related to a family's ability to pay for private facilities. There were very few specialised facilities for the care of the mentally ill. I use the term 'care' deliberately because no effective treatments were available for any of the major mental disorders. Custodial care removed the 'mad' from society. Wealthy patients might receive care at home or in a private madhouse. By the eighteenth century some cities and large towns had established hospitals for the insane. However may 'Pauper Lunatics' were consigned to prisons, workhouses and houses of correction.

Theories about the causation of mental illness abounded and 'treatments' were often similar to those used for physical illness, eg. bleeding, purging, induced vomiting, etc. All had their place in the therapeutic armentarium. Various ineffective medicaments such as camphor and magnesia were tried, as were the use of cold showers or baths designed to induce sanity. Mechanical restraint, now considered cruel, was perhaps the keystone of physical treatment for disturbed patients.

In 1808 an Asylums Act was passed to ensure that each county provided its own asylum for the reception of the mentally ill poor; this was the first attempt to provide a comprehensive system of 'catchment area' care, ie. to ensure that people requiring a service had access to a designated facility where this could be received; and this concept remains in existence in today's psychiatric services. By the mid nineteenth century a proliferation of large country asylums had occurred, many of which are still with us today. These asylums were generally large institutions set in country locations and were often overcrowded, with 'incurable' cases continually being admitted. They provided for patients' basic physical needs but effective treatments were still not available and few patients recovered. However, conditions had improved by the end of the century, following a movement to abolish restraint of the mentally ill, led by Robert Gardiner Hill at Lincoln and John Connolly at Hanwell Asylum.

During the first part of this century may attempts were made to develop effective treatments for the major mental illnesses. There were attempts to use operative treatment, eg. 'the leucotomy' for schizophrenia, and those initial crude operations became the forerunners for modern steriotactic surgical techniques, which are now rarely required, but which can still prove helpful in the most severe cases of intractable depression and obsessive-compulsive illness. In the 1930s attempts were made to treat severe schizophrenia with insulin shock treatment and at around the same time the therapeutic potential of induced convulsions or fits was being explored. Whilst initially advocated as a treatment for schizophrenia, the use of electroconvulsive therapy (ECT) was soon found to be effective in the treatment of severe depression and its use became widespread after the second world war. This was the first really effective cure for severe depression, and in a modified form, given under general anaesthetic, remains a useful treatment for some seriously ill people. 'Malaria therapy' and other methods of inducing temperatures were used to treat syphilis until penicillin became commercially available in the 1940s, although penicillin had been initially discovered by Fleming in 1928. The use of this drug reduced the number of cases of mental and physical deterioration due to the effects of syphilis on the brain (neurosyphilis or tertiary syphilis). Such individuals would have previously spent many years of their lives in the long stay wards of large mental hospitals.

So, to repeat, there were no effective treatments for the most serious mental illnesses until the time around the second world war when electroconvulsive therapy was introduced, initially as a treatment for schizophrenia. However, it was soon noted to be more effective in people suffering from severe depression, which had hitherto been untreatable. In the 1950s the 'major tranquillisers' or 'neuroleptic' drugs were developed, as treatment for schizophrenia and mania, and also at this time antidepressant drugs first came into use. The effect of the development of ECT, antidepressants and major tranquillisers was a wide spread optimism that devastating mental illness had at last been conquered, and health planners were hopeful that the large mental hospitals would be emptied and closed. This move towards closing large mental hospitals was also fuelled by several scandals about the standards of psychiatric institutional care in the 1960s. However a proportion of patients remained treatment-resistant and continued to suffer the devastating effects of longstanding illness on their personality, coupled in many cases with the addictive effects of institutionalisation.

Coupled with the advances in treatment were changes in legislation altering the climate in which mental illness was treated. The emphasis was shifted from custodial care to the importance of prevention and treatment. This was enshrined in the 1930 Mental Treatment Act. The concept of 'voluntary' rather than enforced treatment was formulated and outpatient treatment and the formation of 'observation' or assessment wards encouraged. The Beveridge report was presented to Parliament in 1942 and underpinned the subsequent formation of the National Health Service. It was a plan for social insurance providing medical care and the payment of family allowances and old age pensions. The emergence of Social Service Departments with responsibilities for social welfare and care provision and their interaction with health care services has provided a template for the assessment of needs and provision of services for elderly people and their families. The range of services provided will be discussed further in due course.

In 1959 a new Mental Health Act introduced important new safeguards for those mentally ill patients who required compulsory treatment, safeguards extended and refined in the subsequent 1983 revision of the act. There has been a widespread evolution of psychiatric assessment units incorporated into district general hospitals with a parallel closure of many large mental hospital beds and an increasing focus on community treatment and community care. These moves towards the treatment of psychiatric illness in local facilities rather than distant large institutions have helped to remove some of the stigma associated with major mental illness, although much remains to be done in this area. However the rundown of large hospital beds has not been supplemented with the necessary increase in local community based health and social service resources for elderly people. The last decade has witnessed a burgeoning of private facilities for the care of the elderly, as the availability of hospital beds and old peoples homes places provided by the public sectors have declined, in the face of a rapidly increasing elderly population.

In the post war years Britain has had a relatively low rate of economic growth compared with other industrial countries and this has led to problems of unemployment and inflation. In general, national insurance benefits have failed to keep up with inflation. Beveridge had intended 'supplementary benefits' to be a fail safe mechanism for the poorest people in society, but they have been administratively difficult to claim and have had a relatively low take up rate. In the 1990s, the elderly have remained one of the major poverty groups in this country.

Services for the elderly

Traditionally, specialised services for the elderly mentally ill were provided by the National Health Service and Social Services Departments and these agencies still provide the bulk of specialised services. However, the 1980s and 1990s have witnessed an increasing contribution by the private sector and by voluntary agencies. In addition, the rundown of large mental hospitals with the increasing shift to community care has meant that many elderly mentally ill people now receive the generic support services available to elderly people in the community, in addition to more specialised services.

The range and quality of services available to support elderly people in their own homes vary tremendously from area to area and reflect the commitment of the local elected councils to the elderly. The elderly do not unfortunately enjoy the statutory protection which social services provide for children, eg. the need to maintain 'at risk' registers; and services for elderly people are particularly vulnerable in a difficult financial climate, and have often been adversely affected in areas which have been 'rate capped' by central government. It has recently come to the author's attention that social services departments have a statutory duty to provide immediate assistance to an animal considered at risk, but elderly humans may not enjoy the same degree of protection! It has also become increasingly clear in recent years that elderly people and others in society who require resources and protection often have these resources cut in an unseemly battle for funding between elected local government officials who hold one set of priorities and central government officials who hold another. Services for the elderly and other vulnerable groups are sometimes used as pawns in this deadly 'game'. Despite these problems, the United Kingdom has developed one of the most comprehensive networks of state provided services in existence. In all areas of the country known to the author, the 'meals on wheels' service can bring a hot, or at least lukewarm, daily midday meal to a person unable to cook for themselves through mental or physical disability. A comprehensive network of home helps can assist elderly people with shopping and housework. They will often prepare light snacks or meals, collect pensions and prescriptions and befriend elderly isolated people. Social services departments may also provide specialised 'incontinence laundry services' and 'bathing attendants' to help with washing and bathing, although in some areas district nurses help with this latter function.

The health service too provides a range of professionals to assist elderly people in the community, in addition to the range of services offered through the general practitioner and local hospital services. District nurses, who are often attached to general practices, provide assistance with physical welfare, specialised dressings, and administration of medicine when people are likely to forget to take prescribed medicines, to their detriment. The district nurses may also have close working links with hospital departments of geriatric medicine. Community psychiatric nurses provide similar assessment of and support for elderly people with mental disorders, and generally have close links with specialised psychiatric services for the elderly 'psychogeriatric services'. In addition, many other professionals may visit and support elderly people in their own homes, including physiotherapists and occupational therapists. This latter profession, often employed by health or social services departments, can provide advice on a range of aids and appliances to help to compensate for a person's deficits in physical and/or mental function, and may thus help to ensure safety in the home. In some areas 'day or night sitters' are available to enable the carers of elderly people requiring constant supervision to have a break. In addition, social services departments run a range of 'day centres' which provide a 'club-like' atmosphere and which help to reduce the social isolation experienced by so many elderly people. Luncheon clubs serve a similar purpose. In addition, many local authorities and voluntary agencies such as Age Concern and the Alzheimer's Disease Society have developed specialised day centres for the elderly mentally ill and in particular for those suffering from one of the forms of dementia. Some of the features of this group of illnesses will be described in due course.

Elderly people who are unable to live safely at home either independently or with the range of support services available in their locality have further options open to them. Sheltered housing units are run by the housing departments of local authorities, housing associations or private organisations. These are generally purpose-built blocks of flats in which individuals have their own flat with their own front door. As a minimum, these usually comprise a living room, bedroom, bathroom and kitchenette. A warden is generally in attendance and pays a daily visit to each resident to check assistance in an emergency, and all the community services can visit if required. Thus within this setting an elderly person can enjoy a high degree of autonomy in a supervised setting. In some units, communal areas are available for activities or clubs. Recent financial constraints have caused some local authorities to withdraw the resident warden service and replace this with a radio alarm system. This has meant that some elderly people, with a poor memory as a result of suffering from dementia, are unable to sustain a safe existence in such units as they cannot remember how to use the night call alarm systems. There are an increasing number of private sheltered housing units being developed for those with the means to buy into such accommodation.

Various forms of residential care are available for those people who require 24-hour supervision but not nursing care. Traditionally these residential or Part 3 homes were run by social service departments, but an increasing number of privately run homes are now appearing. Indeed, there has been a massive reduction in the number of new publicly funded sheltered flats and residential home constructions in the last 10 years in the face of our growing elderly population. Social services Part 3 homes were originally for elderly people, but, as a result of the gradual reduction in hospital beds, they now cater for an increasingly physically and mentally ill clientele. Elderly people in residential care tend to have less privacy and autonomy than those in their own homes and generally just have a bedroom of their own, with all other facilities being communally shared. All meals and laundry services are provided and necessary medicines are administered by a 'matron' who usually has a nursing qualification. Care tasks are usually carried out by unqualified care assistants. The homes are in effect mini-institutions and these days significant proportions of the residents suffer from depression or dementia. Generally residents are accepted if they are mobile, faecally continent, able to wash and dress with minimal supervision and do not exhibit severe behavioural disturbance. The public sector residential homes have a good record of continuing to try to provide care for their residents who deteriorate physically or mentally after they are admitted. The milieux in these homes vary between the good homes which have a range of activities and which encourage maximum independence in their residents, perhaps at the expense of some slight risks, to those where elderly residents just sit forlornly in a large unsociable circle around the perimeter of a sitting room, staring blankly at a budgerigar or television, and where no attempt is made by the staff to interest or motivate the residents.

Some elderly people are so physically or mentally disabled that they require 24-hour nursing care. In the past, long stay geriatric medical wards provided most of the care places for elderly people with extreme physical disabilities and such patients were typically immobile, incontinent and in need of assistance with most basic aspects of daily living such as feeding, washing, dressing, and elimination. Psychiatrically dependent elderly people, typically mobile but suffering from severe dementia with associated severe behavioural problems, would receive care on a long stay psychogeriatric ward. Both these sorts of accommodation were and often are rather bleak, with poor patient-to-staff ratios and little staff time available to attend to anything other than basic care needs, though there have been recent moves to set up NHS nursing homes where a more personalised style of care can be given.

The alternative to long stay NHS care is care within the private sector; and the last 10 years have seen a rapid increase in the number of private nursing home places available. This increase has occurred because the decreasing number of publicly funded places has created a market; and coupled with this the State has paid benefits to needy families in order that such care can be provided. The care available within the private sector is, again, of variable quality, but much of the care given is of a good standard. A series of inspections of all registered private nursing home by Health Authorities is supposed to guarantee a reasonable standard of care. However, this system has its flaws, and scandals still occur with monotonous and depressing regularity. Our increasing reliance on the private sector has lead to some heartbreaking situations for families who have to arrange nursing home care for a relative and who are financially reliant on the state benefits system. Generally if a client requires a significant amount of nursing care then a very well staffed home is likely to be required for those who live in areas where there is insufficient hospital provision and such homes obviously charge higher fees than those employing fewer staff. Private nursing homes, whilst offering care, are generally run as businesses and are expected to make a profit for their owners. It is clearly more expensive to purchase a large property suitable for use as a home in a city than in a rural area or a coastal town. The purchase costs of the property are reflected in the fees charged; and many families who live in Inner City areas find that the state benefit will only cover a nursing home place on the coast. Thus elderly ill people who require nursing care may often only receive this care at the expense of being dislocated from their families. Their close relatives, who may be elderly and frail themselves, will find it difficult or too expensive to visit them regularly. The introduction of the purchaser/provider split in the Health Service and ring-fenced community care budgets in Social Services have both heightened these tensions and made them more explicit.

Mental illness in the elderly

The elderly can develop the range of mental illnesses seen in younger people, eg. anxiety, phobias, depression, mania and paranoid states, and indeed some people with a history of severe mental illness will carry their illnesses with them into old age. In addition they are particularly prone to illnesses that are known as 'organic mental disorders'. These organic mental disorders are caused by changes in brain function and sometimes brain structure. The best known of these organic disorders is 'Dementia', which will be described subsequently; another example is 'Delirium', also called 'acute confusional state', which may accompany severe physical illness in the elderly. The commonest serious mental disorders arising in old age are depression and dementia and involvement with these conditions accounts for approximately three quarters of the work of most specialised mental health services for the elderly. It is with the dementias, those often devastating illnesses, that ethical problems most often arise around the provision of care and these issues often interweave with problems of resource provision. The following will serve as a brief introduction to some of these conditions but is by no means a comprehensive guide; for further information the reader is advised to consult more specialised texts cited below. Fictitious case histories have been constructed to demonstrate a variety of problems which may be encountered in clinical practice. The case examples used are those of patients who require hospitalisation and therefore represent the extreme end of the spectrum of disability rather than typical community cases.

Dementia

This is not one illness but a general term for a group of conditions which, whilst most common in the elderly, can in fact occur in middle-aged or younger people. These conditions are characterised by a global loss of higher intellectual function. The core deficit is usually that of memory but other areas of intellect and personality are generally adversely affected. These include language, arithmetical ability, thought processes, visio-spatial function and emotional control. There is an increasing prevalence of dementia with increasing age. It was previously thought that the prevalence was about 10 per cent for people between the ages of 65 - 75 and about 20 per cent for those over 75. However more recent studies have thrown some doubt on these original findings and the true community rates are probably about a half of the figures quoted above. It can be seen therefore that dementia is not an inevitable consequence of ageing.

There are many types of dementia in the elderly, but 'Senile Dementia of the Alzheimer Type' (Alzheimer's disease) accounts for three quarters of all cases. In Alzheimer's disease there is a gradual loss or death of nerve cells across the entire surface of the brain which will not be described here. The effect of these changes however is to produce a brain that is uniformly shrunken. Most other dementias are caused by disease damaging the blood vessels in the brain (cerebral vessels), leading to a series of cerebro-vascular accidents or 'strokes'. Dementia which is caused in this way is not surprisingly called 'cerebrovascular dementia' or 'atherosclerotic dementia' (atherosclerosis is a process of 'furring up' of blood vessels) or 'multi-infarct' dementia. When a person suffers a 'stroke', a blood vessel in the brain becomes clogged up, leading to the death of brain cells which are usually supplied with oxygen by that blood vessel. This process is called 'infarction'. Thus the term 'multi infarct' dementia is used. The processes causing stroke may be changes seen in Alzheimer's disease. There are many other causes of dementia, some of which are reversible or at least can be halted. However the majority of cases are irreversible, as, unlike other tissues in the body, the nerve cells in the brain, once damaged , do not have the capacity to regenerate or regrow. Whilst Alzheimer's disease is generally an illness in which the mental changes arise gradually, the reader may now understand that when dementia is caused by disease of the cerebral blood vessels, the psychological changes will be determined by the extent of the damage caused and the location of the damage within the brain. However, typically in multi-infarct dementia the person's intellectual abilities decrease after each episode; and if an individual suffers a series of small or large strokes, they may deteriorate 'step by step' after each one. It is therefore difficult to describe the clinical features of a 'classic case' of dementia as the mental changes show great variability in their order of onset and severity. However, some of the features of dementia outlined below will be present, and it should be noted that these features may occur irrespective of the underlying cause of the dementing illness.

Often the major clue that a relative is dementing is when the family notices that person's memory seems impaired. Unfortunately, this clue may not be picked up for some time, as there is often the expectation that even severe memory impairment is a consequence of a normal ageing process. Sufferers appear 'absent minded' or 'forgetful' and may take to keeping lists of things which they must do. However as memory impairment becomes more severe the signs that something is wrong become clearer. Individuals may become disorientated within their environment, the gas or cooker may be left on unsafely, saucepans may be burnt out, and there may be other evidence of lack of attention to personal safety and neglect of risk factors within the home. Shopping trips may result in a mass of inappropriate foods and other items being purchased and often the same items are bought again and again as the person forgets that they have already been obtained. There is also a progressive deterioration in the ability to handle money appropriately, eg. working out the correct change which should be received. Poor memory may often lead to a dementia sufferer accusing people of stealing their possessions. They tend to put objects like keys or wallets down and then forget where they have placed them. Anyone who happens to be around whilst the person is looking for these valued possessions is liable to be accused of stealing them. This is because in dementia there is not only a poor short-term memory but also there is a diminished ability to think and reason logically. Life is often lived in the 'here and now'. Therefore whoever is around at the time may be the only person that the suffer can bring to mind and their presence therefore acts as a trigger for the accusation. Devoted carers who spend a lot of time with their ill relatives are, sadly, particularly likely to be subject to such accusations, as they are often the only source of social contact the dementing person has; and such accusations often add to the burden of providing care. It is particularly poignant for carers when their ill relative cannot remember their name or who they are. Disorientation may be evidenced by wandering and failing to find the way home. Incontinence may occur due to various types of physical illness. However, it may also occur due to a failure to find the way to the lavatory or a lack of recognition of bodily signals suggesting that defecation or urination are necessary. A gradual coarsening of personality may occur, with an increased egocentricity, coupled with a lack of awareness of social niceties and failure to recognise the inappropriateness or bizarreness of their own appearance or behaviour. Emotional control may be lost, with rapid switching of mood states, eg. from happy to tearful and back again in the space of a short period of time, often without any clear reason for the alteration in mood. There may be deterioration in the ability to use and comprehend language to its pervious level causing frank difficulties in communication. Suspiciousness and perplexity may occur as the demented person finds it difficult to understand what is happening to them and around them and this coupled with lack of emotional control may lead to episodes of unwarranted verbal and/or physical aggression. Ultimately there may be a total lack of ability to carry out those basic aspects of life necessary for independent survival, as outlined in the beginning of this chapter, and the person may become totally reliant on others for help with all aspects of dressing, feeding, elimination, etc.

Case 1

A GP requested advice on a housebound exasperated man in his 70s who had taken to shouting at and hitting his wife, Mrs B, as she was not doing the shopping correctly and he did not understand the reason for this. The house was filled with pounds and pounds of sweets, a small mountain of cat litter, about 80 tins of cat food and about 2 cubic feet of bags of assorted spices. Essentials like bread, eggs and milk were however purchased on a more haphazard basis. In addition, the wife had been speaking in a peculiar and childlike way, adding the sound 'eeee' to many words, resulting in the phrases like 'I'm going shoppingeeee', 'put the kettle onseeee' etc. The husband, always a rather prickly character, felt driven way beyond his level of tolerance and had contacted his GP to have his wife 'taken away'. The psychiatrist duly arrived with the mental health social worker and the GP to make an assessment. After obtaining the history and examining the lady it was abundantly clear that Mrs B was dementing and had an extremely poor short term memory, which explained the unusual collection of shopping in the flat. She was emotionally disinhibited and wanted to hug the social worker and the psychiatrist even though she did not know them. Her language function had deteriorated markedly and she was unable to name simple everyday objects. She was physically well and a battery of blood tests recently carried out by the GP had been normal. The history suggested that this lady had probably been dementing for a year to 18 months. The husband had put up with his wife's increasingly eccentric behaviour without understanding the reason for it until a few weeks before the visit, when he had starting slapping her in exasperation.

It was clear that Mrs B could not stay at home if the situation remained unchanged, as her behaviour, coupled with the husband's reaction to it, put her at risk of harm. At the same time it was also clear that Mrs B wished to stay in her own home and was blissfully unaware of the chaos she was causing. It would have been possible to section or commit this lady to hospital against her will, but what would have been the outcome? Her condition was almost certainly incurable and her husband would have definitely refused to have her back at home. She would have to go into institutional care, against her will. In the event, it was decided to try to adopt a different strategy. The nature of Mrs B's illness was explained to the husband.

In particular he was told that her poor memory, eccentricity and peculiar language were all due to dementia. He immediately became tearful and remorseful as he understood the situation, and asked for help. The social services agreed to send him a home help to go shopping with the wife. Meals on wheels were also offered but the husband said that he would prefer to do his own cooking. An offer was made to provide a telephone to decrease his isolation and social services agreed to try and provide a day centre for Mrs B to give her husband some respite. The mental health community team would visit to give Mr B further chances to ask questions and receive practical advice about his wife's management. Health and social services agreed to monitor the situation at home until it was that clear that it was stable. In this way an unnecessary admission, which would almost certainly have resulted in this couple being permanently separated and the lady losing her home, was avoided, albeit at the slight risk of potential further abuse. However, the situation had been radically altered by the husband developing an understanding of his wife's condition and the reason for her odd behaviour and it was felt the situation, whilst needing monitoring, was safe. In this way it was possible to address the needs of both partners. If an explanation had failed to alter the husband's understanding of the situation and/or he had refused offers of help, then there would have been no alternative but to remove the lady from her home and make other arrangements for her accommodation and care.

Case 2

A 76-year-old man, Mr K, was referred by his GP, as his wife was concerned about his memory loss over the previous six months. Mr K had not noticed any changes in his memory but his wife reported that he had seemed rather more worried about minor household matters recently. Mrs K had realised that something was definitely wrong when she started speaking about a recent wedding to Mr K and she realised that he did not recall it at all. On examination of Mr K's mental state, it was clear that Mr K was in the early stages of a dementing illness. He was disorientated regarding the month and the day although he could recall his name and address. He was given a five-item address to learn and completed this task successfully, but after five minutes could not remember any of the items and could not recall being given an address to learn. When asked questions to which he did not know the answers, he tended to try and compensate for his memory gaps by giving irrelevant information, a process called 'confabulation' which commonly occurs in people with memory deficits. Physical examination and a battery of blood tests did not reveal any treatable cause for Mr K's problems. Mr K had always been a physically active man, who had always enjoyed travelling around the city, visiting historical monuments. Over the next few months, on several occasions, Mr K failed to find his way home and the police eventually brought him home. When his wife attempted to persuade him not to go out he became upset, and on occasion verbally aggressive. Matters came to a head when Mr K wandered forty miles from home and was found walking along a dual carriageway. His wife finally agreed to allow referral to social services for day care at a specialised day centre. This was tried for 2 months, unsuccessfully, as Mr K was insistent on leaving the day centre and the staff felt that they were keeping him inside against his will illegally. However, they were aware that if they allowed him out without supervision, he might wander and be at risk. Reluctantly, the staff terminated his day centre placement, leaving his wife without respite. Mr K became increasingly difficult to manage at home as his behaviour became more and more aggressive. He was ultimately admitted to hospital and from there to an NHS nursing home in close proximity. This was possible because Mr K's ultimate level of disturbance would not have been tolerated by a private nursing home and therefore the only placement possible was NHS care. Had Mr K been less behaviourally disturbed, however, then it would have been necessary to seek a private nursing home placement, as the all too few NHS long stay beds have to be reserved for those whose needs cannot be met elsewhere. As the couple had no private means, they would have been dependent on state benefits to pay for a nursing home placement and inevitably, with the high costs of property around London and therefore high nursing home fees in the city, Mr K would have probably had to be placed in a home 50-100 miles away from his wife, thus splitting up a couple who were devoted to each other! Thankfully in this case, such a split did not occur, although in many other cases there is no alternative, given the relative dearth of long stay hospital or NHS nursing home places.

Delirium

This condition is often termed 'Acute Confusional State' and is a sudden deterioration in mental function caused by general illness. Any illness may precipitate a delirium and elderly people are particularly prone to becoming delirious when physically ill, although younger people may also become delirious if they are seriously unwell. Some examples of illnesses which may precipitate delirium in elderly people are check and urinary infections, heart failure, strokes, poor control of diabetes and many others. Mentally, the patient deteriorates rapidly over a short period of time, typically a few hours or a few days. The hallmark of delirium is a reduced or fluctuating level of consciousness, generally manifesting itself as tiredness and then drowsiness. The person becomes increasingly disorientated and may appear frightened, perplexed, or emotionally labile, often finding it difficult to understand what is happening to him and what is happening in his environment. This may lead to suspicion, and frank paranoia. Hallucinations may occur in any sensory modality but commonly the sufferer will experience visual hallucinations - 'seeing things' - which may be extremely frightening. The treatment of this condition is the treatment of the underlying physical illness; and delirious people require admission to an appropriate physical (and not psychiatric) unit for this purpose.

Case 3

The psychiatrist was called to see a 78-year-old lady, Mrs J. Although she was previously independent, she had been living with her son for 4 days prior to the visit. She had endured a difficult year, having fallen and fractured her hip at the beginning of the year, which required an orthopaedic operation. Three months prior to the referral she had become caught in the doors of an underground train, subsequently falling to the ground when released. This required yet another operation. Despite these two setbacks, Mrs J had rehabilitated well and for the previous month had been living independently in her own flat, walking stably with a walk frame. There was no history of mental confusion. In the preceding week her son noticed that Mrs J had become mildly confused and seemed suspicious that neighbours were going to break into her flat. Mrs J's GP examined her fully but could not find any sign of medical illness. The family grew increasingly worried about their mother and moved her in to live with them. When seen, she was only mildly disorientated but appeared labile in mood. Her family informed the psychiatrist that she had been talking to people who were not present and that she had been seeing objects on the floor which were not present. She was clearly short of breath, and on physical examination she was in heart failure and had an underlying abnormality of heart rate and rhythm.

81

Admission to the local medical unit was arranged. Her son was relieved that his mother was not dementing and was reassured that if his mother made a full physical recovery, her mental state would be likely to return to normal.

Depression

This is a common condition in elderly people and community surveys suggest that its prevalence is around 15 per cent. Whilst all of us are prone to feeling depressed when faced with adverse events, the type of depression presenting to mental health workers is generally more severe that this, and may indeed be a life-threatening illness. It may or may not be triggered by an understandably depressing event happening in the person's life; but where an adverse event has occurred, the degree of depression is greater than would be usually expected. Typically the depressed person feels intensely miserable and this depressed feeling becomes the predominant mood. Sometimes the mood lightens towards the end of the day but often the misery is unremitting. Accompanying these feelings of depression are poor sleep, often as little as 3-4 hours a night, with typical waking in the early hours of the morning. This poor sleep adds to the general feelings of lassitude and lack of energy caused by the depression. Appetite is often reduced and depressed people often feel they have to force themselves to eat. Weight loss is generally marked and can lead to complete emaciation if the illness is untreated. Concentration is reduced and severe depression is often accompanied by slower mental processing. Depressed people may take a long time to reply to a question for this reason. Pastimes and hobbies may be given up completely and a depressed person may just sit at home, doing nothing, neglecting themselves and neglecting their surroundings. Sometimes the depression is accompanied by gross agitation where the person feels so wretched that they just cannot sit still and they pace about incessantly, often wringing their hands. Sometimes depressed people develop feelings of guilt which have no basis in fact and inevitably they take an overpessimistic view of themselves and the world. Occasionally the depression may be so severe that they develop frank delusions, which are false beliefs which have no basis in fact. They may believe that they are responsible for the ills of the world, or that they deserve to be put into prison or die. They sometimes believe that they are terminally ill, often with cancer, when there is no evidence to support this. Occasionally people feel so wretched that they attempt to take or successfully do take their own lives.

Severely depressed people may develop hallucinations, typically voices which tell them how wicked they are and which generally disparage them.

Fortunately, depression in the elderly is usually amenable to treatment and most mildly depressed people can be successfully treated at home using one of a variety of antidepressant drugs now available. The antidepressants work by increasing the levels of transmitter chemicals released from nerve cells in the brain, levels which are known to be lowered in people suffering from depression. If the depression is of life-threatening severity or the sufferer is unable to cope safely at home then hospital treatment may be required. Many severely depressed people will improve on antidepressant medicine alone and most of those few who do not respond to drugs will respond to ECT (electrical treatment) which in certain cases can literally be life saving. In these days it is generally used when other treatments have failed or when the person's life is threatened by the illness. The treatment is given under general anaesthetic and can be safely given to most elderly people who require it. Most elderly people with depression respond to treatment but a significant proportion are liable to have repeated episodes throughout their life and the outcome is generally held to be less favourable than in younger patients, particularly if there is evidence of vascular or stroke disease in the brain.

Case 4

Mr W, a widower in his early 70s, was admitted to hospital after unsuccessfully trying to take his own life. He had a long history of depression from his early 20s, with four previous admissions, usually treated with ETC. There was a strong history of mental illness in the family; Mr W's father had been an alcoholic, and his sister had suffered depression and had killed herself. He was happily married from his early 20s until 15 years previously when his wife had died from cancer. He had little contact with his two children who were both married and who lived many miles away. His depression had always responded to treatment and he had a good work record, having retired seven years previously. He had been well for the four years prior to his admission.

Mr W had gradually become depressed again over a period of three months. His mood was worse in the mornings. His appetite was reduced and he had lost two stone in weight. His concentration was poor, his energy levels reduced and he had given up going out and reading books and watching TV, his previous hobbies. Approximately one month prior to admission to hospital he had started thinking about suicide and gradually his suicidal thoughts became more intense.

In the week of admission he had tried to stab himself in the neck with a kitchen knife and on the day of admission he had tried to strangle himself and when this was unsuccessful he then cut his leg with a knife. He eventually presented to the casualty department from which he was admitted to hospital. On the ward he appeared depressed and agitated and was preoccupied with the fact that he had once wet the bed when he was in the navy as a young man. He believed that because of this, he was a bad person and had let everyone down. He felt that he deserved to die as a punishment for his past deeds and had therefore tried to take his own life. Physical examination and all blood tests were normal. He settled quickly on the ward and antidepressant drugs were started. However after one month's treatment there had been no improvement and he agreed to a course of ETC. He improved rapidly with this treatment and was discharged home after an admission of 10 weeks.

Case 5

A 72-year-old married woman, Mrs L, was admitted with a three months history of increasing depression accompanied by poor appetite and sleep, poor concentration and low energy levels. The reason for her depression was clear cut. Her relationship with her husband had always been poor, as he was, and always had been, a bad tempered man. However, she had become adjusted to this from early in their marriage and had decided to put up with her 'lot in life'. In recent years she had become increasingly incapacitated by arthritis and was relatively housebound, being reliant on transport to take her to a day centre once a week. Apart from this outing she could only move around her home slowly with a walking stick. Only one of her four sons lived near enough to visit occasionally (50 miles away) and he visited his mother every three or four weeks. Mrs L was a sociable woman who was keen to have friends in the house, but Mr L, an unsociable character, refused to allow visitors, social workers or home helps to enter their home. Mrs L's arthritis became progressively worse, to the extent that she was no longer able to pursue her favourite hobby, knitting. At the same time Mr L became increasingly aggressive to his wife and in addition to losing his temper and being verbally abusive, which he had been for many years when angry, he hit his wife on several occasions and on one occasion knocked her to the floor. It was not surprising therefore that she presented with depression in the face of such adversity.

Mrs L was admitted to hospital. She was initially assessed without medicines being given to see if her mood, sleep and appetite improved in less stressful surroundings. It was clear two weeks after admission that Mrs L remained significantly depressed; so an antidepressant drug was started, and by a month later Mrs L was sleeping and eating well and had good concentration and energy. She was much less depressed, though understandably worried about the future with her husband. She was given the opportunity to discuss matters extensively with one of the ward nursing staff and a social worker. The ward team were of the opinion that Mrs L should consider leaving her husband and, in view of her disability, moving into a residential home. After detailed consideration Mrs L decided not to accept this advice. The ward team could certainly not enforce their views on Mrs L, and she was discharged after an eight week admission. The hospital team and social services tried to provide the best supervision with their resources after her discharge. She was visited by a community psychiatric nurse once a week, and a social worker also visited her at home twice a week. Mrs L and her son had been informed of the social services' willingness to admit her to a residential home immediately if her husband again became violent, and they were given emergency telephone numbers to contact if necessary. Four weeks after her discharge, Mr L again started hitting his wife. She requested a transfer to a residential home and this was accomplished immediately. Whilst she was initially ambivalent about leaving her home, when seen one month later she was cheerful and had no regrets about the decision that she had taken.

Paranoid states

Paranoid states can arise *de nova* in the elderly or may be the continuation of a life long psychiatric illness persisting into old age, such as schizophrenia. Where these illnesses occur for the first time in the elderly, they are found more commonly in those individuals who suffer from sensory deficits. It is possible to understand that a person who suffers from a sensory deficit such as deafness or blindness may find it more difficult to make sense of the world around him and may therefore be increasingly prone to a degree of paranoia anyway. Occasionally this becomes extreme and manifests itself as a frank illness. There is also an association between alcohol abuse and the development of paranoid states in elderly and younger individuals. In addition these illnesses are associated with a degree of structural change within the brain. The illnesses may take several forms but are often labelled as Paraphrenia or Paranoid Schizophrenia. Sufferers are generally reclusive individuals who isolated themselves from families and neighbours. They are often floridly deluded, with ideas that people are trying to harm them or spying on them without any evidence to support these claims. They often misinterpret events in their environment as evidence for their beliefs. They may hallucinate, commonly hearing voices which threaten them. They are generally reluctant to receive treatment and often only get admitted to hospital when in a state of extreme self neglect. These illnesses respond variably to treatment. Some patients lose their hallucinations and/or delusions with major tranquilliser drugs but others prove resistant to treatment. Such illnesses are relatively infrequent, accounting for 5-10 per cent of referrals to most psychiatric services for the elderly.

Case 6

An 81-year-old widow, Mrs N, was admitted to hospital from home complaining that people were trying to harm her. She had first come to the attention of the social services eight years previously, when she persistently complained to the council that her flat was infested. She believed she had fleas in her flat and was insistent that there were 'flea droppings' on her floor. The council officer removed several samples of these 'droppings', which were found on analysis to be shreds of tobacco However, despite evidence that there was no infestation present, this lady insisted on being rehoused. Although she no longer complained of flea droppings in her new flat she came to the attention of the mental health services because of her paranoia towards her neighbours. She had been admitted to hospital as a voluntary patient four times in the previous three years and her paranoid beliefs would disappear on treatment with low doses of major tranquilliser drugs. Inevitably she would then refuse to take medication after a few months and her symptoms would return. In the week before admission she became extremely frightened. She experienced auditory hallucinations in the form of voices which she believed were those of her neighbours shouting through the letter box. These voices told her that she would be murdered. So convinced was she that her life was in imminent danger that she went round to the local police station to seek their help. Her neighbours were elderly people like herself, who clearly had not been shouting though Mrs N's letter box and who had no knowledge of any disturbance in the vicinity of Mrs N's flat. Mrs N was only too willing to come into hospital to escape from the perceived threats and her symptoms disappeared rapidly over a period of a month. She refused offers to reduce her isolation and provide support by arranging attendance at a day centre. After a successful trial leave of a week at home she was discharged with home follow up arranged and arrangements to supervise her taking of medication.

Summary

Mental health services are an integral part of our welfare state and specialised services for the elderly mentally ill are now available in most parts of the United Kingdom. They cannot operate in isolation from other parts of health and welfare services and ultimately the quality of service which is provided for elderly people with mental health problems is dependent on the overall levels of funding in health and social services. There is currently an escalating reliance on the private sector for the provision of long stay care, which is of variable quality. Elderly people without private means who require care are increasingly being relocated from their local communities to places where they required level of care is affordable within the state benefits system. This mirrors the changes in mental health services generally, with the large scale closures of mental illness beds in large mental hospitals, which have not been accompanied to date by the adequate provision of local mental health community services. Given the increasing numbers of elderly people who will require services in the next 10-20 years it remains to be seen whether current or future governments will rise to the challenges ahead.

References

Lishman, W.A. (1997), *Organic Psychiatry*, Blackwell, London.
Murphy, E. (1986), *Affective Disorders in the Elderly*, Churchill Livingstone, Edinburgh.
Pitt, B. (1982), *Psychogeneriatrics. An Introduction to the Psychiatry of Old Age*, Churchill Livingstone, Edinburgh.
Pitt, B. (1987), *Dementia*, Churchill Livingstone, Edinburgh.

6 Ending lives: age, autonomy and the quality of life[1]

GAVIN FAIRBAIRN

Prologue: Wolfensberger and death-making in the human services

In *The New Genocide of Handicapped and Afflicted People* Wolfensberger (1987), introduces us to his deeply disturbing view that we live in a 'death-making society', one in which many people die as the result of human acts and actions carried out in the name of welfare and health. The death-making on which he focuses is accomplished by a number of means including killing, allowing to die, encouraging to die and failing to engage in life enhancing activities. It is:

> ...any action, especially by services and social agencies, that causes or hastens or makes more likely the death of a disadvantaged, handicapped or devalued person, or that is an expression of a wish that such a person, or such persons in general, should die or should not exist. Illustrations of death-making might include many human service practices, 'euthanasia', 'non-treatment' of newborn handicapped babies, dumping people out of institutions without adequate support, and abortion (*Speak Out*, Issue 5, December, 1988, p1).

Wolfensberger's ideas about death-making represent a new and in my view more aggressive approach to societal problems that he had addressed earlier by developing the 'Principles of Normalisation' (Wolfensberger, 1972). Normalisation offered a new and helpful way of thinking about the position in society of a range of people who are often disadvantaged in a world in which they are devalued. It aimed at the development and adoption of practices in the human services which used:

> ...means which are valued in our society in order to develop and support personal behaviour, experiences and characteristics that are likewise valued (O'Brien, J. and Tyne, A, 1981).

Though they were originally developed to analyse and explain the processes of devaluation to which people with learning difficulties are often subjected in modern society, the principles of normalisation soon found a place in thinking about services for other groups, including older people, people with severe mental health problems and people with physical disabilities. They have been hugely influential in many countries including the UK, in helping to shape both thinking and practice in organisations and institutions which are involved in caring for members of such groups.

In setting forth his views about normalisation, Wolfensberger was concerned to speak of the ways in which value is attributed to people. He was also concerned to discuss ways in which clients within human services may be devalued and marginalised. In setting out his views about death-making, he was again concerned to draw attention to the marginalisation of people which may arise when they are devalued both consciously and unconsciously. *The New Genocide of Handicapped and Afflicted People* is a contentious and shocking analysis, not only of some of the less savoury possibilities of the human character but also of the human services - social work, medicine and so on. Wolfensberger's claims are far reaching and demand attention even (perhaps especially) from those who would seek to deny their truth, because the human services, of which they are a part, come in for critical and unflattering consideration.

The canvas upon which Wolfensberger paints his picture is a broad one; he speaks of ways in which the deaths of members of devalued groups are systematically arranged or in which they are encouraged to die socially or physically. His use of the expression 'socially dead' is intended to draw attention to the way in which caring for devalued individuals such as people with intellectual or psychiatric problems in impersonal and depersonalising institutions (some might say incarcerating them in such places) makes them 'as good as dead' to the rest of the world. The point is that while they are accommodated in such institutions, such individuals are not really in the world but rather exist in a kind of annexe to it, and since they have no place in the world they might as well be dead as far as those of us who live in the outside 'real' world are concerned.

Some people might wish to argue that in the UK at any rate, the move towards a care system in which individuals of this kind are assisted to live in the community, in domestic sized accommodation, means that this particular accusation cannot stick. But however large scale the move to close down large institutions for people with learning disabilities and chronic mental health problems has been, many still do live in large institutions; and some local services even seem gradually to be sliding back into a situation where the average size of 'community care' settings is growing larger again. And even if it really was true that the transformation to care in smaller units had been achieved, other accusations of a death-making kind might be levelled at services and governments that fail to fund such care adequately. One of these might rest on the contention that the failure to fund the move to community care adequately means that rather than bringing about the 'mainstreaming' of citizens with learning disabilities and severe mental health problems in helpful ways (that is, bringing them into the mainstream of life), what has often happened would be better described as the 'maindumping' of vulnerable people into situations where not only their mental and spiritual health but their physical existence is under threat. And in cases where inadequate support contributes to the death of such individuals the charge of death-making would certainly not be misplaced.

It is important to distinguish Wolfensberger's use of the expression 'socially dead' from its use to refer to people who are said, however loosely, to be in what has become known as a 'persistent vegetative state' as the result of brain injury, or who as the result of brain deterioration due to conditions such as Alzheimer's disease have ceased to function in recognisable and understandable ways. The idea that such individuals are 'as good as dead' can lead to actual or physical death-making if those labelled 'socially dead' are killed, or their deaths achieved by others 'allowing them to die'. It would, for example, be easy to view the death of Tony Bland (see Dyer, 1993) as a case of physical death-making following the social death-making brought about by the way in which many people view individuals such as him who, as the result of traumatic injuries, have a greatly reduced capacity for personal human life. Bland, a victim of the disaster at the Hillsborough football stadium in 1989, died physically in March 1993, after a landmark legal decision in which his feeding was defined as 'medical treatment' from which it was said he was not benefiting, leading to the decision to allow him to die by withdrawing it.

Wolfensberger discusses a wide range of devalued groups, from the unborn to the very old, paying particular attention to those with intellectual or physical disabilities. A wide range of activities come under scrutiny, from the abortion of disabled babies to the mass murder of whole populations; and from the encouragement of those who are very ill, very disabled, or very old to think of themselves as being as good as dead, to ways of treating groups of such individuals that encourage them to die if not physically, then socially. Activities that Wolfensberger would consider to be death-making include:

i.   Sending elderly or chronically ill people, who have been receiving treatment or care in hospitals or other institutions, home to care for themselves before they are able to do so.

ii.   Encouraging terminally ill people to plan for their deaths - by finishing business, writing wills and so on.

iii.   Placing institutions offering care to devalued groups such as people with learning difficulties or severe mental health problems, or elderly people, near buildings or sites that are associated in the public imagination with death; for example abattoirs, graveyards, crematoria or funeral parlours. Wolfensberger claims that this is very common.

iv.   The use of language that interprets people who are devalued as if they are already dead, for example by referring to them as 'living corpses', 'living cadavers', 'vegetables', 'geeks', 'empty shells', as 'socially dead', and in other similar ways.

The story Wolfensberger tells about our death-making society is both fascinating and appalling; it is tempting to sweep it under the carpet of one's mind. It is anxiety-provoking and likely to anger those who care for, and have devoted their lives to the care of, those he claims are victims of the practices that together make ours a death-making society. Some such practices are consciously engaged in by their perpetrators with the intention of arranging the deaths of those who die; examples would be the abortion and infanticide of disabled babies, though those who engage in these practices believe that they are justifiable. However, it is important to note that other practices that he claims are death-making are engaged in by workers who have not reflected on the fact that what they do might bring about or encourage the deaths of clients; examples here would include certain aspects of the care of the elderly and terminally ill, such as encouraging them to come to terms with death by taking an active part in planning for their own funeral. Indeed those who engage in such practices are likely to see them as life enhancing and to be horrified by the suggestion that engaging in them might be viewed as encouraging their clients to die, rather than facilitating their lives by enabling them to make sense of life and to approach death in a dignified way.

Wolfensberger's ideas about death-making are deeply shocking and upsetting. Nevertheless some of what he has written about this topic is, I think, so obvious, when one comes to think about it, that it is difficult to believe that someone had to point it out. Its weight lies not in whether any particular aspect of it is true or easy to comprehend, but in its power to force us to reconsider what we do as people faced with the need to relate to and care for those who are or may be devalued. If we take him seriously there are very few areas of human life that will not be affected.

I find Wolfensberger's ideas about death-making fascinating, and though I am by no means convinced by everything he has to say, I believe these ideas have enormous importance for services like medicine and social work, that are concerned with human health and welfare. In spite of this very few people that I know have come across them, perhaps because of the way in which they have been publicised; and this is one reason that I have chosen to begin this chapter by placing them central stage. But I have also done so because I want to use them in looking at some issues that arise in relation to treatment decisions that are made at the beginning and end of life. At the end of the chapter I will try to draw together what I have had to say, in some observations about autonomy, ageing and the allocation of resources.

The main event: Quality of life at the beginning and end of life

'Quality of life' frequently figures in discussions of life and death in medical and other contexts where enhancing human health and well-being is the primary aim. For example, at the beginning of life it may be argued that a disabled infant's life is likely to be of such poor quality that it can be justifiable (even merciful) to allow him or her to die by withholding treatment and/or sustenance. I want to contrast the importance frequently attached to such speculative estimates about quality of life, with the way in which considerations of quality of life seem to be laid to one side in the care of people who are terminally ill and would rather die than live with the poor quality of life they are experiencing. In doing so I will draw attention to the possibility that death-making in each of these circumstances might mean very different things.

Let me focus, first, on the relative unimportance which seems to be attached to quality of life in deciding what it is right to do at the end of life.

The end of life

Many years ago I attended a meeting at which a committed and experienced doctor spoke of her work in a hospice and about her belief that dying people should be helped to enjoy the life left to them in the best way possible. She believed that her work in the hospice increased the quality of people's lives - sometimes dramatically in their last days and weeks and months, and she illustrated this by reference to cases that she had worked with. She also spoke about euthanasia and her passionate belief that it can never be right to kill those who are dying even when they ask to be killed. This doctor is, I think, typical not only of the hospice movement but more generally of those who are specialists in palliative medicine. I have no doubt about the dedication of those who share her views because their experiences in working with terminally ill patients lead them to believe that in most circumstances pain can be controlled with good enough care, so that lives can be lived fully till they end.

That those who work in palliative care are motivated to provide the best possible quality of life for their terminally ill patients, is clear from their actions. However, there is a sense in which it seems to me that at times many, if not most, palliative care staff are willing to abandon their commitment to quality of life, because their commitment to the absolute rule against killing is even stronger. Thus, even in circumstances where a patient's quality of life had dropped to the point at which he, the patient, would rather die than live, and had asked to be helped to die, many (dare I venture to guess *most*?) palliative carers would be unwilling even to contemplate killing him. Faced with a patient for whom life has become intolerable, and who asks to be killed rather than live with the quality of life he is presently living with, most would thus refuse to kill. And this would be so even in cases in which their considerable skills in palliative care could not help a person's pain any longer without making him unconscious or non-autonomous, or in which they could do nothing to relieve his distress because of other unpleasant and life-destroying aspects of his condition. Apparently such carers do not want to be involved in death-making. Apparently such carers are adhering to a positive model of human care which seems opposed to death-making.

Of course, this position is not unusual. Many, if not most, doctors in this country would refuse to kill their patients even when they ask to be killed. This is true of those who are willing to 'allow patients to die' when they judge that it would be in their best interests to die. And it is true even of those who are willing to end a person's pain using drugs in quantities that they are aware will kill him.

Those doctors who are willing to kill patients in the course of treating their pain most often take moral and legal refuge in the idea that the death of those they kill is not aimed at and intended, but is merely a side effect of drugs administered and prescribed for the purpose of relieving pain; one might wonder whether at times the adoption of such a rationale involves self-deceit. Those who are willing to allow patients to die yet refuse to kill them, take refuge in the common view that while killing is morally wrong, allowing to die is acceptable because it does not involve actively bringing about the death of the person, but merely allowing it to occur naturally. It might be argued that holding this view also involves self-deceit (or at any rate a failure to think clearly about the matter) because the moral importance of both killing and allowing to die surely depends upon the circumstances in which they take place and on the intentions of the agents involved, rather than on the fact that one is active while the other is passive. After all, for those who end up dead there is no difference between being killed and being allowed to die; that hinges merely on whether they died as the result of an act of commission or rather of one of omission. In relation to the selective non-treatment of severely disabled infants, Harris (1985) has observed that '...non-treatment is a death-dealing device' (p34). Allowing a person to die deals death whatever we call it, and if we allow him to die because we want him dead (however noble our purposes in wanting this), allowing him to die has a flavour not of passivity but of activity about it.

In my view, where we deal death for morally justifiable reasons we are morally right to do so, however we do so. And it seems to me that protecting the dignity and the life of one who would rather die than suffer the pain of a death he is already dying, or who would rather die than suffer the indignity of living to his biological end devoid of the autonomy and self-control that constitutes, for him, a large part of his personhood, is as morally good a reason for killing as may be found, provided that the means used do not involve the imposition of suffering so great that the value of dying now rather than later is overcome.

It seems odd that doctors, who believe that quality of life is important, should deny death when the quality of life a person is experiencing is so bad that he sees death as an advantage and there is no prospect of things changing so that the quality of life will improve. One reason for this, perhaps, might be that they cannot imagine themselves being the kind of person who would actually kill a patient, because they see their role as being about preserving life. However, while the preservation of life seems to be thoroughly laudable in most circumstances, I do not believe that it should be pursued at the expense of the quality of life of the patients whose lives (and deaths) are in question.

Doctors who refuse to kill their patients seem to be making a bid for the moral high ground, and with good reason. In general doctors should not kill. However, to my mind, adherence to an immovable belief in the sanctity of life, to the idea that doctors must never kill their patients, carries moral dangers. In order to be consistent, doctors who hold to the view that killing must never be allowed, even in the case of terminally ill patients who have rationally asked to be killed, must be willing to commit such patients to lives of pain so great that they would rather be dead then live with them. In a sense doctors who act thus are guarding their own quality of life at the patient's expense, because they are willing to see others suffer in order to maintain their personal integrity as people who do not kill. This would be rather like the position in Bernard Williams' example of Jim and Pedro, if Jim refused to kill one person to save the lives of nineteen even though the one he could have killed was bound to die anyway (Williams, 1973).

Jim, who has accidentally stumbled upon a situation in which twenty innocent people are going to be killed, is given the opportunity to save nineteen of them by shooting one himself. Most people who come across this story react immediately, as they expect Jim will, by saying that they could not kill the one, because they believe that killing is wrong. Nonetheless, after some consideration, most persuade themselves that provided that killing the one would have no side effects such as increasing the likelihood that Pedro or some as yet unknown and unnamed others will act in similar ways in the future, Jim should kill the one person because by doing so he can save nineteen who would have died anyway. And what's more, they believe that if Jim refused to kill the one he will be protecting his own integrity as one who does not believe in killing innocent people, at the expense of the lives of those he could have saved. In a similar way, it seems to me that doctors who refuse to kill their patients, even in circumstances such as I have described, do so to protect their own integrity and as a result allow patients who could have died comfortably, and at a time of their own choosing, to die less good deaths than they could have done. And just as I believe that someone in Jim's position would be wrong to refuse to kill, however much he believes that killing is usually wrong, I believe that doctors (and others) who refuse to kill those who are dying in terrible pain and/or distress, who wish to be killed and ask to be killed, are wrong to refuse to help them even when helping them means killing them.

95

James Rachels (1985), a philosopher whose writing shares with that of many others working in this area a tendency towards 'death-making'[2], makes an interesting distinction between 'living a life' and 'being alive'. Biological life, which is what 'being alive' refers to, is a necessary substrate for living a life in the personal sense; but one could be alive in this biological sense without having any kind of life in the sense of 'living a life'. Consider, for example, individuals who are irreversibly brain dead or anencephalic babies; do they live lives? or are they merely alive? Notice that I am making no claim here about whether individuals who are brain dead or anencephalic are persons, about whether they have value or about whether they should be killed, allowed to die or kept alive.

A person who knows he is terminally ill and close to death may not wish to live any longer. He might, if he has read Rachels' book, wish to say that he considers that remaining alive is now a question merely of being biologically alive and no longer of living a life. Or he might claim that, though he is both alive and living a life, the life he is living is so bad as to be worse for him than death. For such a person death might seem preferable. In such a case there is a paradox for Wolfensberger's death-making hypothesis. Couldn't killing in such a case be seen as life-enhancing, as respecting and even venerating life, because it allows the individual to exit gracefully while he still has some vestige of dignity? By contrast, isn't imposing life on a person that is for him, worse than death, when one could help him to die, to disregard the things that make life valuable? It seems to me that in such circumstances killing the person could be construed as life-enhancing, while refusing to kill him might, paradoxically, be seen as death-making.

Possible misconceptions of, and objections to, my position.

Some people might consider my view that refusing to kill a person who is in irremediable and terminal pain may justifiably be considered as a species of death-making, to be absurdly liberal. On the contrary, my position is actually quite conservative because I believe that killing another for humanitarian reasons will only be morally acceptable in very special circumstances and where that person has asked to be killed. Furthermore, I do not believe that euthanasia should be legalised. I should therefore attempt to deal with some ways in which my position could be misconstrued. I will also reply to some possible objections.

First of all, I should reject the idea that some people have developed, that I am in favour of all forms of euthanasia. On the contrary my sole concern is with what I would term 'voluntary and requested euthanasia', in which a person arranges his own death in order to avoid another form of death. Indeed, my preference would be to limit the use of the term 'euthanasia' to such instances. What is important here is the stress I want to lay on euthanasia being an act of the person who dies, even when it is performed through the agency of another or others. Nothing that I have said, or will say, is intended to offer support for those who advocate what are often referred to as 'non-voluntary euthanasia' and 'involuntary euthanasia'. Nor am I suggesting that whenever a patient thinks that his life isn't worth living any longer and asks to be killed his doctor should kill him; to say this would be to suggest that anyone who is depressed with life has the right to be killed, and I certainly don't believe that. However, I strongly support the idea that when it is requested by those who are terminally ill and in great pain or distress, euthanasia is morally justified; and in some circumstances I would go so far as to say that it would be morally wrong to refuse to kill another person.

Of course there may be difficulties in telling whether a person who asks to die really wants death rather than an interlude from intolerable pain or distress. It is not uncommon for people who are terminally ill, and in great pain, to become so depressed that they protest that they wish to die, when doctors and other carers know from experience that, given a few days and some modifications to their drug regime, they will be glad to find that they are still alive. I do not believe that patients in such a period of depression should be killed even if they ask to be killed. My contention is simply that if occasions arise when doctors and others caring for dying people can do nothing further to help, short of rendering them unconscious or non-autonomous, it would be morally right to kill individuals who are dying and who ask rationally for death at that time, and morally wrong to refuse to do so.

Though I believe that it is morally permissible and even morally required, at times, I believe that to legalise voluntary and requested euthanasia would be to set foot upon a slippery slope towards a situation where euthanasia of a death-making kind became acceptable. By 'euthanasia of a death-making kind' I mean those acts usually referred to as non-voluntary or involuntary euthanasia, which are often if not always aimed at enhancing the lives of others rather than the lives, and the meaning of the lives, of those who die, whatever the rationalisations that are presented as justification for killing. So, for example, they can be about increasing the quality of life of relations and loved ones, or of other citizens, by freeing up, for other purposes, time and money, emotional energy and professional expertise that is being spent on the care of those who are marked for euthanasia. Though I am arguing that voluntary and requested euthanasia can be morally acceptable and even morally required, my belief in the dangers of the slippery slope towards a situation in which these other so-called and in my view death-making forms of euthanasia become acceptable, is such that I think it would be unwise to allow those who kill others, even in the kinds of circumstances where I believe killing is justifiable, recourse to the law to justify their actions. I would rather that it was left to their own conscience to justify what they do, in the face of laws that make their actions illegal even when they are morally right.

The second possible misconception is that I believe that the responsibility for killing patients rests solely with doctors. Although most of the time I refer to 'doctors' as if they were the only people who are involved in making decisions about the lives and deaths of terminally ill patients, that does not mean that I think that they are the only people involved or who should be involved. Nor indeed does it mean that I believe that they are the only people who might be involved in arranging for the deaths of those who are to die. Nothing about my argument would change if 'nurses', 'close relations' or 'friends' were substituted for 'doctors' as appropriate, provided that the named individuals had the required knowledge of the patient's condition and the ability to kill him or to assist him in dying easily and with dignity. Anyone who was asked by a terminally ill patient for help in dying would occupy the moral space I suggest is occupied by doctors, provided that she had the necessary skill and knowledge to arrange that person's death, and had access to the means by which she could do so.

Objections to my position

First, it might be objected that my case is misplaced because there never are situations in which pain cannot be controlled, even in cases, say, of cancer involving the nervous system. Some people would claim that uncontrollable pain never occurs. I do not believe it; or at any rate, I do not believe that there are no occasions where pain occurs that cannot be controlled without at the same time rendering a person non-autonomous. Even if it was true, however, there would still be cases where I would suggest that killing was morally acceptable, or even at times morally required. For example, where pain cannot be controlled without dosages of painkilling drugs so high that the person will lose consciousness or otherwise be rendered non-autonomous, I believe that this should be made clear to him, and if he prefers to die rather than ending up like this I think it would certainly be right to kill him. Another instance would be where the reason that a person would rather be dead related, not to the amount of pain he was experiencing, but to distress caused by irremediable symptoms, such as nausea, constipation and hair loss, which might be associated with chemotherapy; or the incontinence and bleeding from the nose and mouth which may accompany conditions such as lung cancer. In such cases I again believe that it would be right to kill a person who rationally asked to be killed.

A problem arises, of course, in trying to say how one might be sure that a person who asks for euthanasia is rational and serious in his wish. No doubt if euthanasia of any kind was legalised some formula would be laid down against which individual cases could be measured in order to allow decisions to be made about whether an individual's request to die was rational and resulted from circumstances which justified killing; it might, for example, be decided that the candidate had to have asked for death in certain circumstances and in certain ways. But even if such criteria were decided upon and their presence or absence was judged by a panel of experts from relevant disciplines such as law or ethics, psychology or psychiatry, we could never be sure beyond any possibility of doubt that a person rationally and seriously wished to die rather than to live (similar problems arise in deciding, in relation to a person who has brought about his own death apparently as the result of intentional actions aimed at bringing it about, whether he actually intended to die). I therefore do not believe a legally agreed procedure for making this decision would be particularly useful. What would be helpful, of course, would be a series of guidelines developed following discussions among experts, about the kinds of things that might or even should count as evidence that a person's wish to die was serious and rational. Such criteria are beyond me to dictate but might include, for example, his having made the request on many occasions and to different people; his having given what appear to be cogent reasons for wishing to be dead rather than alive, and perhaps the fact that he has expressed the desire to live but not to live in the state he is living in (where the state in which he is living is by all accounts irremediable). Reference needs, of course, also to be made to the objective evidence of the case - to whether the individual is suffering a condition that is causing him pain and distress of a kind that he claims to be suffering.

Secondly, it might be objected that my proposals do not allow for differences between doctors with specialist skills in pain control such as work within the hospice movement, and those who do not have such expertise. As a result of such differences, patients in painful terminal conditions who do not have access to specialist palliative care might want to die under circumstances such as I have argued would justify euthanasia, when, had they been in a hospice, or had they lived in an area where good palliative care was available, it might yet have been possible to do something further for them. Among other things this fact leads me to believe that there is an injustice done to those who cannot gain access to the highest standards of palliative medicine - because, for example, an accident of geography means that it is not available in the area in which they live. It is clear that if such care is available in some areas, it should be available to everyone, so that everyone suffering from painful terminal illnesses has the possibility of living as comfortably as possible until they die. However, it also means that I feel compelled to support the requested euthanasia of those individuals where it is not possible to transfer them to a hospice or to arrange good palliative care at home; the fact that, at another time or in another place, they might have been helped, is no reason for depriving them of the help that we could give them now, even when that help involves killing them at their request.

Those who work in hospices and other palliative care situations are committed to offering the best quality of life to those for whom they care and to helping them to live as well as possible until they die. And yet, as I have argued, if they refuse to kill patients who wish to die and who have good reason for wishing to die, then their attempts at life-enhancing care could become a kind of death-making for those who have life enforced on them. In the case of terminally ill patients who are being cared for in medical settings which are not run on the hospice model, there is another problem which arises, because of the temptation in such situations to pursue, and attempt to deal with, every pathological condition. This temptation can lead to death-making interventions that are apparently about preserving and prolonging life. This is well illustrated by a story related by Christiaan Barnard (1986, pages 174-6).

Eli Kahn, who is dying of cancer, has told his doctors that they mustn't try to save his life. 'I am ready to die. The machine is worn out, and the mechanic must now give up.' The doctors assure Mr Kahn that they do not work in a hospital where patients are simply allowed to die. He protests. 'But doctor, what is wrong with death? I have lived a very happy life and a very proud life. My children have all been proud of their father, and I want them to remember me as a *Mensch*, a human being.' Mr Kahn is not asking to be killed, but simply to be allowed to die, and the doctors want, no doubt with the best intentions, to protect his welfare. However, they fail to see that his welfare does not simply consist in his physical life continuing for as long as possible; it also consists in his making a good death.

Despite Mr Kahn's requests that they should not perform useless investigations or treatments on his dying body, the doctors pursue an aggressive course of action. In the next bed there is another patient with inoperable cancer of the stomach; he has tubes through his nose, coming from his abdomen, his bladder; he is being fed artificially and is on an intravenous drip; he is unconscious. Mr Kahn tells the doctors that he has no wish ever to end up looking like that man and a few days later, when the man dies following unsuccessful attempts by all possible means to resuscitate him after a cardiac arrest, he says 'Doctor, please promise me that you will never let that happen to me, because I am a proud man, and I don't fear death'. A few days later Mr Kahn develops problems with his lungs and as a result is put on an artificial respirator. The following morning a nurse finds him dead; he has disconnected the respirator. In the bed beside him is a note written in a shaky hand which reads 'Doctor, the real enemy is not death - the real enemy is inhumanity'.

Not to allow Eli Kahn, and patients like him, to die with dignity when they wish to do so, is death-making, because it treats the quantity of a person's biological life as more important than the quality of his personal life. Those who put quantity before quality are likely to think that what matters is their answer to the question 'How long did the patient live?' rather than the questions 'How did the patient live?' and 'How did the patient die?'[3] This seems to me to be a mistake for those who care about people and the quality of their lives. It is never justifiable to pursue treatment beyond the point at which it is personally beneficial to the patient but begins rather, to harm him. To do other than this is, I think, death-making because it is to pursue biological life at the expense of, rather than for the sake of, personal life, and to treat being alive as the aim, rather than living a life.

Of course, Mr Kahn's story is not about euthanasia as it is usually conceived - as a merciful but active act of killing. It is not, that his doctors did not, by killing, grant him release from life at his request. Eli was not that kind of man; he simply wanted to be allowed, when his time came, to pass quietly away rather than be subjected to the abuse that can occur when a yet living person is treated like an object in order to preserve his biological life. On the other hand, his story is pertinent to my case because it is about the extension of biological life at the expense of human life; it is about enforcing life on those who do not wish to live it beyond a certain point.

Someone might object that a person who asks for euthanasia might have been subjected to just the kind of death-making pressure that Wolfensberger has suggested is all too common, that they might, for example, have been subjected to pressure by relations and professionals who made it clear, either in words or by body language, that they believed death would be a benefit. Such a person might then request death because he had picked up the implicit message that others expected him to die soon, and that the sooner he died the better it would be for everyone concerned, rather than because he himself actively wished for death. Messages of this kind might be conveyed in both subtle and not so subtle ways. Though it is possible that this could happen, it is hardly likely to be the case in hospice settings, where emphasis is likely to be placed on the positive benefits of living as well as one can until one dies. On the other hand, however, some individuals being cared for in such settings might conceivably experience the care they were receiving as pressure to live as fully as possible until they died, and paradoxically this in itself could perhaps be viewed as death-making in the case of those who did not wish to put in the effort necessary to live well until they died, but preferred, rather, to give in gracefully, believing at a certain point, that 'enough is enough'.

The danger that, for example, people who stand to gain financially or personally from the death of their relatives might consciously (or even unconsciously) attempt to make their terminally ill loved ones wish for and ask for death, is clearly a problem. However, given my belief that euthanasia can only have a place within a culture in which life is valued and living is valued- a culture, in other words, that mirrors most of what is good about the ethos of the hospice movement, in which treatment is aimed at enhancing life, rather than at detecting and dealing with pathology, I think all that those who might contemplate assisting a dying person to die will have to do is to find ways of reassuring themselves that the will to die comes from the person concerned and is uninfluenced by anyone else, particularly anyone who might stand to gain from his death.

Another objection that might be raised to my position relates to the question of who should be responsible for killing those who wish to die. It might, for example, be argued that it would be wrong to expect doctors, who have been trained to preserve life and the quality of life, to do the killing, because of the ambivalence and resultant stress it would cause them. But more important than that, the argument might continue, if doctors in palliative care were at times given the duty to kill, their patients would develop anxiety about whether they could trust their physicians to care for them. They might, it could be argued, develop a fear of being put to death against their will. Inducing such a fear could be construed as death-making, since it would reduce the extent to which dying people would enjoy their remaining life, and might even induce in them a wish for death to remove the anxiety that resulted from worrying about whether and when they were going to be killed.

But my suggestion is simply that when patients who are terminally ill and in irremediable pain or distress ask to be killed, it would be the mark of someone who cared to kill them. I am not suggesting, for example, that doctors in hospices and other branches of palliative medicine should kill everyone for whom they are caring who they believe would be better off dead; I am suggesting that, when death is more attractive for the person whose life is in question, not to kill is a death-making refusal, which diminishes the value of the life of the one who is forced to live on.

One possible way of getting over the problem of who should do the killing would be to accept Roger Crisp's proposal for a new medical specialism to be known as 'telostrics' (Crisp, 1987). Telostricians would be trained in both hospice care and in euthanasia and hence would be specially skilled in helping patients to die good deaths. It seems to me that rather than inducing fear in patients in a way that might in itself be construed as death-making, it might well enhance the life of a terminally ill person to be secure in the knowledge that, if necessary, and at the time of his choice, he could request, with the certainty of a positive answer, that his telostrician should kill him.

The beginning of life

Having said a little about the way in which quality of life considerations seem to pay little part in the deliberations of those who refuse to participate in the euthanasia of those who are terminally ill and ask to die. I want to turn now to considerations about quality of life in relation to babies with disabilities. In particular I am concerned to address the reasons for the different ways in which we regard small people and big people when we come to make life and death decisions about them, so that, while terminally ill big people who wish to die find it difficult to arrange their deaths, the deaths of small people who have not asked to be killed seem easy to arrange.

References are often made to 'quality of life' in attempting to justify the abortion of babies who either are, or may be, disabled, and also in relation to the 'selective non-treatment' of newly born infants with disabilities. The idea is that if estimations of the quality of life they are likely to experience do not match up to the standards expected by or aimed at by those who arrange their deaths, they may be killed. In the case of abortion, of course, this justification is also at times applied to babies who, in themselves, show no signs of disability. In Wolfensberger's terms, this use of the notion of quality of life leads to death-making for many babies who could have lived happy lives, and may, in itself, constitute a species of death-making. Death-making by infanticide on the grounds of disability is as fine a display of the disablist views which are rife in society, as we could hope to meet, because it would never be the case that able-bodied and able-minded infants would be allowed to die on the grounds that the quality of life they were likely to have in the future would be poor, since to act thus in relation to such children would be considered wrong, and probably as murder; it is also an example of ageism and sizeism, because similar acts would not be acceptable were they regularly to be carried out in relation to bigger and older folk. Though I do not wish to pursue this here, I should point out that I also believe that abortion, whether of disabled or non-disabled babies, rests upon ageism and sizeism, whatever the explanations that are made by those who support its practice.

I often tell a story, when I am teaching, about a newly born child with Down's syndrome and a life threatening condition which can be remedied by a routine and simple procedure. However, the parents are asked whether they want the doctors to bother or not. I ask the members of groups with which I am working, 'Should these parents be given this choice? Should they be allowed to choose whether their baby is given a routine procedure that will save its life? Or should the procedure be carried out whatever their views on the matter?' A large percentage of people I come across think that the parents should be given the choice. Their reasons range from the (mistaken) belief that all people with Down's syndrome live miserable lives, to the belief that it is for the parents to decide whether their child should live or die, because it is they that will have to care for him, and their lives that may be made miserable as a result. After discussing this story, I often move on to a story in which the parents of another child, who has been born with the same physical problem, but who does not have Down's syndrome or any other, similar condition, are asked whether they wish the same routine life-saving procedure to be performed on their child. Again I ask, 'Should these parents be given this choice? Should they be allowed to choose whether their baby is given a routine procedure that will save its life? Or should the procedure be carried out whatever their views on the matter?' Oddly, in my view (though I understand something about why it happens), most people protest that in this instance the parents should not be given the choice, arguing that the procedure should be carried out regardless of the parents' wishes.

One argument that is often made out in favour of arranging the death of disabled babies goes something like this: 'Since this baby would have such a poor quality of life it would be better off dead.' The cases most likely to come to public attention involve babies with spina bifida and babies with Down's Syndrome. References to 'quality of life' in deciding on courses of action in such cases are often illicit because they serve no purpose other than to make the decisions in question look as if they are about the quality of life of the baby when really they are about the quality of life of someone else.

Killing a baby, or allowing him to die, necessarily involves acting without taking account of his views. Of course it would not be possible to ask a newly born, or yet to be born, baby whether he or she wanted to live. There are, however, a variety of things that could be done:

i   Firstly, rather than guessing, in a more or less informed way, at the quality of life disabled babies are likely to have in the future, people with disabilities could be asked whether, given their disabilities, they would rather be dead then alive. Such information could then be extrapolated to the lives of babies: if they are suffering from a disability of a kind and of a degree that adults commonly insist makes their lives so miserable that they wish that they never have lived, they could be killed. This possibility would have some similarity with the way in which Quality Adjusted Life Years, or QALYs, are calculated, and shares with them the disadvantage that different people with the same disability will experience that disability as more or less of a handicap and as more or less detrimental to their quality of life. The fact is that though we might be able to guess at the level of physical pain or of mental disability which an individual would experience, the 'quality of life' that she will experience is not open to measurement. 'Quality of life' is a subjective notion. I cannot tell what your quality of life is, you cannot tell what my quality of life is, and neither of us can say what the quality of life experienced by a disabled baby will be. This strategy therefore seems to be a non-starter because though it may

105

enable us to predict with reasonable accuracy the percentage of infants with a given disability who will grow up into adults who would rather be dead than alive, it could never allow us to say with certainty that any particular infant will grow up into such an adult.

ii   An alternative would be for doctors to wait until the disabled baby had grown enough, and matured sufficiently, to be able to express his own preference - to live or to die? If he turned out to be severely disabled, such that others found it hard to believe that life for him could be tolerable, he could be asked whether he wished to live with the quality of life he had at that point. If he expressed what seemed to be a rational preference to be dead he could be killed or assisted in killing himself. This would require a commitment to the notion that it is morally permissible to kill, or help to die, at least some people who do not wish to live.

Some people might think this possibility rather ghoulish. This is understandable; the idea of killing those who respond positively to the question of whether they wish to die is quite shocking. On the other hand, it seems to me to be a good deal less horrific than killing babies, or allowing them to die, before they are able to express any opinion about whether they would like to live or die.

One reason this possibility may be thought shocking, whereas the killing of unborn babies is less so, concerns the ways in which, as a society, we think about babies. For example, many people (and philosophers who by Wolfensberger's analysis would be considered as death-makers are among the most vocal of these) do not believe that babies are people like you and me. The idea of killing humans who have grown up past the stage of babyhood and ask to be killed, or even of arranging that they may be allowed to die, sounds horrific. It sounds horrific because they are likely to look like us, they will have been living for some years in relationship to others, and so it will be harder to do the deed because their personhood will either be established or at any rate more difficult to deny.

The range of positions that people espouse about whether and when and in what ways the deaths of disabled babies may be morally arranged - specifically whether they may be killed or merely 'allowed to die', is wide and the reasons that individuals hold their particular beliefs on this matter are more complex than I could discuss in detail in this chapter. For example, they depend not only on their moral beliefs but on their personal history - on whether, for example, they grew up with disabled siblings or at least in contact with disabled people, and if so, what the severity of the disabilities was. However, the most important factor seems to be their beliefs about the nature of the baby - whether at different stages it is indeed a baby person, or yet to become a person. Many who believe it is morally acceptable to kill babies before they are born believe that after they are born they may not be killed although they may be 'allowed to die'. For many people birth seems, in other words, to be especially significant in dictating how they think it is permissible to act in relation to small people. Among those who believe that abortion and infanticide are at times permissible, a common view seems to be that before birth babies are not people, and therefore they may be killed, while after birth they are people but only just; so we may 'allow them to die' but not actually kill them.

iii A third, and better, alternative, would be for doctors to wait until a person who had been born with a serious disability with which he had lived for some years, indicated that he was unhappy with life and wished to die; then, as in the last alternative, he could be killed or assisted in killing himself, provided that his preference seemed to have been seriously and autonomously made. This alternative would have the advantage over the last, that doctors could not be accused (by asking direct questions about the wishes of their patients) of putting ideas into the heads of those who were satisfied with their lives, or at any rate would rather put up with them than die.

Problems with these three strategies

All three strategies that I have considered share the disadvantage that they could not take account of the views of people who are born with disabilities such that they are incapable of expressing any view on the quality of their lives, some of whom might rather be dead. Of course it would be regrettable if a person for whom life was intolerably awful was compelled to live simply because he could not let others know about his wish to die. However, it seems no worse then the current practice of aborting disabled babies or allowing them to die after birth, because this cannot take account of their views either. Similar concerns might be expressed in relation to those who are born with disabilities so severe that

107

they are incapable, not only of expressing any view on the quality of their life, but even of formulating any such opinion.

Another problem with my second and third alternatives is that each might result in situations in which some babies would be condemned to live lives that they would rather not live, until they were able to opt out. However, I do not think that this would be any worse than allowing to die, or killing, those babies who, had they lived, would have been glad to be alive. My guess is that such cases are quite common, because however much they try to be objective, those making the life and death decisions will inevitably compare the projected quality of life of the disabled baby with their own quality of life; the leap of imagination into considering what it would be like to be living a life with greatly reduced possibilities such as a severely disabled neonate might face, without ever having experienced a richer and easier life, is perhaps too much to expect of most able bodied people. Of course, since disabled babies who have been killed or allowed to die cannot be interviewed about their views, there is no empirical way of proving that had they been allowed to live, they would have preferred life to death. On the other hand reference to the experiences of other individuals, equally disabled in an objective sense, whose parents perhaps rejected abortion or infanticide as a solution to their own problems or the problems they guessed their children might experience, lends some support to this claim. A particularly poignant and forceful example may be seen in a letter by Alison Davis to the *Journal of Medical Ethics* (Davis, 1983, but see also, Davis, 1992) in which she discusses a proposal that legal measures should be put in place to make it legally permissible to allow babies with certain degrees of disability, to die. In that letter she notes with interest that with respect to the criteria for quality of life that had been put forward in an earlier article (Brahams and Brahams, 1982) she fails to fulfil most of them. She goes on to refer to aspects of her life, including her need for many, often life saving, operations; her double incontinence; her confinement to a wheelchair; her school life in an ordinary school and university degree; her work defending the rights of disabled people; her marriage to an able bodied man, and the extent to which she has travelled outside the UK. Her letter ends with a question: 'Who could say that I have no 'worthwhile quality of life'?'

What I have said so far may seem simplistic, because I haven't taken account of the wide range of disabilities with which a baby can be born. Whereas some disabled babies will have disabilities of a very minor kind, some will be seriously handicapped by their disabilities and some will be so severely disabled that they are unlikely ever to experience life in any sense that we can relate to. To use Rachels' distinction between 'being alive' and 'living a life' to which I have already referred (Rachels, 1985), such babies it might be argued, might be kept alive without living lives. The argument might then be made that since they cannot experience life in any way, there is no reason why their deaths should not be arranged. Such a case might, for example, be made out in relation to some anencephalic or microcephalic babies, on the basis, not that they would experience a poor quality of life, but on the basis that they could not have lives of any kind. Questions about the allocation of resources may come into discussions about the treatment or disposal of such infants in two ways. First, it might be argued that it is wrong to use resources to keep them alive that could have been used in saving or enhancing the lives of others, perhaps other severely disabled infants, who do have lives that they can live. Leaving aside the question of its validity, this argument carries moral dangers because of the possibility that, if accepted, it might be extended, for example, to both older people with similar disabilities, and to babies whose disabilities were much less extreme, or indeed, to any individual whose condition was such that he was likely to require sustained and expensive medical treatment. It is a clear example of how utilitarian thinking is likely to lead to death-making decisions. The second way in which resource allocation may creep into discussions of such infants concerns the widespread view that since they are not living and will not live lives, they have no need for their organs and may thus justifiably be considered as a source of spare parts for patching up the bodies of others. This again seems to me to be an example of the way in which utilitarian thinking is likely to lead to death-making decisions.

Allowing babies to die or killing them makes more sense in relation to infanticide than it does in relation to abortion, because at least a more accurate picture of the extent of an individual's disabilities is possible after birth than before. Though I can imagine cases where I might be persuaded that death would be best for such a baby, I think the deaths of such babies should not be arranged simply on the grounds that they will have very limited lives. In any case, I think it is important that discussions about how such babies may be treated must be made on the basis of proper information about the possibilities that exist for them, and such discussions are often ill-informed.[4]

An easier case could perhaps be made in relation to the allowing to die, or killing, of babies who because of gross abnormality or genetic disorder were unable to live for more than a very short time and were likely during that time to suffer greatly. Again I will not enter into this here except to say that the argument would hinge on the amount of suffering caused to such a child during a short and fruitless existence which we cannot imagine brings any compensatory benefits to the child, who may be loved but cannot love, and who is unable to develop relationships with others, though others may relate to him. It is considerations of this kind that have led me to wonder for many years whether it would have been better for my first child, whose condition was incompatible with life, to have been killed rather than being left to die. In at least some cases it might even be argued that it was morally wrong not to bring death to the baby on the grounds that to continue treatment, when it is pointless and does nothing other than to cause suffering for no purpose, is a death-making action. There is some similarity here to the death-making that, in discussing the case of Eli Kahn, I suggested occurs when those at the end of life who wish either to be assisted in dying, or at least to be allowed to die in peace, have life enforced upon them.

Though I accept that infanticide, however achieved, may be the right thing to do in a very small proportion of cases, I believe it would be a mistake to legalise it, for reasons similar to those that make me against the legalisation of even voluntary and requested euthanasia. In any case, I am reticent about admitting that I might be persuaded even in extreme cases, that the quickest and least painful route to death, was the best option for both the child and the parents, because I already feel the weight of critics bearing down on me with cries of inconsistency. I have no defence against such criticisms, though I only believe that it could be morally acceptable to arrange the deaths of babies who, because of profound defects, had no possibility of living biological lives.

It is important to make clear that I do not think that arranging the deaths of babies may be justified merely by referring to the quality of life of the baby concerned. I have already pointed out that references made to the 'quality of life' of a baby may sometimes be used to justify actions that in truth are intended to protect the quality of life of their families or of society. Let me offer some support for this contention by looking again and in more detail, at the draft bill on the treatment of disabled infants to which Alison Davis was responding in her letter in the *Journal of Medical Ethics*, to which I have already referred (Davis, 1993). Had this bill become law, blanket permission would have been given to fail to treat very young patients if certain conditions about the baby's quality of life were fulfilled, specifically if his disability was:

> ...of such gravity that the patient (after receiving all reasonable treatment) would enjoy no worthwhile quality of life.

Clearly this refers to the quality of life of the child in question, (though as I have argued earlier, references to quality of life are destined to be rather fragile because of the subjective nature of quality of life decisions). However, in expanding on this criterion, the Brahams want on to refer to '... the degree of suffering (both mental and physical)' it is likely to suffer. And it is in their attempt to say what this means that support for my contention lies.

For example, in 3)(ii) they refer to :

the ability and willingness of the parents of the patient to provide the care and facilities appropriate to the patient's condition.

and in 3)(iii) they refer to:

the likely effect on the mental and physical health of the parents and other members of the patient's family of the need to provide such care and facilities to the patient during his probable lifetime.

Notice the echoes here of the 1969 Abortion Act. My point is that 3)(ii) and (iii) have nothing directly to do with the quality of life of the child; and although it may be argued that 3)(ii) is indirectly concerned with the child's welfare because, if parents are unwilling to provide the care and facilities the child needs, the child's quality of life will be adversely affected, this fails to take account of the possibility that the child might be cared for very well outside its family of origin.

Enforcing death and enforcing life: Two species of death-making

From what I have said so far, I hope it is clear that there is an inconsistency in the way in which the concept of 'quality of life' is used at the beginning and at the end of life, and further that this inconsistency is likely to lead to harm for two groups of people, one large and one small. The large group is made up of those babies born or unborn, who suffer, or seem likely to suffer, from disabilities so severe that others judge that their lives will be of such poor quality as to make them not worth living. The smaller group is made up of people who are suffering from terminal conditions so severe, so painful or so distressing, that they themselves judge their lives to be worth living no longer.

111

The harm that may be done to disabled babies will come about because, at the beginning of life, quality is likely to be treated as so important that the absence of certain features, thought by some people to be necessary before an individual can have a worthwhile quality of life, may be used to justify enforced death whether by abortion or 'allowing to die' after birth. This contrasts markedly with the way in which harm is likely to be done to terminally ill people who wish to die, In this case, although quality of life is considered important, at times when it comes to life and death decisions it is overlooked, because the imperative against killing seems to be regarded as stronger than the imperative against bringing about or allowing suffering; dying patients may thus be made to suffer enforced life. It is clear that the enforced death of babies with disabilities is a death-making activity in Wolfensberger's terms. And as I have already suggested, more surprisingly and paradoxically, perhaps, the enforced life that terminally ill people may be made to suffer, because doctors adhere to the notion that killing is something they must never do, may also be viewed as death-making.

Postscript: Autonomy, ageing and resources

I began this paper by saying a little about Wolfensberger's ideas about death-making and in what I have had to say about the way in which quality of life is regarded at the beginning and at the end of life, I have suggested that some human acts that aim to extend or preserve life may, perhaps paradoxically, be viewed as death-making while some that are aimed at bringing death may, paradoxically, be viewed as life enhancing. In drawing what I have to say to a close I want, finally, to try to relate what I have been saying to the three main topics of concern for this book. I shall say something about each in turn.

Ageing

When people are very little - when they are fetuses or babies or newly born infants, we seem, as a society, to have different views about how it is appropriate to act towards them than when they are older and rather more like you or me. One example of this is the acceptance of the notion that it can be right to bring death to fetuses and neonates who are found to have severe disabilities without asking them whether they would like to die. In a way I think what is going on here is a kind of ageism: we wouldn't do that with older people.

112

Indeed, as I have argued, it is most likely that, when big people ask to be killed because they do not wish to lead the lives that they are leading, their request will be turned down. I guess it could be argued that they are then subjected to a form of ageism also, because at least some babies who it is thought will suffer miserable lives may benefit from the early death that others prescribe for them, while most of those nearer the end of life, who wish to be killed, will have this possibility withheld from them. Whether the deaths of babies who die because others decide that their lives will be of low quality, is painless or not will depend upon the way in which those delivering the 'death-dealing device' (Harris, 1985) think about the distinction between killing and letting die. Whether it is construed as a benefit will depend on one's opinion about the future state of the baby and about how likely he is to have a life worth living, and hence to have a life whose ending is to be regretted. No matter what the answers we give to these questions, to those terminally ill folk who wish to be dead, and would like to be dead, it might seem that they are being discriminated against merely because they are older and bigger.

Autonomy

Turning now to autonomy, it seems that what I have said impinges upon this also. At the beginning of life, when little babies are as yet unable to make autonomous decisions, many people demonstrate a willingness to take decisions on their behalf, even, as I have indicated, when this involves deciding that they should be killed or allowed to die. At the end of life things aren't so different, even though big people in general have more autonomy than baby ones. I guess that an aim of those who claim to wish to help people who are terminally ill to live as well as they can until they die would be to help them to remain autonomous as long as possible; to wish less than this seems to me to deny quality of life to such people. But this seems to conflict with a refusal to accept, and act upon, the request of such a person, acting autonomously, to be killed rather than to live miserably with a painful life till it ebbs naturally from him. And where a person who would rather be dead than live in pain until he dies cannot have his pain relieved except by measures that will render him less autonomous by taking away his possibilities for straight thinking, or even any kind of thinking, those who are unwilling to accept his wish to die, and insist that all they can do is to render him painfree at whatever cost, choose to neglect his autonomy in favour of their wish to avoid killing.

Resources

Finally to resources, in relation to which I want to share two final thoughts.

First, at the beginning of life, it seems likely that some of those who are in favour of the killing or allowing to die of infants who may have miserable lives may support a policy of death-making as much because they are intent on lessening the call such infants may make upon resources in the future, as because they are concerned for the welfare of the children in question. Utilitarian arguments in favour of the permissibility of infanticide in the case of very disabled babies would draw both on the fact that maintaining the lives of very disabled babies is a very high cost enterprise, and on the fact that the money used in doing so could be usefully used in pursuing treatments for others who are equally in need of attention and who some people at least will assume are more likely to benefit from it. As far as I can see such an argument would also count against all those whose call upon resources is likely to be high for some considerable time, unless, that is, cogent reasons could be given for treating small people differently from big ones in the matter of resource allocation, and I can see no general reason for arguing that they should be given less access to treatment.

Secondly, at the end of life, it seems to me that to force unwanted treatment on, or to deny death to, a person who wishes to die because he cannot bear to live the life he is living is not only death-making, but involves an abuse of resources. To pursue aggressive treatment in relation to someone who would rather die as a person, a *Mensch*, like Eli Kahn, or to continue to offer hospice care to a person who would rather be killed, is not just to offer a personal affront to such individuals; it is to waste resources that could be used helping those who wish to live the lives they have for as long as they can with as much quality as possible.

References

Barnard, C. (1986), 'The Need for Euthanasia' in Downing, A.B. and Smoker, B. (eds.) *Voluntary Euthanasia: Experts Debate the Right to Die*, Peter Own, London.
Brahams, M. and Brahams, D. (1983), *Journal of Medical Ethics*, vol. 9, no. 1, pp.12-16.
Crisp, R. (1987), 'A good death: who best to bring it?', *Bioethics*, vol. 1, no. 1, pp.74-9.
Davies, A. (1983), 'Right to life of handicapped', letter to the Editor, *Journal of Medical Ethics*, vol. 9, no.3.
Davies, A. (1992), 'The right to life: the right to education', in Fairbairn, G. and Fairbairn, S. *Integrating Special Children: some ethical issues*, Aldershot, Avebury.

Dyer, C. (1993), 'Lords lift last bar to mercy death', *The Guardian*, 4th March, p.1.

Fairbairn, G.J. (1987), 'When a baby dies - a father's view,' *Nursing Practice*, pp.167-168.

Fairbairn, G. J. (1991a), 'Enforced death: enforced life', *Journal of Medical Ethics*, vol. 17, pp.144-9.

Fairbairn, G.J. (1991b), 'Complexity and the value of lives: some philosophical dangers for mentally handicapped people', *Journal of Applied Philosophy*, Vol 8, no. 2, pp. 211-217.

Fairbairn, G. (1992), 'Response to Saunders and Singh', *Journal of Medical Ethics*, vol. 18, no.3, pp.162-3.

Harris, J. (1985), *The Value of Life*, Routledge and Kegan Paul, London.

McCullagh, P. (1993), *Brain Dead, Brain Absent, Brain Donors: Human Subjects or Human Objects?* Chichester, John Wiley and Sons.

O'Brien, J. and Tyne, A. (1981), *The Principles of Normalisation - A Foundation for Effective Services*, Campaign for Mental Handicap, London.

Rachels, J. (1986), *The End of Life*, Oxford University Press, Oxford.

Saunders, C. (1991), 'Enforced death: enforced life', letter to the editor, *Journal of Medical Ethics*, Vol 18. No., p.48.

Singh, S. (1992), 'Enforced death: enforced life - another response', letter to the editor, *Journal of Medical Ethics*, vol. 18, no.1, p.48.

SPEAK OUT, Issue 5, Dec, 1988, Community and Mental Handicap Educational and Research Association, 12a Maddox Street, London, W1R 9PL.

Williams, B. (1973), 'A Critique of Utilitarianism' in Smart, J.C.C. and Williams, B.

Utilitarianism: For and Against, Cambridge University Press, Cambridge.

Wolfensberger, W. (1972), *The Principle of Normalisation in Human Services*, published by NIMR, Canada. (Available in Britain from CMH publications, 5 Kentings, Comberton, Cambridge, CB3 7DT.)

Wolfensberger, W. (1987), *The New Genocide of Handicapped and Afflicted People*, New York, Syracuse University Training Institute. (Available in Britain from CMH publications, 5 Kentings, Comberton, Cambridge, CB3 7DT.)

Notes

1. A version of part of this chapter appeared in the *Journal of Medical Ethics* (Fairbairn, G.J. 1991a) and was followed up (Fairbairn, 1992) by a reply to critical letters by Saunders (1991) and Singh (1991).

2. See, for example his distasteful and poorly argued remarks about complexity of life in p.57-8 of his book *The End of Life* which I discuss in some detail in Fairbairn (1991b).

3. The first two of these questions come from Christiaan Barnard (1986, p.177) who relates how they are the most frequent questions he is asked when he speaks to audiences about transplantation.

4. Though there is a tendency to regard microcephaly and anenephaly in a simple way that is then used to justify not only medical decisions in relation to, but moral decisions about the status of babies with these conditions, they are each much more complex and varied than most of us believe. For a full discussion of this area, see McCullagh, P. (1993).

7 Therapy abatement
DAVID LAMB

Introduction

Many arguments in favour of euthanasia rely on examples of life-prolonging therapy applied to unwilling patients in circumstances which suggest that a dignified death is being denied to those whose suffering is needlessly extended. In this respect requests for the withdrawal of certain life-prolonging procedures is presented as an inseparable issue from requests for euthanasia or 'mercy killing'. Similarly, a patient's expression of an autonomous decision regarding therapy options is frequently regarded as morally equivalent to an autonomous decision in favour of assisted suicide. With increasing public demand for greater control over therapy options at the end of life, is it possible to separate current interest in legal directives which specify options to forego various forms of life-sustaining therapy from the 'right to die' and 'right to kill' objectives frequently expressed by pro-euthanasia pressure groups? Is an enlightened attitude towards autonomous decisions regarding therapy abatement likely to encourage steps towards voluntary or non-voluntary euthanasia?

Treatment abatement

Fears of medical technology out of control are well-expressed in Robert F. Weir's (1990) appraisal of therapy options for the terminally ill. He speaks of the need to 'establish reasonable ethical limits to the technological prolongation of life lest we become unthinking and uncaring slaves to that technology' (Weir, 1990, p.viii). Weir's arguments and case studies should be placed in the context of recent legislation in the USA on Living Wills, Advanced Directives and legal directives on treatment abatement cases, including decisions to abate technological feeding and hydration. But these are also ethical issues of universal concern. Of particular importance to the question of separating euthanasia from withdrawal of therapy is Weir's concept of 'treatment abatement', which means - in one crucial sense - 'decisions to withhold', or not to initiate a form of treatment, and also a 'reduction in degree or intensity' or 'a

116

progressive diminishing of treatment' (Weir, 1990, p.10). A further meaning is 'nullification' or 'termination', which encompasses 'decisions by autonomous, critically ill or terminally ill patients (or the surrogates of non-autonomous patients) to refuse all forms of life-sustaining treatment' (*ibid.*, p.10). Whilst this latter case is close to euthanasia, it nevertheless embraces those conditions where inevitable death is recognised - and hence the futility of life-prolonging therapy is apparent - whilst a moral imperative to provide comfort and care is uppermost. Withdrawal of some - but not all - forms of therapy need not be synonymous with euthanasia, especially when treating the terminally ill.

The withdrawal or withholding of therapy which has proved to be useless in the face of inevitable death has always been an aspect of 'good medical practice' and should not be construed as mercy killing' - either by act or omission. It is sometimes misleading to speak of 'letting die' by withdrawing certain forms of therapy from the terminally ill. In some cases there is nothing else a doctor can do. The expression 'I let him die' has a meaning only if there is a possible chance of maintaining life. When facing inevitable death the choice is not between life and death, but how the patient shall die. For this reason outmoded distinctions such as the 'acts-omissions' distinction, or that drawn between extraordinary and non-extraordinary therapy are of little relevance to therapy options for terminal patients. It should be stressed that 'therapy abatement' is not synonymous with 'termination of all therapy'. Properly understood it captures that aspect of sound medical practice which recognises that there are times when the dying process should be rendered more comfortable. Is there an ethical imperative to subject a patient to repeated attempts at resuscitation, a futile regime of intravenous alimentation, dialysis, drug-dependent maintenance of the blood pressure 'prophylactic' antibiotics, and control of the heartbeat by electrical means in order to maintain survival for a couple of days, or even a week? Is it not more important to concentrate on physical comfort where therapy might involve more emphasis on oral hygiene, and care of skin in a family environment outside the ICU? Thus to avoid confusion between therapy abatement and euthanasia (passive or active) it is important to recognise an alternative distinction between 'treating for living' and 'treating for dying' (Kennedy, 1989). There are times, in the course of treating terminally ill patients (or anencephalic infants with no hope of any future), when treatment for dying is the only appropriate course, and where the infliction of life-prolonging therapy is morally unjustifiable. This point is expressed by Robert Twycross and Sylvia Lack in their study of therapy options for patients suffering from advanced cancer.

Nasogastric tubes, intravenous infusions, antibiotics, cardiac resuscitation and artificial respiration are all primarily supportive measures for use in acute or acute-on-chronic illness to assist a patient through the initial period towards recovery of health. To use such measures with patients who are close to death and have no expectancy of a return to health is generally inappropriate, and therefore bad medicine (Twycross and Lack, 1986, p.7).

Under appropriate conditions it is good medical practice to treat severely brain-damaged infants (for example, anencephalics) for dying rather than engage in hopeless and futile attempts to prolong their lives. Such a course should not be confused with proposals for the 'mercy killing' of newborns. (Singer and Kuhse, 1985). There is, however, an urgent need for open discussion and guidelines regarding the categories of handicapped newborns for whom treatment for dying should supersede attempts at life-prolongation. This was apparent in the case of Baby J.

In 1990 an infant boy, known as Baby J, was born in England. He was 13 weeks premature, weighing two and a half pounds, was brain-damaged, paralysed, probably blind and deaf, incapable of spontaneous breathing such that life could only be maintained with the aid of a ventilator. Because of conflicting ethical opinions on the right course of treatment Baby J was made a ward of court, and in October 1990 the Court of Appeal ruled that he should be allowed to die if further life-threatening conditions occurred. Lord Justice Taylor said that the case had created a 'hideous dilemma', but he emphasised that the courts could never sanction steps to terminate a life (Reported in *The Independent*, October 20, 1990, p.6). An editorial in *The Sunday Correspondent*, (October 21, 1990, p.18) saw that judgement as an endorsement of 'current medical practice'. On the other hand, pro-life organizations expressed fears that the courts were actually endorsing euthanasia and offers were made to provide life-prolonging therapy for Baby J. The case showed a clear need for an informed debate on this issue which raised moral issues which went beyond disputes over medical knowledge, such as the value society places on the quality of life. In this instance, however, an injunction was imposed and further reporting of the case was prohibited.

The context in which therapy is provided often determines the ethical imperatives regarding therapy options. In hospices and nursing homes for the elderly the moral imperative to prolong life is not uppermost - as it may be in an ICU or accident unit. Yet even here treatment abatement, in the sense of 'not initiating' or 'diminishing' therapy, does not amount to euthanasia. The central philosophy of the hospice movement is the need to maximise the quality, not necessarily the quantity, of remaining life, and if life-prolongation involves the infliction of suffering it is not regarded as an ultimate good to be sought at all costs. The point of hospice care is not the addition of more days but the prolongation of an ability to make each day count for something. A similar imperative is relevant for nursing homes for the elderly where 'Do not resuscitate' orders and 'Do not hospitalise' orders may be morally acceptable. Given the average age of 82 years in nursing homes for the elderly, removal to a hospital may be so confusing, and unsettling, that ending one's days in comfort may have greater value than life-prolongation. Thus in the context of geriatric care 'appropriate medical practice does not always mean employing all the guns of medical technology' (A physician cited by Weir, 1990, p.50).

Advance directives

In March 1976 the New Jersey Supreme Court ruled that the 'right of privacy' permitted termination of therapy in the case of Karen Quinlan. This ruling initiated a new era in treatment abatement which recognised an ethical requirement to limit therapy. The Quinlan decision was followed within seven months by the Californian Natural Death Act and similar legislation in several other states, according to which patients, under certain stringently defined conditions, could forego life-prolonging therapy. (Keene, 1978, Lamb 1988) During the next ten years an increasing number of American court decisions acknowledged that autonomous patients may refuse therapy on the legal grounds of 'privacy' - even when refusal may result in death. Emerging case law also reveals that an adult's right to refuse therapy may be upheld even though he or she has lost the capacity to make such a decision.

In 1985 attention focussed on the removal of life-sustaining nutrition and hydration when the New Jersey Supreme Court ruled that technological nutrition and hydration (a nasogastric tube) could be removed from a non-autonomous patient, Claire Conroy, an 84 year old woman with serious mental impairment and a limited life expectancy, on the authorization of a surrogate. That same year saw considerable legislation concerning advance directives, living wills and Natural Death Acts, with statements on nutrition and hydration. At present some 40 states and the District of Columbia have legislation on advance directives which allow for the removal of 'medical treatment'. Further steps which firmly establish the legal basis of advance directives include the Patient Self-Determination Act which from 1 December, 1991 tied Medicare and

119

Medicaid reimbursement for hospital and nursing homes to the provision of information about the use of living wills and advance directives. Hospitals and nursing homes who do not have a system in place for educating patients and staff about advance planning are excluded from Medicare and Medicaid funding. This clearly extends the scope of patient refusal and will benefit the taxpayer. Ironically there are no provisions for the extension of health-care funding for those whose capacity for choice is restricted in the face of under-provision of health care. Although living wills have not been widely discussed in the UK until recently, there are signs of public interest in them. In 1988 the Age Concern Report under the title, 'The Living Will, Consent to Treatment at the End of Life', generated interest in the subject. The question addressed by proponents of living wills and advance directives is the right to direct treatment during the end stages of one's life, especially when a stage is reached where one is no longer competent to make a rational decision. There is widespread fear of painful death in institutional isolation in circumstances where the disease process has severely limited the ability to make decisions concerning treatment options. A living will, or advance directive, is a document upon which individuals can indicate in advance a preference not to be given various forms of therapy to prolong life. Many caring and compassionate institutions and individuals have supported them as a means of providing a patient with some means of control over his or her death.

There appears to be widespread support for living wills and advance directives among bioethicists, especially for prior decisions concerning incompetency. Following the Patient Self Determination Act, 1991, there is a growing demand in the US for their recognition in the Constitution. Their moral and legal basis is the autonomy interest in avoiding bodily intrusions. Their alleged benefits are bound up with a sense of control over future decisions regarding the end points of life. John A. Robertson (1991, p.6) outlines the two foremost benefits of living wills:

i   The living will thus empowers people, by extending the scope of personal autonomy to situations in which autonomy cannot be directly exercised.

ii.   ...living wills, if specific enough, provide a worthwhile rule for nontreatment decisions that appears to respect autonomy without compromising respect for incompetent patients.

There are two closely related ethical problems with advance directives. First, there are problems of abuse, in the sense that many proponents of euthanasia (both voluntary and non-voluntary) support them as part of a strategy to relax existing prohibitions on euthanasia. Some pressure groups in favour of euthanasia see no distinction between therapy abatement and euthanasia and would welcome an extension of therapy abatement to include 'merciful release'. Second, there are problems concerning the potential abuse of autonomous decisions to abate life-prolonging therapy.

To appreciate the potential for the abuse of advance directives it is necessary to examine some of the earliest proposals for living wills where therapy abatement was not so clearly separated from directives to kill. The earliest proponent appears to be Luis Kutner, a Chicago attorney who drafted a living will in the 1930s in response to 'barbaric' medical treatment inflicted against the protests of a dying friend (Weir, 1990, p.181). The document was circulated and the first person to sign it was Bishop Fulton Sheen. The second was Errol Flynn. In the 1960s the document was taken up by the United States Euthanasia Education Council. In 1969 Kutner published a paper in *The Indiana Law Journal* under the title 'Due Process of Euthanasia: Living will, A Proposal'.

Although Kutner did not openly advocate euthanasia in his paper it was clear that this was what he had in mind. In his concluding remarks he said, 'as of now a doctor cannot be directed to act affirmatively to terminate a patient's life' (*ibid.*, p.553).

The fear that, once legalised, advance directives concerning treatment abatement may lead to a more permissive attitude towards euthanasia explains much of the pro-life opposition to them. In giving expression to these fears pro-lifers have been accused of adopting doctrinaire attitudes in favour of the curtailment of patient autonomy. Where possible pro-lifers have secured restrictive amendments to NDA's and Living Will legislation, which have been accepted by proponents of a more radical position in the belief that these amendments can be changed through 'clean up' legislation at a later time (Weir 1990, p.197). In this context slippery slope predictions from pro-lifers have considerable significance. Proposals were put forward by the Hemlock Society of the USA for two advance directives not limited to the Living Wills' criteria for therapy abatement. The first is a 'Request for Help in Dying' which calls for acceleration of one's dying in the event of terminal illness; the second is a 'Request for Help in Dying by Proxy', which is a written directive for securing a physician's help by intentionally killing the patient. The Hemlock Society has also tried, so far unsuccessfully, to promote a Humane and Dignified Death Act, as a substantial modification of the NDA. Its most controversial clause is an advance directive calling for a physician to 'administer 'aid in dying' in a humane and dignified manner'. The Hemlock Society interpret the expression 'aid in dying' as any medical procedure that will 'swiftly, painlessly and humanely terminate the life of the qualified patient'. This would include the use of a lethal injection or lethal overdose. If accepted the proposal for an 'aid in dying' would not only legitimise euthanasia; it would incorporate a legal obligation to kill. Moreover, it would initiate a new departure in defensive medicine. If a living will grants immunity from civil or criminal liability to those who remove 'life-sustaining procedures' but gives no protection to those who act in the belief that it is in the patient's best interest to provide maximum care, erring on the side of death would be the safest course in any questionable situation.

In November 1991 voters in Washington were given a chance to express a preference over Initiative Measure No. 119 following a petition organised by Citizens for Death With Dignity containing 223,000 signatures of registered voters. It was defeated. But if passed Initiative 119 would have amended Washington's 1979 'Natural Death Act' to the 'Death With Dignity Act', and would have specified that 'artificially administered nutrition and hydration' could be legitimately refused by competent adult patients, or withdrawn from incompetent patients who have made an advanced directive to physicians. The initiative also proposed a loosening of the definition of 'terminal condition' to include PVS patients, and provided the option of a voluntary 'aid in dying' as 'aid in the form of a medical service, provided in person by a physician, that will end the life of a conscious and mentally competent qualified patient in a dignified, painless and humane manner'. Opponents of Initiative 119 contended that the proposal would make it legal for doctors to administer a lethal dose on request.

At present pressure groups in favour of extending the scope of living wills embrace both those who favour greater patient autonomy over therapy options and those who have an interest in killing. This is further complicated by the fact that the same movement can contain those whose interest in killing arises from compassion and those whose interest is grounded in fiscal or eugenic reasons.

Can abuse be prevented?

Can proposals for autonomous treatment abatement be kept distinct from proposals for the right to kill? An affirmative answer would depend on NDA's and advance directives being framed in such a way that they do not support the long-term objectives of euthanasia societies; on 'aid in dying' amendments being recognized as proposals for the right to kill and consequently rejected; and on statutes based on the right to refuse or rights of privacy clearly addressing the question of refusing nutrition and hydration and placing restrictions on the decisions of surrogates.

Nutrition and hydration

The moral justification for advance directives is the right not to have unwanted therapy inflicted on one, a right possessed by those who have clearly and autonomously indicated such a preference. In many cases advance directives are an understandable response to the threat of unlimited technical prolongation of life but it has been argued that nourishment and hydration is not a therapy, even if it is provided on the instructions of a therapist in a therapeutic environment. Among the differences between nourishment and hydration and medical treatment is the fact that only the latter is withdrawn when the patient recovers. Food is not medicine; it is not like antibiotics or blood-transfusions, and it is somewhat absurd to treat it as such. Medicine is administered as a cure, or relief, for diagnosable pathological conditions. Food is provided to meet the body's need for basic resources. Even when food has some medical significance - for example, to alleviate pain or combat certain deficiencies - this function is indirect. A patient may surprise physicians and live or even recover after the withdrawal of medicine, but will certainly die if food is withheld. If it is maintained that withdrawal of nutrition and hydration is not equivalent to the withdrawal of therapy then the withdrawal of food from patients in persistent vegetative states will be seen as a form of euthanasia, not as a policy of 'treating for dying'. According to this argument, if persistent vegetative state patients are not dying and if they are hungry there is a human duty to feed them. Giving food to the hungry also has an important ethical symbolic role such that those who deny food to the hungry represent a paradigm case of a denial of fundamental human relationships. The revulsion against the denial of food to patients in persistent vegetative states is not based on crude emotion but is grounded in a

123

long-standing moral tradition in which food has a basic symbolic role in the expression of human compassion. On these terms it is as wrong to withhold nourishment and hydration as it is wrong to kill the innocent.

Of course there are exceptions; for example, nutrition may cause such pain and discomfort that the distress caused by feeding outweighs any potential benefit. But if it is withdrawn for non- therapeutic purposes those who authorise this course should state clearly that they are engaged in euthanasia.

It should make no difference whether the food is served on a tray, spoon fed, eaten with the aid of artificial dentures or administered through a tube. The intentional denial of food for non-therapeutic reasons is nothing other than euthanasia. Withdrawal of nourishment and hydration is not strictly akin to the abatement of useless therapy because (1) in many cases food is not therapy and (2) even when it does not assist in a cure it may still bring comfort.

Autonomy

Demands for greater patient autonomy reveal a desire by individuals to achieve greater levels of self-management against professional paternalism and bureaucracy. Yet in much of the literature of recent bioethics support for autonomy has become an ideology which many support without reflection on the range of choices that can be freely sought by an individual. Most discussions, for example, focus on the autonomous refusal of therapy, reflecting fears of over-treatment. This is how autonomy has been championed by euthanasia societies. It is easily forgotten that the greatest problem for the majority of the world's population is that of under-treatment. Even in the wealthiest countries health-care resources are too thinly stretched to provide all of the population with adequate care. At present thirty seven million Americans have no health cover; forty five million are under-insured. Opinion surveys on the reluctance to donate organs reveal that fear of under-treatment ('the doctors might give up before I'm really dead') is one of the main reasons for not carrying donor cards. As a corrective to the view that large-scale public-opinion support for treatment abatement is an indication of support for euthanasia it might be suggested that such demands are simply part of a wider movement in favour of more control over a whole range of informed therapy options, which are not reducible to slogans concerning the 'right to die'.

It is sometimes argued that a patient should have the right to refuse therapy - and possibly life-prolongation - on the grounds that it is too costly, or burdensome on relatives, to continue. This, however, is not a question of autonomous choice as the conditions under which the choice is expressed may not have been autonomously chosen. Some disabled people may exercise their 'right' because of lack of adequate services, support and money. Given a free choice few people would opt for circumstances in which financial restrictions limited their range of free expression. Moreover, the cost of therapy should be recognized as a social or political problem with a collectivist solution. A situation in which a patient dies in a state of anxiety over payment for therapy can be seen as an immoral outcome of a society which has adopted a restricted and distorted individualist perspective.

The concept of autonomy is not always adequately represented in decisions concerning treatment abatement. There is more to the exercise of autonomy than mere refusal. In April, 1986, a 28-year-old American woman, Elizabeth Bouvia, successfully established her right to refuse therapy despite the fact that such a course was life-threatening. She was quadriplegic. Except for a few fingers of one hand and some slight head and facial movements she was immobile. She suffered degenerative and severely crippling arthritis. She was in continual pain. A tube permanently attached to her chest automatically dosed her with morphine which relieved some, but not all, of the pain and physical discomfort. She had previously sought the right to assisted suicide, requesting care in a public hospital whilst she intentionally starved herself to death, but the courts refused her request. However, when the state of her health declined to the point where she could not be spoon-fed without vomiting and nausea a drastic decision was taken. Noting the court's ruling against her suicidal intentions the hospital authorities decided that when her weight loss reached a life-threatening level a nasogastric tube should be inserted, even though it was against her will and contrary to her express instructions. Acting on legal advice Elizabeth Bouvia took her case to the California Court of Appeal where she sought 'the removal from her body of a nasogastric tube inserted and maintained against her will and without her consent by physicians who so placed it for the purpose of keeping her alive through involuntary forced feeding' (Report of the California Courts of Appeal, 24 April, 1986, p.1317).

The Court ruled in her favour. In his twenty-five page ruling, associate justice Edwin Beach, said: 'She has the right to refuse the increased dehumanising aspects of her condition created by the insertion of a permanent tube through her nose and into her stomach' (Beach, 1991, p.49). The question of passive euthanasia or assisted suicide was clearly ruled out when the Court stated that it was immaterial whether or not the removal of the tube caused her

125

death. 'Being competent, she has the right to live out the remainder of her natural life in dignity and peace' (Report, 1986, p.1317).

Having established her right to forego her life-sustaining therapy, a victory secured after a two year long legal battle, Elizabeth Bouvia decided not to have the tube removed. The real issue was not whether she should live or die but how she could control her destiny.

In some recent discussions on autonomous refusal of therapy idealised models of autonomy have been borrowed from political discourse and applied to health-care with devastating results. The policy of restoring autonomy to mental patents in the United Kingdom over the past decade is one unfortunate example. Releasing patents from institutional confinement without adequate community support has not enhanced their capacity for autonomy. In the political context liberal individualist values have stressed the freedom of persons from state authority and the restraint of tyrants. But these models of autonomy have entered into medical decision-making without allowing for the fact that they have a very different meaning in the area of health-care. In the political sphere restraint of government has been the hallmark of liberal values. With government withdrawal from public welfare commitments the right to opt out of state-run health provisions has been presented as an extension of personal liberty against paternalistic intervention. But freedom from care and medical intervention is not, in itself, a characteristic of autonomy like freedom from political tyranny. The concept of autonomy means more in the moral sphere. As George J. Agich argues:

> The abstract liberal concept of autonomy has its proper place in the legal political sphere, where protection of individuals from tyranny and oppression by powerful others is rightly defended, but not in the moral life, where a fuller conception is required, one that acknowledges the essential social nature of human development and recognises dependence as a nonaccidental feature of the human condition (Agich, 1990, p.12).

The goal of autonomy in the provision of health-care, especially in Agich's (1990) account of the needs of patents requiring long- term care, is not reducible to the removal of obstacles and state interference. It may also require a maximisation of options and community support. Dependence is not antithetical to autonomy in the moral sphere, where autonomy might well be compatible with dependence upon a nurse or helper. There has been too much emphasis on resistance to unwanted care and paternalistic abuse with little recognition that, for many patients, including the very young and the old, some form of

126

dependence is the condition upon which autonomous decision-making rests. Agich's analysis of autonomy is important in this respect: although correct in the political and legal sphere the abstract liberal concept of autonomy should not be uncritically extended into the moral sphere and limits on the ideal should include recognition of 'the essential historical and social nature of persons', especially in 'the development aspects of becoming and being a person' (Agich, 1990, pp.12-13).

There are many limits on the right to refuse therapy which are compatible with respect for autonomy. A paradigmatic case here would be a twenty-one-year-old anorexic suffering from depression. Should she be allowed to starve herself to death? The answer is a resounding no: her condition prevents an autonomous rational choice.

The fact that there is more to autonomy than the right to refuse has not been fully appreciated by many philosophers and lawyers who have expended large amounts of energy in arguments for the withdrawal of therapy and accelerated death. That there is more to autonomy than the right to an early death was recognized in a decision reached by the Nevada Supreme Court, following the death of Kenneth Bergstedt in 1991.

Kenneth Bergstedt was a 31-year-old ventilator-dependent quadriplegic who was cared for by his father. When facing the imminent death of his father Kenneth petitioned the court for the withdrawal of life-sustaining therapy. But whilst the legal proceedings dragged on Kenneth died in circumstances which suggested that his death had been planned. The toxicology report revealed a high level of barbituates in his system and the respirator clamp had been unfastened so that he could remove the tube from his mouth. Nevertheless, the Court went on to issue a 'decision' in order to 'provide guidance to others who may find themselves in similar predicaments'. The Court expressed a 'state interest' in preserving life, but recognized that an individual's 'right to decide' will 'generally outweigh the state's interest in preserving life', even if the condition is not terminal. But, most important, the Court required that all competent patients be informed of available health-care alternatives before ending life-sustaining therapy. This is interesting because it maintains the crucial link between therapy abatement and autonomy whilst isolating arguments exclusively based on appeals for the right to an early death. Too frequently autonomy is paraded in slogans bound up with the right to die. The Nevada Supreme Court, in this decision, placed autonomy back in the centre.

A precedent which might have influenced the Nevada Supreme Court was a ruling by the Supreme Court in the State of Georgia on a 33-year-old quadriplegic, Larry James McAffree, who pleaded for the discontinuation of ventilatory support. After winning his case, and repeatedly insisting that he would exercise his right-to-die he was offered residence in various institutions with the intention of making his life more productively tolerable. He consequently chose to remain alive. This case would appear to justify the Nevada decision, as it illustrates that patients who opt for discontinuation may do so without knowing all the options available to them.

The potential for dramatic decision-reversals has not been fully appreciated by the architects of living wills and advance directives. For despite their popularity with the media and the bioethicists living wills have not been enthusiastically accepted by those who are supposed to benefit from them. Opinion poll surveys have indicated that few people actually make them out (Emanuel and Emanuel, 1989). Even when they are made out many physicians are reluctant to follow them. John A. Robertson (1991) in a critical commentary on the living will juggernaut, speaks of a distrust and ambivalence among ordinary people and policy-makers. He sees the roots of this distrust in 'conceptual confusions and contradictions that inhere in the use of an advance directive to control a future situation' (Robertson, 1991, p.7). It is not clear, argues Robertson, that a prior directive made by a competent person is the most accurate indicator of a person's interest when she becomes incompetent. There is a different framework in the latter case; the rational standpoint on which the prior decision was made is missing. The values and interests of the competent have no meaning to the incompetent. These interests can be distinct. It is the competent person who does not want to be maintained in an incompetent state; we cannot speak authoritatively of the wishes of the incompetent, which do not rest on any rational basis. Although it is still the same person the patient's interests have radically changed. 'Yet the premise of the prior directive', says Robertson, 'is that the patient's interests and values remain significantly the same' (*ibid*, p.7). But we cannot know this. What we do have, however, is an increasing number of cases, like Bouvia and McAffee, where a strongly held preference is freely reversed. The difference is that in these cases the authors were competent at the time of the reversal. Merely because incompetents cannot express a reversal does not guarantee that their interests remain identical.

One objection to this argument may lie in an appeal to the wholeness of the self; that the self has a unity that exists over one's entire life, and that if previously competent persons have a history of preferences and values they should be treated - when incompetent - as still having those values. This, however, is a weak argument which overlooks the fact that people can change their interests and values throughout their lives. At the very least any course of action based on an appeal to the autonomy of persons must respect their capacity to change their interests.

It is this potential for conflict between the interests of the competent and the incompetent person which weakens the appeal to autonomy in advance directives which specify abatement of life-sustaining therapy. Admittedly it is difficult to verify or assess the extent of this conflict, as in most of these cases the patient remains incompetent until death. But there is plenty of anecdotal evidence of patients being treated, despite a contrary directive, and then recovering with gratitude. Perhaps the most informative thing that can be said about advance directives is that they are a device for measuring a person's interests, not an expression of certainty, which is a characteristic of the will of a deceased.

Autonomy and surrogacy

The dangers of the abuse of autonomous refusal are beginning to emerge. Another serious problem concerns the employment of surrogates to express a patient's 'autonomous' choice. There are, for example, problems regarding who is an appropriate surrogate. Although it is accepted that surrogates should be close family members there are many who do not live in 'recognized' families, such as members of the gay community. There is also what Americans describe as 'the Florida syndrome', where elderly retired parents have lost contact with their offspring, although the latter may be called upon to make decisions without appreciating their parent's desires regarding therapy options. A similar problem occurs if it is the parents in such circumstances who are called upon to make decisions on behalf of estranged offspring.

Even if these practical problems can be resolved the objection remains that autonomy is not always the highest virtue, and that autonomous refusal may have to be weighed against a presumption in favour of life, especially in cases involving an alleged change of mind, as indicated by the following borderline example by James F. Childress.

A twenty-eight-year-old man decided to terminate chronic renal dialysis because of his restricted life-style and the burdens on his family - he had chronic diabetes, was legally blind, and could not walk because of progressive neuropathy. His wife and physician agreed to provide him with medication to relieve his pain while he died and agreed not to put him on dialysis even if he requested it under the influence of uraemia, morphine sulphate, and Ketoacidosis (the last resulting from cessation of insulin). While dying in hospital, the patient awoke complaining of pain and asked to be put back on dialysis. The patient's wife and physician decided to act on the patient's earlier request that he be allowed to die, and he died a few hours later (Childress, 1990, p.14).

Childress argues that he should have been put back on dialysis where it could then have been determined whether he had autonomously revoked his earlier decision. If it was then deemed that his earlier decision was uppermost they could have proceeded with more confidence. 'Present revocation', argues Childress, 'takes priority if it is autonomous' (p.14).

Why is it that there is concern, in cases of this kind, over which decision counts? Surely, both were taken by the agent concerned. One obvious answer is that it is the truly autonomous decision that is being sought. But there is another answer which reveals the importance of a presumption in favour of life in doubtful circumstances: a decision in favour of life-prolongation can always be annulled if it turns out that this was not autonomously desired by the patient, but steps taken to end a life cannot be revoked if it later turns out that this was not autonomously desired.

The limits to surrogate refusal were tested in the controversy surrounding the Cruzan case in 1990. Following a motor accident in 1983 Nancy Beth Cruzan remained in a persistent vegetative state. Convinced that there was no hope of recovery and that she would not have wished to go on living in that condition, Nancy's parents sought to withhold nutrition and hydration which was being artificially supplied through a tube. A court authorised removal but this was overruled, in November 1988, by the Missouri Supreme Court, which maintained that Nancy's parents could not exercise the right to refuse treatment on her behalf and that the state's unqualified interest in preserving life should prevail. The case was then taken up by the United States Supreme Court, on June 25 1990, which upheld the decision of the Missouri court in a 4 to 3 decision. One of the arguments advanced in support of the withdrawal of nutrition and hydration was the claim that prior to the accident she had made several remarks to the effect that she would not wish 'to face life as a vegetable' and that she believed that 'some conditions were worse than death'. Although she had not signed an advance directive it was argued that these prior statements amounted to an informed refusal. The court, however, did not accept this as sufficient evidence for an autonomous refusal. It should be stressed that the cost of life-prolonging therapy was not at issue in this case and there was no undue financial strain on the relatives. Nancy's daily food supply cost $7.80 and the cost of therapy was paid by the State of Missouri.

The arguments for and against unlimited life-prolongation in irreversible persistent vegetative states will not be addressed here, although it must be said that no constitutional rights are violated by maintenance of therapy for such patients. In a state beyond pain, unaware of her situation, Nancy Beth Cruzan could not be said to have been harmed by continuing medical treatment. She was certainly not in the same category as a pain-racked terminally ill cancer patient who has expressed an interest in foregoing further attempts at life-prolongation.

Yet those close to her maintained that her plight was intolerable, and in September of 1990 the State of Missouri withdrew its interest in prolonging her life. Shortly after her legally appointed guardian concurred with the family wishes and her feeding tubes were removed. Nancy Beth Curzan died on December 26 1990. Her death was reported in England, in the *Guardian* (27 December) in the context of a euthanasia decision. Under the heading 'Euthanasia woman dies' the report described how her parents satisfied the high court's 'euthanasia criteria'. The distinction between treatment abatement and euthanasia was apparently ignored.

There is, however, serious concern over a tendency in cases like Cruzan to amalgamate surrogate decision-making with autonomous refusal. Nancy Beth Cruzan's wishes were not abundantly clear and if a surrogate had been appointed any decision made on her behalf would not have been her autonomous decision. It may be necessary in such cases to appoint a surrogate to act in a patient's best interests, with powers to refuse therapy. But the decision to authorise a surrogate cannot be based on an appeal to patient autonomy and self-determination. The introduction of a legal fiction that autonomous decisions can be made by others is incompatible with the principle of autonomy and would involve the re-introduction of paternalism. Before long it could be claimed that the state provided the best mechanism for making autonomous decisions on behalf of its citizens.

Conclusion

An individual's right to therapy abatement can be protected from abuse in the context of a full understanding of autonomous choice; not merely the right to refuse but the opportunity to consider alternatives. Limits are also required on the role of the surrogate in the refusal of therapy, and further clarification is required concerning the status of nourishment and hydration as forms of therapy. Further safeguards should require that advance directives are not framed in such a way that they can be later hijacked by euthanasia societies. It should also be noted that fears of unlimited life-prolongation could be greatly exaggerated. In an atmosphere of governmental indifference to the plight of the sick, with the notion of welfare tuned to market forces, there is a danger that self-determination can have a restricted meaning; the option of death in the context of an underfunded health service. This may not be the time to campaign for the right to refuse therapy, but rather the time to campaign for improvements to existing therapy.

References

Agich, G.J. (1990), 'Reassessing autonomy in long-term care', *Hastings Center Report*, Nov/Dec., pp.12-17.
Beach, E. (1991), Quoted in *Medical Ethics Advisor*, vol. 7, no. 4, April, p.49.
Beach, E. (1986), Report to the California Court of Appeal, April 24th.
Childress, J.F. (1990), 'The place of autonomy in bioethics', *Hastings Center Report*, Jan/Feb, pp.12-17.
Emanuel, L. & Emanuel, E. (1989), 'The medical directive: a new comprehensive care document', *The Journal of AMA*, vol. 261, pp.3288-3293.
Keene, B. (1978), 'The Natural Death Act: a well-baby check-up on its first birthday', *New York Academy of Sciences*, vol. 315, pp.344-355.
Kennedy, I. (1989), *Treat me right*, Oxford, Clarendon.
Kutner, L. (1969), 'Due process of euthanasia: the living will, a proposal', *The Indiana Law Journal*, vol. 44, pp.539-554.
Lamb, D. (1988), *Down the slippery slope*, London, Routledge.
Robertson, J.A. (1991), 'Second thoughts on living wills', *Hastings Center Report*, Nov/Dec, pp.6-9.
Singer, P. & Kuhse, H. (1985), *Should the baby live?*, Oxford, OUP.
Twycross, R.G. & Lack, S.A. (1986), *System control in for-advanced cancer: alimentary symptoms*, London, Pitman.
Weir, R.F. (1990), *Abating treatment with critically ill patients: ethical and legal limits to the medical prolongation of life*, Oxford, OUP.

8 The global distribution of health care resources

ROBIN ATTFIELD

Introduction

There has been a salutary increase of late in the study of medical ethics, and many philosophers have been applying their skills to themes such as informed consent, *in vitro* fertilisation and choices between lives in matters such as the allocation of kidney machines. This study has probably already been of assistance to individual physicians and health administrators, and, even if it has seldom been of assistance to national governments, this has not been the fault of the philosophers.

Much less, however, has been heard about international priorities in health care, and this despite the well known disparities between facilities in the poorest countries and those in more developed ones. This could be because, besides the staff of the World Health Organisation, there are few professionals liable to be influenced by such a reflection. Or it could be because problems which are difficult enough at local and national levels seem to become mind-boggling and intractable when writ large and considered in their international version. Thus the *Journal of Medical Ethics* in particular has carried little or nothing on international disparities of health and health care, to judge from its own 'Thematic review of past issues'.[1] Yet health and sickness know no boundaries, any more than morality and justice do; and it is high time for some of the global aspects of medical ethics to be explored and debated, as well as more circumscribed and familiar issues. Indeed the task of defending the tendency among medical ethicists to limit themselves to the problems of wealthier societies would be an unenviable one, were anyone bold enough to attempt it.

In this essay I shall therefore be investigating the requirements of justice in health care at an intersocietal and international level. After reviewing some of the current imbalances in health care, I shall investigate what various different accounts of justice involve, and what policies, in present circumstances, those agents and agencies capable of affecting health care provision might, accordingly, be expected to adopt. While attention is not paid directly to the distinctive needs of the elderly, the adoption of the conclusions thus derived would bring it about that many more people would have the opportunity to reach that stage in life; for plausibly one unacceptable aspect of life in much of the Third World is that far too many people die young, and that there simply are too few elderly people. But as little more than an exploratory excursion can be made into these subjects here, my principal aim is to stimulate others to develop these themes much more thoroughly and in much greater detail.

The gravest problem of medical ethics

Currently life expectancy in most of Africa, at about 50 years, is considerably lower than in most of Northern Europe and North America, where it is over 70 years. As the life-prospects of individuals depend to no small extent on life-expectancy, this already constitutes a serious and, on almost any account, an unacceptable imbalance. There again, this imbalance is accompanied by others: by imbalances, that is, in the infant mortality and infant morbidity rates of those regions, in their immunisation rates, and also in the ratios of doctors, of hospitals and of dispensaries to potential patients. Further, many Asian and Latin American countries fare not too differently from most of Africa with regard to these various rates and ratios. Granted also the prevalence of diseases like schistosomiasis and of the various famine-related diseases in the poorer countries, the impression of radical inequalities in health and health care between most developed and most Third World countries is readily confirmed.

Now these inequalities are, of course, related to more fundamental imbalances between levels of wealth and of development, which are attested further by differential rates of literacy, productivity, investment and trade; and this is sufficient warning against regarding the problems as relating to the distribution of medical resources and facilities alone. Yet these health care imbalances are considerable enough in themselves to constitute what must be considered by those with a sense of proportion as the gravest of the many problems of medical ethics.

Justice: Rawls, Nozick and needs

The most influential theory of justice of recent years, that of John Rawls, as presented in *A Theory Of Justice*[2], has relatively little to say about a just international order. Rawls envisages a contract being made between self-interested but rational individuals who, from a behind a veil of ignorance about their own life-prospects, choose rules for their shared life in society. But these individuals are assumed to be potential members of the same geographic community, rather than potential members of international society. Now Rawls occasionally recognises that the principles which the contracting parties are said to chose are appropriate to societies where basic material needs can in general be met, implicitly allowing that different principles might be chosen for other circumstances. But little or nothing is specified about the principles which would be chosen to govern intersocietal relations, whether of diplomacy, communications, trade or mutual aid.

The deficiency is, however, attended to by Brian Barry in *The Liberal Theory Of Justice*[3]. There it is urged that Rawls's contractors would select rules for international relations which would preempt the need for them to live in an underprivileged society, and which would provide, as far as possible, for basic needs to be met in general in every society. Without endorsing Rawls's fundamental but questionable assumption (the assumption that the rules which self-interested but rational contracting parties choosing behind a veil of ignorance would select will be just ones) Barry here points the way towards a development or extension of Rawlsian contractarianism which would both cope with international relations and, if implemented, have a world-shaking impact on global health-care provision.

By contrast the rival theory of justice supplied be Robert Nozick's *Anarchy, State and Utopia*[4] appears systematically at odds with the kind of redistribution which contractarianism is capable of advocating. This historical theory of justice, with its concern for the upholding of entitlements and with its defence of a minimal, night-watchman state, leaves little room for redistribution within any one society, let alone for international redistribution. Indeed it explicitly rejects appeals to non-historical grounds for redistribution, such as current needs.

Admittedly Nozick's theory calls for a revision of holdings where present holdings result from violence or deception in the past, as long, presumably, as the claim that this was so can itself be proved; and certainly there would be a basis here for the advocacy of reparations between societies, as long as present deprivations could be clearly ascribed to past exploitation. But if this were the only allowable basis for international redistribution, the prospects of poor countries would be poor indeed, granted the scope for challenges to such historical explanations of poverty. As long as needs are not counted as in themselves grounds of obligation, the obligations of rich countries would often be exhausted well before the lack of health care resources in poor countries had been as much as alleviated. But the implication that there is nothing unfair or unjust about people in their millions inheriting wretched life-prospects which are far worse than those of millions of others, and through mere accidents of birth at that, puts a great strain on the credibility of any theory which carries it. Indeed it puts a great strain on the credibility of Nozick's theory in particular.

This in turn suggests a theory of value which locates high value in the satisfaction of basic needs. Things are here understood to be of value when there are interpersonal reasons for promoting or preserving them. This granted, a theory of obligation and of justice is readily suggested which requires agents to maximise the satisfaction of basic needs. Or rather, such a theory is readily suggested unless, as is surely implausible, other goods outstrip the satisfaction of basic needs in point of value. The resulting theory is of the consequentialist type, but is much more plausible than positions requiring the maximisation of happiness or the minimisation of unhappiness, or again the maximisation of the satisfaction of preferences (utilitarian positions which theorists such as Rawls understandably reject). On such a theory, if there are unsatisfied basis needs in one country, however far away, their satisfaction would generally take priority over other goods, even if the other goods would arise much closer to the agent's home.

Further, this form of needs-consequentialism can justify obligations to conform to various rules or practices. These are rules or practices overall compliance with which would enhance appreciably the satisfaction of basic needs, and can do so for the reason that where people act together and conform to such rules, a greater difference is made to the satisfaction of needs than would otherwise be made. (Accordingly this theory is not a version of act-consequentialism, or open to the standard objections to which that kind of theory is liable.) Good examples would include rules of trade which take into account the interests of primary producers as well as those of consumers and entrepreneurs; rules such as these would be upheld by this kind of consequentialism, every bit as much as by the extended contractarianism introduced earlier.[5]

There again, rules requiring reparations on the part of the agents or the beneficiaries of unjustified violence or deception would again be upheld by this kind of theory just as much by historical and libertarian accounts such as that by Nozick. This type of theory can thus account for justifications of policy such as appeals to reparations, appeals which are apparently a strength of Nozick's theory. (By contrast, Nozick-like theories cannot consistently be revised to find room for non-historical considerations such as needs.) By combining the justifications of redistribution found in other theories of justice, and through its capacity to appeal without inconsistency to basic needs, consequentialism thus supplies a strong basis for tackling international obligations in the matter of health care, deserving thereby to receive a readier acknowledgement of its own intrinsic merits as a theory of obligation and of value.[6]

Some implications

It follows from such an account of justice that much more effort is called for, in the forms both of treatments and of prevention. More doctors and nurses, more hospitals and dispensaries are needed in much of the Third World; but also much more effort should be given to ensuring for people everywhere clean water, adequate sanitation, improved nutrition and the control of pollution. These issues, indeed, interact with ones of health care, and in at least two ways; for they are in many cases preconditions of improved health, and, there again, improved health prospects often form a necessary condition of the success of population policies, and thereby for progress in economic and social development in general.

But it does not follow that hospitals and health systems should be transplanted from the more developed countries to the less developed, either literally or as models. On the one hand the basic needs of people of the former countries matter too; and on the other hand these institutions will not easily transplant, and will not function at all unless supplied with sufficient recurrent resources. Agents have to take account of the world as it is; and only if large numbers of agents or if powerful agencies cooperate are the contexts and the limits of possible action likely to change. Until that happens the typical ethical problem confronting agents is how, while resources remain inadequate, to make the most difference to the ocean of unsatisfied basic needs; and at the same time how to foster self-help among the people concerned, so that the fruits of intervention are multiplied and development becomes self-perpetuating. If the likeliest way of achieving this is through training paramedics and 'barefoot doctors' (rather than, eg., through building modern hospitals) then that is how action should be shaped; and the same applies if the likeliest way consists in supporting a new and more just social order, and leaving the citizens of that order to confront their health problems without further intervention.

Yet health care is an international project in more ways than this would suggest, and concerns more than the bilateral relations of any pair of countries. Infectious diseases are an international and sometimes a global threat; while much medical research is and perhaps must be of an international character. (This applies also to research into the sociology of medicine, and the study of, for example, why doctors all over the world prefer on average to ply their trade in cities rather than in the countryside, and of how, in the face of such problems, to provide for rural health care.) In such matters, whatever the merits of self-help and local autonomy, collaborative effort is often vital, as well as being in the interest of each and every country; and, even if a creaking international bureaucracy must be endured, each of them has an obligation to take part in one way or another. International divisions, barriers and hostilities obviously inhibit and sometimes prevent such collaboration; but this is but one of the many reasons for eroding them.

How obligations 'To our own people' can be overridden

So far, the activities delineated may suggest that greater effort on the part of (and support for the efforts of) international organisations such as WHO and charities such as Oxfam is the greater part of what theories of justice call for, if supplemented with some amount of aid from governments of the more developed countries. But this is to ignore some of the ethical dilemmas facing both individuals and governments. For where the same outlay of effort or resources would make more difference to the satisfaction of basic needs if directed to a poor country rather than to one's own rich country, consequentialism apparently calls for it to be directed to the former; and this holds good of the agency of governments as well as of individuals.

Now it is widely held that the first duty of either an individual or government is to assist one's own family, district or country; and indeed if everyone belonged to a family, district or country where concerted action was viable and enough people assisted their relations or their fellow-citizens, there would be much less call than there is for assistance to strangers and aliens.

Indeed this is, perhaps, enough to justify effort to provide for one's family at least as far as the satisfaction of basic needs is concerned. But the world is such that in some countries concerted action, eg. in matters of health care, is not viable, whether because of famine, poverty or corruption, and also, for these or other reasons, not enough local people are capable of showing solidarity with one another. But this suffices to bring out fatal defects in the view that agents may quite generally give priority to their own family, district or country.

Admittedly the pressures on agents will often be so great that giving priority to the basic needs (health care needs included) of faraway people is out of the question. But often it is not. There are governments which would have the support of a sufficient proportion of their electorate to be able to dedicate at least one per cent of the gross national product to aid Third World countries, or to negotiate better terms for these countries in international trade or (eg. through participation in the counsels of IMF or the World Bank) in negotiation to reschedule international debt. And the resulting changes could make enough difference to satisfy unsatisfied health needs on an enormous scale. These governments lack the excuse of inability to act, and should accordingly do so as justice demands, as many individuals and voluntary organisations (such as churches) do already, and many more individuals and organisations should also do.

For some medically qualified individuals, then, this could well mean practising in the Third World, where the need is great, rather than in the West, where need is sometimes less great. For others, granted their situation, abilities and the medical needs of their own community it would not mean this, but it would mean reviewing intelligently one's sphere of operations from time to time to discover where, in the circumstances, most differences can be made.

The inescapability of commitment

Those who reject the kind of consequentialism advocated above might be thought to be under no obligation to adopt these conclusions, and free, perhaps, to regard medical ethics as limited to individuals and intrasocial dilemmas rather than to the problems which I have been discussing. Yet any theory which recognises the importance of the satisfaction of needs, whether consequentialist or not, is likely to generate the same conclusions; and, there again, any contractarianism which does not insist that the contract is a purely local one is likely to yield them too, as has been seen. Only a theory restricted to the defence of current entitlements and liberties is likely to be able to resist these conclusions; but such theories diverge so far from the widespread moral beliefs of humanity both about right and wrong and about justice that theorists who defend them risk loss of credibility and governments resort to them at their peril.

Thus any credible account of obligations or of justice upholds the above implications for action, which apply to agents and agencies able to make a difference, whether they recognise all this or not.

Conclusion

I have argued for the relevance of medical ethics to international and intersocietal issues, and maintained that the most plausible normative theory, a kind of consequentialism, and indeed other normative theories besides, generate far-reaching obligations with regard to meeting the unsatisfied basic health care needs of people of all ages in poor countries. Given these obligations, there are far-reaching practical implications for governments, for international bodies, for companies (which often have the power of international bodies), for voluntary organisations, and for individuals. In addition there are special implicit obligations for medical ethicists to ensure that the international aspects of medical ethics are in future much more extensively pursued, and that the practical implications are more explicitly drawn and publicised.[7]

Notes

1. (Author anonymous) 'Thematic review of past issues', *Journal of Medical Ethics*, 15, 1989, pp. 99-106.
2. John Rawls, *A Theory of Justice*, Oxford University Press: London, Oxford, New York, 1972.
3. Brian Barry, *The Liberal Theory of Justice*, Oxford: Clarendon Press 1973.
4. Robert Nozick, *Anarchy, State and Utopia*, Oxford: Basil Blackwell and New York: Basic Books, 1974.
5. I believe this point to survive such objections as that rules like these would remove salutary incentives.
6. Such a theory (including an attempt to specify basic needs, including self-respect, and to locate the boundary between acts of obligation and of supererogation) is elaborated and defended in Robin Attfield, *A Theory of Value and Obligation*, London: Croom Helm, 1987. A related theory of nature and limits of supererogation is supplied in 'Supererogation and Double Standards' *Mind*, 88, 1979, 481-499.

7.   I am grateful to Martyn Evans, to participants in the Eighteenth World Congress of Philosophy (Brighton, 1988) and to the referees of *Journal of Medical Ethics* for comments on an earlier draft of this essay, which appeared in that *Journal* in Volume 16, no.2, 1990, pp.153-6. I am also grateful to the editor of *Journal of Medical Ethics* for his permission to republish it (in slightly revised form) here.

9 Population ageing, social security, and the distribution of economic resources

PAUL JOHNSON[1]

All the major industrialised countries are now experiencing a common economic and social transformation - the ageing of their populations. The fall in the birth rate in the 1970s means that twenty years on there are relatively few young adults entering the workforce, and meanwhile the post-war 'baby-boomers' are moving into middle age, and the baby boomers' parents are moving into retirement. The consequence is a general rise in the average age of the population and in the proportion of the population aged over 65 - in Britain the median age of the population in 1901 was 24 years and since then it has risen in steps to 30.3 years in 1931, 34.7 years in 1981 and will be around 40 years by 2011. This upward restructuring of the population age profile which is common to almost all industrial societies is having a profound effect on the way in which resources are distributed between individuals, generations and age groups, and on the social institutions - such as the family and particularly the social security system - through which much of this resource distribution is effected.

A number of commentators have identified the distributional imperatives that are a concomitant of population ageing as a cause for economic concern. Both the International Monetary Fund (Heller et al., 1986) and the Organisation for Economic Cooperation and Development (OECD, 1988) have conducted major investigations into the long-term costs of population ageing in the developed economies, and they have reached the broadly similar conclusions that social security costs will inevitably rise as the size of the ageing pensioner population increases relative to that of the working age population. The rate of projected cost increase varies enormously between countries, because of differences in their age structures and the workings of their social security systems, but the direction of change is uniform. The preferred responses advocated by these international upholders of economic rectitude are a reduction

142

in pension levels, an increase in normal retirement ages and a close control of escalating health care costs.

These policy recommendations are based upon a clear (though partial) economic logic, but they have obvious and important implications for the welfare of all parties affected by policy changes. Such welfare considerations are not the primary concern of economists, whose purpose is, typically, to find an administrative solution to social security funding difficulties; yet they are in fact central to any fundamental reform of social security systems. Although social security may be viewed simply as a sophisticated system for economic redistribution, it should also be seen as an essentially political construct rooted in pluralist collectivism, and both the pluralism and the collectivism impose constraints on the scope of social security reform. Pluralism requires that reform does not reduce the welfare of the majority of the participants in the social security system (in pluralist democracies, of course, the participants are the voters); collectivism requires that no particular interest group controls or manipulates the system in order to reap 'unfair' rewards. The reforms proposed by the IMF and the OECD may violate the first of these requirements since the ageing of the population increases the electoral power of older age groups who would be disadvantaged by the reforms. But to do nothing may violate the second requirement, since it is argued that the impact of population ageing on current social security structures is to present certain older generations with very large, unfair, windfall gains at the expense of other less fortunate younger birth cohorts who have to pay for these intergenerational transfers.

There is, in fact, no simple and unambiguous solution to the problem of fitting existing systems for redistributing resources to the novel conditions of a rapidly ageing society. Economists, social administrators and philosophers have all attempted to grapple with the problems from their own standpoint, but they have done so within narrow perspectives which seem to ignore (or at least undervalue) the dual constraints of pluralism and collectivism. The next three sections of this paper will review these attempts made from within different social science traditions to develop solutions to the distributional problems caused by population ageing. The final section will show how this search for solutions is structured and compromised by the manner in which the problems are identified and phrased.

143

Economics and population ageing

Most of the (small number of) economists who have considered in depth the issue of population ageing have focussed on the implications of this demographic restructuring for the financing of social security systems. This concentration on social security arises not simply because of the financial and fiscal importance of social security systems, though these are important. In 1980 total government expenditure (on pensions, health care, education, unemployment benefit and poverty relief) in the United Kingdom was approximately 23 per cent of gross domestic product, a figure which put Britain below France, West Germany, and Italy in the public expenditure league, but above the United States, Canada and Japan. (Heller *at al.*, 1986:17) With pensions in Britain alone accounting for about 6 per cent of GDP, and with over half of health service expenditure being directed to people aged 65 and over (Johnson and Falkingham, 1988), redistribution through government agencies to the elderly accounts for around 10 per cent of GNP. It is not surprising to find, therefore, that in 1985 social security benefits (primarily the state pension) provided almost 60 per cent of pensioners' total incomes (Dawson and Evans, 1987). In terms of both its macro-economic importance and its personal significance in determining the living standard of welfare recipients, the social security system rightly dominates economic concern about future government expenditure priorities.

However, the size and function of the existing social security system is not generally viewed as a pressing problem, except by those who believe that the system has over-expanded and reduced individual liberty to an unacceptable degree. Although this view has been canvassed widely by some 'new right' politicians and analysts throughout the 1980s, public opinion has remained firmly in favour of maintaining the social security status quo (Taylor-Gooby, 1985). Economists in general concur that the present social security system works reasonably well at relatively low cost. Benefit rules undoubtedly create perverse incentives for some poor workers caught in the 'poverty trap', administration could be made more cost effective here and there, but compared with most of our European partners, Britain pays miserly public pensions, runs a cheap health service, and has a low net rate of tax. Economic concern about social security arises, therefore, not from unease with the existing performance of the system, but from a belief that the current system will interact with future demographic trends in such a way as to create large additional costs which will be distributed very unequally.

Crucial to the understanding of this economic argument is knowledge of how social security systems are financed. From an individual's perspective, paying into a social security scheme is rather like saving for a private pension, except that participation is compulsory and administration is conducted by large government departments rather than large banks or insurance companies. Contributions are paid regularly throughout working life, and the majority of benefits and services are received after retirement. But whereas saving with a private organisation involves the accumulation of a stock of assets which are then drawn on and run down in old age, social security runs on a 'pay as you go' basis, with this year's contribution from workers being used to pay this year's pensions to the retired. Although many pensioners may feel they have been accumulating a pot of gold - their state pension - throughout their working life, in practice they have accumulated nothing; their past contributions were used to pay then current pensions.

The social security system is, therefore, based on the principle of intergenerational transfers. It is as if there were a contract between generations, with current workers agreeing to transfer resources to former workers who are now retired, in the expectation that future generations of workers will likewise transfer resources to their elders. The contracts are implicit rather than explicit, both because the social security system is based on the principle of collective participation rather than contractual entitlement, and because the current workforce cannot formally contract with the as-yet-unborn generations who in the future will be expected to participate in the system of transfer.

If each successive generation is of the same size, the intergenerational transfer system is 'fair' because, in aggregate, each generation will receive in benefits an amount equal to its own contributions. But if changes in fertility and mortality rates alter the size of different generations in different ways, 'unfair' transfers can result. Take the case of people born in the second decade of the twentieth century and now around the age of 75. The life-time contributions of these people to the social security system have been relatively low, because in the past the ratio of benefits to average earnings was lower than it is today, and because the size of the pensioner population relative to the tax paying population was smaller in the past than now. The combined effect of these two factors was to make the net social security tax rate (or national insurance contribution rate) relatively low for most of the working life of today's 75 year olds. Yet their receipts from the social security and health care system are large because of improvements in the real value of the state pension since the early 1970s, in the health care facilities which are consumed disproportionately by the over 65 population, and in mortality experience during the twentieth century, which means more adults live to pensionable age, and more pensioners now live into their ninth or tenth decade, than ever before. All these developments which have led to an overall increase in the welfare of the retired population are entirely praiseworthy, but they result in the social security system effecting a net transfer of resources from younger generations.

There is, of course, little sign that this transfer has been resented by the younger, paying generations. As already mentioned, although social security tax rates in Britain (and most other counties) have risen over the last twenty years, public support for social security systems in general and pensions in particular remains strong. What concerns economists is that in the future the scale of these intergenerational transfers will increase substantially because of the interrelationship of two distinct demographic events - the high fertility of the post-war 'baby-boom', and the abrupt decline in fertility rates (or 'baby-bust') of the 1970s. The retirement of the baby-boomers in the decade from 2010 will lead to a sharp increase in the public transfers towards the retired population. At the same time the workforce - the potential tax-payers and contributors - will be declining in size because below-replacement fertility leads to each new cohort of young adult workers being smaller than the cohort for 65 year olds leaving the labour force. The consequence, in the absence of changes in the structure or function of the social security system, will be rapidly increasing tax rates. In West Germany, the country with the most adverse demographic outlook, the necessary contribution rates in the statutory social insurance system will need to rise from around 18.5 per cent today to over 41 per cent by 2030 simply to respond to the financing requirements of demographic change (Schmahl, 1989: 141). In France a similar rise in the contribution rate, from 16.3 per cent today to around 40 per cent by 2040 is also projected (Verniere, 190: 33). In Britain the post-war baby-boom was short lived and the 1970s fertility decline was modest by international standards; so the transfer claims of the retired population will grow relatively slowly, and the size of the working population (the tax base) will barely decline. Even so, if the value of the state pension relative to average earnings is maintained in the future, national insurance contributions will need to rise from 17.5 per cent today to 26.4 per cent by 2030, with most of this increase occurring after the baby boomers begin to retire around 2010 (Government Actuary, 1990:31).

The scale of these projected transfers concerns economists for at least three distinct reasons. First, they argue that high marginal tax rates on workers create strong disincentives to greater production and increase labour costs, and so may reduce both the dynamism and the international competitiveness of the economy. Second, they suggest that massive resource transfers to older people may lower

146

the net investment rate (and in the long run the overall rate of growth of the economy) because older people tend to be risk-averse and more interested in immediate consumption than long-term investment. Third, and most importantly, they show that many current and future social security contributors will never receive in return from the system a sum equivalent to that which they have paid in.

By looking at the expected lifetime flow of contributions to and receipts from the social security system it is possible to calculate the realised rate of return on contributions. For early participants in social security the rate of return was very high; for those joining in the 1950s and 1960s, the rate of return was lower but still strongly positive; but for young adults now entering the labour force the expected rate of return is negative (Hagemann and Nicoletti, 1989). Forty years ago new entrants to the social security system could expect a rate of return far higher than that offered by private savings institutions; so they were happy with the social security bargain even though net resources were being transferred to older age groups. Today, however, younger workers would be better off saving for their own private annuity or pension rather than contributing to the social security system. This system has worked like a chain letter, with each new generation of entrants willing to make large payments to previous entrants in the expectation that in the future they will receive equivalent rewards. But the social security system, like a chain letter, can only provide something for nothing if it keeps on expanding, and population ageing now precludes such future expansion. With the intergenerational contract becoming so manifestly unfair there is a very strong disincentive for younger generations to attempt to renege on the implicit contract to support their elders and instead take the more advantageous free-market route to provision for old age.

There are a number of ways of ameliorating the social security funding problem associated with population ageing, and they are defined by the accounting identity of a pure pay-as-you-go system:

$$W. (t.w.) = P. (p.w.)$$

where W is the number of contributing workers, t is the average social security tax rate, w is the average wage, P is the number of pensioners, and p is the pension replacement rate (ie. the value of a pension as a proportion of the average wage). An increase in P, the number of pensioners, can be balanced by an expansion in the tax base (W), an increase in the tax rate (t), or a reduction in the relative value of the pension (p). In practice, only two of these possibilities are open to governments, since there is little scope in most countries for extending the tax base by incorporating more contributors into social security systems, which are now virtually comprehensive in their coverage of the occupied population. Furthermore, the rapid expansion of female paid employment which did serve to expand the tax base for much of the post-war period can provide few further increases in revenue because female participation rates, in Britain at least, have now reached virtually the same level as those for men. Since the aim of policy adjustment is to avoid or at least limit the increase in the tax rate, the main area of compensation for an increase in the number of pensioners has to be a reduction in the pension replacement rate (p), so called because it shows what proportion of average income is replaced by the state pension when a worker retires. The unequivocal advice coming to governments from the OECD and the IMF is that the value of the social security retirement pension relative to wages must be reduced. In addition, since the root of the problem is the future rate of increase in the number of pensioners, a second string to the policy proposals is simply to make it more difficult for older people to qualify for a pension by raising the age of entitlement.

The economic logic behind these reform proposals is straightforward, but the pluralist basis of social security systems may well make the proposals politically untenable. A direct reduction in expected pension income is likely to win little support from current pensioners or from people within reasonable striking distance of retirement - say those over the age of 50. But the over-50 population already constitutes a substantial proportion of the potential electorate in the developed economies - 40 per cent in Britain, a figure which will rise to 50 per cent by 2025 (Office of Population Censuses and Surveys, 1987). Furthermore, older people tend to have a higher level of political participation and electoral turnout than the young - in the 1986 US mid-tem election, for instance, the turnout rate for voters over 65 was 61 percent, compared to 22 per cent for those aged 18-25 (*Guardian Weekly*, 1990). Although it is not clear that median voter models are the best way to account for the direction of transfers within social security systems, it requires a strong assumption of altruism or stupidity to believe that the majority of the electorate, those aged over 50, will enthusiastically vote for a massive reduction of their income.

Already legislation has been introduced in both Britain and the United States to bring about just such a reduction in the cost of pensions and the transfer of resources to older people, but significantly the changes will have little effect until well into the twenty-first century. In the US the age of entitlement to a full social security pension will rise in small steps from 65 to 67 years between 2003 and 2027. In Britain the indexing of the state pension to prices rather than wages since 1980 means that pensioners are now losing out on all real income growth -

it is projected that this will lead to a relative fall in the value of a single man's pension from an ungenerous 16 per cent today to a trivial 7 per cent by 2050 (Government Actuary, 1990:18). It is, of course, one thing to legislate for distant cuts in pension entitlements but quite another thing to carry these out. In the United States the American Association of Retired Persons has a membership of over 30 million, fifteen full-time lobbyists on Capitol Hill and the ability to mobilize the most powerful and cohesive voting block in the country. Recent attempts to make wealthy American retirees pay health insurance surcharges have been deferred in the face of organised pensioner opposition. The combined economic logic of OECD and IMF reform proposals will come to naught unless the process and mechanics of redistribution away from the elderly can be negotiated within the pluralist welfare state. If economic reform is imposed by administrative fiat, there is a strong possibility that it will be overturned by electoral pressure.

Social administration and population ageing

Social administrators and social policy analysts have long had a particular interest in the elderly population, since this group is the largest constituency for the receipt of medical and personal social services and for financial transfers through the pension system. Interest in the elderly is not, of course, the same thing as an interest in population ageing, although there is an association between the two since population ageing results in an increase in the relative number of elderly people in a society. In consequence social policy analysts have tended to take a less mechanistic and generally more compassionate view of population ageing than have economists, because their original point of reference is the broadly-conceived welfare of older individuals rather than the rate of change of economic aggregates. While this emphasis makes them aware of and responsive to the pluralist pressures in social security systems, it leads them to undervalue or even ignore the equity considerations that are essential to the long-term stability of collective social security.

In Britain this tendency is particularly marked because of the Fabian origins of so much social policy analysis, which in the case of pensioners sees them as a disadvantaged, dependent and essentially helpless group whose needs can best be provided for and living standards improved through the advocacy of state welfare provision by social administration experts. This is probably not a bad characterization of the way the social position of older people has evolved through the twentieth century. In Victorian Britain to be old meant to be poor, except for those few and fortunate individuals who had either acquired or inherited sufficient wealth to sustain themselves in retirement or who remained physically fit enough to continue in full-time paid employment until their death. The first state old age pension was introduced in 1908 primarily because of the advocacy of social investigators and progressive politicians such as Charles Booth and David Lloyd George. Although pensioner groups have made efforts to redirect pensions policy in both the inter-war and post-war periods (MacNicol and Blaikie, 1989; Harper and Thane 1989), subsequent reforms have continued to be handed down from on high, particularly by William Beveridge and Barbara Castle. Campaigning charities such as Age Concern and Help the Aged reinforce the idea, in their actions and in their very names, of elderly people as a dependent population, a social problem, to be protected and ministered to; this is very different to the militant self-assertion of the American Association of Retired Persons. Social policy analysts have compounded this image of helplessness by stressing the pronounced poverty of many sections of the retired population and, among some more radical writers, by developing a neo-Marxist concept of 'structured dependency' which unintentionally carries implicitly pejorative overtones (MacNicol, 1990:39). The net effect is to construct an image of the elderly as constrained by their poverty to a limited social world, allowed only so much freedom of choice and action as the state pension grants them. Inevitably, therefore, increasing the size of pension payments is seen as a necessary first step to expanding the economic and social horizons of older people, and something that should be undertaken by any advanced industrial society that makes even a passing reference to equality and civility.

A strong *a priori* justification for higher pensions can be drawn from current statistics of pensioner poverty. In 1986 over 1.7 million pensioners were in receipt of supplementary benefit because their incomes were below the official poverty line, and several million more had incomes barely above this level (Annual Abstract of Statistics, 1988). This is a clear indication that most pensioners are not living a life of milk and honey, with winters in Benidorm and summers in Florida. An emphasis on the scale of pensioner poverty has led many social administration advocates of higher pensions to treat economists' concerns about future pension costs as irrelevant or pernicious. A typical response is to castigate economists for presenting a pessimistic view of population ageing when what needs to be emphasised is the positive aspects for both society in general and for aged individuals in particular of a fundamental shift in the age structure and in the distribution of economic resources in modern society (Jeffreys, 1990). The distributional tensions will be resolved, it is suggested, not by changes to the social security system, but through the fruits of future economic growth which will allow more resources for everyone (Midwinter, 1989).

This argument about the beneficent effect of future economic growth in solving any distributional problems caused by population ageing is made frequently and with great confidence by people who do not seem to understand that it deserves to be examined carefully. Although seldom spelled out, the implicit line of argument seems to run as follows. A growth rate of, say, two per cent per annum will increase national income by over 50 per cent in just 21 years, which is far faster than the expansion of the pensioner population or any likely increase in health-related expenditure on older people. Society therefore has or will have the resources to ensure that pensioners have a much improved standard of living while at the same time making sure that no-one, including workers and tax-payers, is worse-off in real terms. The distributional conundrum is resolved!

In practice, far from resolving the conundrum, this formulation merely restates it in more obscure terms. This is clear from an examination of the pay-as-you-go pension scheme accounting identity presented above. In this identity the average real wage (w) appears on both sides of the equation since the pension level is set as a proportion (p) of this wage. Economic growth - an increase in average real income - will therefore automatically affect both sides of the equation (through an increase in w), leaving all other variables unchanged. In this formulation, therefore, economic growth alters the absolute level of both wages and pensions, but not the relative value between the two which is defined by the pension replacement rate (p). If the size of the workforce is fixed, an increase in the value of pensions relative to wages or a rise in the number of pensioners necessarily involves an increase in the tax rate regardless of what is happening to real wages and economic growth. The contention of those who see economic growth as the solution to distributional problems appears to be, therefore, that as long as the post-tax real income of the working population (defined as $w-(w.t)$) does not decline, there will be no difficulty in transferring a growing share of their pre-tax income to the pensioner population. Far from addressing and answering the distributional question raised by an economic analysis of public pension systems, this appeal to the benefits of economic growth simply ignores the issue, and it does so on grounds that seem implausibly optimistic and frankly unhistorical. It is possible to dream of a future world in which tax-payers will not object to an increase in the tax rate as

151

long as their real post-tax income does not fall, but it is not possible to find examples of such a world in the past. A simple overview of economic development since 1945 shows clearly that four decades of rapid economic growth have done nothing to lessen disputes about how (and how much of) the real income of tax-payers should be redistributed to other groups in society. There is little sign that as the economic cake grows larger people care less about how it is cut.

The common social administration response to population ageing - more money for more pensioners - may have growing appeal for an ageing electorate, but it seems to fall foul of the equity considerations that need to be preserved in a collectivist system. One favoured counter to the equity objection is that Britain is sufficiently different from other countries in its demographic, economic and social security structures for it to be able to ignore, at least for the time being, the concern about the scale of intergenerational transfers that is surfacing elsewhere. Some of the emphasis here is placed on the advantageous demographic ratios that Britain has compared with most of her economic partners, but more important is the structure and function of the British state pension system which has made it less effective than its continental counterparts in equalizing incomes between the retired and the working population.

Comparisons between the living standards of pensioners and non-pensioners are notoriously difficult to make, in part because of a tremendous dispersion around the average for both groups, but also because their household structure and consumption patterns differ quite markedly. However, a crude indication of relative changes in Britain is shown by the fact that the basic state retirement pension for a single man rose from 20 per cent of average net male manual earnings in 1951 to 33 per cent in 1981, since when it has fallen back slightly because of the indexation to prices rather than earnings. In France, by comparison, the growing generosity of the earnings-related pension scheme over the same period has led to the per capita income for households headed by a retired person to rise above the national average for all households (Cribier, 1989). If the present value of pension entitlements is included in a measure of effective per capita wealth, then the wealth of the 60+ population in France has more than trebled since 1960, whereas for the 15-60 age group per capita wealth has increased by only 19 per cent (Verniere, 1990). So while it appears to be true that in many European countries and in the US the elderly have improved their relative economic standing compared with the working population (and so some analysts claim, at the direct expense of the working population (Longman, 1987)), in Britain the high-spending fast-living well-off older person (WOOPIE) is more media myth than social reality. Therefore, it is argued, Britain has a good deal of catching up to do before it experiences the sort of intergenerational transfers and tensions now seen in other countries.

This is a somewhat perverse argument. If the car in front is heading for a precipice it surely makes more sense to brake or change direction rather than accelerate along the same route. As well as being of questionable logic, it is also premised upon a probable misreading of the available statistics. Although many current pensioners in Britain have near-poverty incomes, recently-retired pensioners have incomes well above the average for all pensioners. This is because they have been able to accumulate substantial assets over their working life, particularly in the form of housing and occupational pensions. It seems likely that in twenty years time the baby-boomers will be entering retirement with even greater per capita assets than today's newly retired pensioners, because they have experienced even wider property ownership and pension scheme membership. A general increase in the relative value of the state pension is a long-term response to a problem that will simply not exist in the same form or to the same extent in the long-run. But once higher pensions have been introduced it will become increasingly difficult in the future to find electoral support for pension reductions, even if such reductions are required to prevent grossly iniquitous transfers from workers to pensioners. There is, it seems, a profound conflict between the policy preferences of social administrators who wish to improve the lot of today's elderly population, and of economists who wish to prevent the imposition of an unfair intergenerational transfer on tomorrow's workers. There appears to be little scope for reconciliation of these divergent views which derive from the distinct perspectives of economics and social policy. But attempts have been made to order and resolve these differences by resorting not to further empirical investigation but instead to the philosophical principles of distributive justice.

Philosophy and population ageing

Philosophers look at the provision of income security for the elderly in an ageing society by posing a number of ethical questions. How far is the individual's right to the product of his labour to be qualified in order to ensure desired social goals? (MacDougal, 1988). What is a just or fair distribution of social resources among the different age groups competing for them? (Daniels, 1989: 57) Is the implicit welfare contract that binds members of successor generations

153

fair to all participants, regardless of their birth date? (Thomson, 1989: 34-5) The first of these questions refers to broader issues of taxation and redistribution than those considered in this paper, but the other two are central to the policy issues that economists and social administrators have to face when considering the consequences of population ageing for existing social security systems.

The most detailed and sophisticated discussion has been provided by Norman Daniels who takes to task social scientists for 'merely describing' the pattern of transfer of income, power and other social goods from one age group to another rather than trying to search for the normative principle which implicitly governs such a distribution (Daniels, 1988:11). Daniels begins this search by distinguishing between the concepts of justice between birth cohorts (or generations) and justice between age groups, two distinct issues which are commonly conflated in discussion of intergenerational equity. He argues that of these two concepts, justice between age groups is the more general, because everyone ages and (given average life expectancy) passes through the successive stages of life, whereas people born at different times are members of unique birth cohorts which acquire their own, distinct, historical experiences and legacies. Therefore, he suggests, the general age-group problem logically needs to be solved before the particular birth cohort problem can be addressed in a considered manner.

To solve the age group problem he takes a Rawlsian position. Differential and unequal treatment by age does not generate inequality in life prospects (as long as the differential is consistent) because we all pass through the successive stages and ages of life. In fact, from the perspective of institutions that operate over a lifetime (such as education, health care or pension systems) unequal treatment may be exactly what we want, because our needs vary at different stages of our lives. Although it appears in a health care or pension system that it is the young who pay hefty premiums and the elderly who consume the services or benefits, we should see, says Daniels, that each group represents a stage of our lives; unequal treatment of people by age is a kind of budgeting within life. If we can determine what form of prudential reasoning individuals use to allocate resources over their own life-span, we can generalise from this to specify what transfers between age groups actually improve prospects for everyone.

We cannot, however, simply ask fully-informed rational agents this question about the resource allocation over the life-span, because their responses would reflect their existing personal and economic circumstances, and would necessarily exclude the voice of infants and children. So the rational deliberator has to be behind a 'veil of ignorance' which prevents him knowing his age (certain other conditions restricting the range of choices also need to be imposed to conform with the more general principles of distributive justice). Daniels calls this schema the 'prudential life-span account' - a way of establishing an ethical solution to the problem of distribution between age groups which can provide a principled set of criteria for reforming existing transfer systems. This is a way of cutting through the differences between economists and social policy analysts about the appropriate level of financial support for older people, or at least of getting them to focus on the same issue, rather than pursue different issues and objectives while confusedly using the same language, as tends to happen now.

However, the prudential life-span account can provide a guide to the distribution of resources between age groups only if the differential treatment by age is consistent for successive cohorts, and it is this condition of stability that rapid population ageing appears to be undermining. Daniels notes that birth cohorts have to co-operate to develop a stable solution to the age-group problem, and that in a world in which the rate of growth of population, income and inflation is subject to uncertainty there will need to be some sharing of risks across cohorts (Daniels, 1989:71). The possibility of net transfers between birth cohorts is an inevitable consequence of trying to solve the age-group problem in a non-ideal context. What needs to be aimed at, therefore, is approximate rather than absolute equality in benefit ratios for successive birth cohorts. The upper and lower bounds of this approximate equality are, however, very much a matter of individual judgement, and therefore a potential source of conflict.

The prudential life-span account certainly allows arguments about the relative expenditure of public funds on children and the elderly to be addressed in a clear and direct manner; this is an age-group problem, and the inequality in expenditure may be just what rational deliberators positioned behind a veil of ignorance would chose. The cohort problem, on the other hand, remains a matter for judgement about how far a society can deviate from approximate equality of benefit ratios without undermining the intergenerational contract on which social security is built. And when solutions to the age-group and birth cohort problems appear to conflict, as the arguments of economists and social administrators suggest they do today, it is not clear which goal should be prioritised. One response is to 'fine-tune' the solutions. For instance, if the social security system solves the age-group transfer problem but creates an inter-cohort transfer that leads the system to deviate from the principle of approximate equality of benefit ratios, this can be compensated for by intergenerational transfers within the family, from parents to children. There is no doubt that this happens - recent retirees with high pension incomes and substantial assets increasingly are transferring resources to their (adult) children to assist with property purchase and school fees (Cribier, 1989). But this resort to private transfers, a reliance on the whim and fortune of parental wealth, sentiment and survival, is the antithesis of the assured stability and entitlement that social security systems were designed to provide.

A further challenge to the prudential life-span account comes from those who believe that generations will and do cheat. Thompson (1989) claims that, in New Zealand at least, the generation which received the first fruits of the modern social security system as young adults in the 1950s is now managing to use its growing electoral power to continue to monopolise social security expenditure as it enters retirement. The system has been captured by what Thomson calls the 'welfare generation', a cohort that refuses to accept the fundamental rule of membership that benefits have to be matched by contributions. Others have argued more generally from public choice theory that the willingness of elders to transfer resources to their own children will not generalise to the transfer of resources to other people's children included in a comprehensive social security scheme. In consequence, cohort self-interest overrides the desire to find a stable solution to the age group problem (a desire which is a fundamental premise in Daniels' account). Thompson believes that the actions of such selfish generations may undermine the implicit contract on which social security systems are based, just as, in another context, their actions may de-stabilize the world's environment. In both cases the responses are disconcertingly similar - grand pronouncements and promises to change things in fifteen or twenty years time, when the costs will fall on others. In sum, therefore, despite the elegance with which philosophical analysis has allowed age-group and birth cohort issues to be distinguished from each other, it is far from clear that, at least in Daniels's formulation, it enables a joint solution to these problems to be developed when populations are ageing rapidly. Is any such solution possible?

Conclusion

Comprehensive solutions can be proposed only for fully specified problems. The distributional impact on the social security system across generations when populations age is only one of a multitude of economic effects that arise from societal ageing and it may not be the most significant in either quantitative or subjective terms. Perhaps the most important transfer from one generation to the next is the stock of assets, the physical and cultural capital which underpins our economic and social system. This capital stock is expanded and enhanced by the investment behaviour of a society at any particular time, but the effects extend across several generations. If one generation foregoes a certain amount of consumption in order to sustain a high net investment rate, thus bequeathing to its successor generation a highly augmented stock of capital, then it could be argued that it deserves recompense in retirement in terms of large net transfers from the (augmented) income of the working-age population. On the other hand, if the social security transfers from the current workforce to finance the consumption expenditure of today's retirees are paid at the direct expense of net savings, the costs will fall not just on current workers but also on future generations who will inherit a capital stock diminished by present low saving and investment rates.

A large literature has developed in economics around the questions of whether the social security transfers diminish net saving and investment, whether population ageing affects this process, whether the accumulation of a social security reserve fund can compensate for the transitional effects of population ageing, and whether any such issues matter in an international economy in which goods and funds flow rapidly between countries. The complexity of the questions, and the limitations of economic analysis, have led one group of US researchers recently to conclude that America needs a substantial increase in its net savings rate over the next thirty years to cope with the economic effects of population ageing (Aaron et al., 1989) while another group has found that the best response to population ageing would be a decline in the savings rate (Cutler et al., 1990). This inability of economists to agree on the nature, let alone the scale, of the economic consequences of population ageing once the level of analysis is raised beyond the specifics of the social security system to the economy in general must cast a shadow of doubt over the search for technocratic solutions to the distributional problems of population ageing.

At a more subjective level, it is not obvious that distributional equity as defined by equality of benefit ratios between generations is the criterion by which people in fact judge the performance and the acceptability of the social security system. Four distinct objections exist. First, intergenerational relationships tend to be observed most intimately within family structures, where economic issues of equitable distribution are qualified by non-economic (or less overtly economic) sentiments of obligation and desert. Secondly, the actual intergenerational inequity of the social security system may be perceived less clearly (and therefore given less weight) than the specific generosity of the social security system to one's own parents. Third, the complexity of the social security benefit and tax regimes means that few people other than social security economists are ever aware of the net direction of inter-cohort transfers in social security systems. Finally, equity is not necessarily judged by the ratio of contributions to benefits. Equity can be couched in terms of equal inputs (each generation paying the same absolute or proportionate tax rate) or outputs (each generation receiving the same absolute or proportionate pension) or welfare results (each generation of retirees having the same living standard as workers). If any of these concepts of equity is stronger than the concept of approximate lifetime equality of contributions and benefits when averaged across cohorts, the collectivist underpinnings of social security systems will not be violated by a violation of a strictly economic interpretation of intergenerational equity. This point has been elaborated by Verniere (1990) who suggests that the only viable concept of intergenerational equity for social security systems to aim for in a period of population ageing is that of a fixed parity between the average pension and net real income. If an automatic rule along these lines could be incorporated in social security systems, this would prevent their capture by a particularly selfish generation, although within any pluralist system rules made against the interest of an (ageing) majority can be unmade by that majority.

The search for a simple and complete solution to the distributional problems caused by population ageing is severely compromised by the difficulty, perhaps the impossibility, of adequately specifying the problem. Economists, social policy analysts and philosophers advocate responses that suit their own interpretation of the distributional issues, but none of these proposals appears to take full account of the political constraints that pluralism and collectivism jointly place on social security reform. Perhaps this is inevitable, because we have little idea of what in practice individuals in different cohorts regard as an equitable intergenerational social security transfer. Arguments from the first principles of economic logic or distributive justice are elegant, but they are neither necessary nor sufficient for the development of politically acceptable proposals for social security reform.

References

Aaron, H. J., Bosworth, B.P., and Burtless, G (1989). *Can America Afford to Grow Old?* Washington, D.C., Brookings Institution.

Annual Abstract of Statistics, 1988, London HMSO.

Bury, M., and MacNicol, J. (1990), *Aspects of Ageing*, London, Department of Social Policy, Royal Holloway and Bedford New College, Social Policy Papers 3.

Cribier, F. (1989), 'Changes in Life Course and Retirement in Recent Years: the Example of Two Cohorts of Parisians', in Johnson et al. (1989),181-201.

Cutler, D.M., Poterba, J.M., Sheiner, L.M., and Summers, L.H. (May 1990), 'An Ageing Society, Opportunity or Challenge?', Boston, National Bureau of Economic Research.

Dawson, A. and Evans, G. (1987), 'Pensioners' incomes and expenditure, 1970-1985', *Employment Gazette*, May, 243-53.

Daniels, N. (1988), *Am I My Parents' Keeper? An Essay on Justice Between the Young and the Old*, New York, Oxford University Press.

Daniels, N. (1989), 'Justice and Transfers Between Generations', in Johnson et al. (1989), 57-79.

Government Actuary (1990), *National Insurance Fund Long Term Financial Estimates*, London, HMSO.

Guardian Weekly, (1990) 'Pensioner Power puts fear into Congressmen', October 28, 1990

Hagemann, R., and Nicoletti, G. (1989), 'Ageing Populations: Economic Effects and Implications for Public Finance', Paris, OECD Department of Economics and Statistics, Working Paper 61.

Harper, S., and Thane, P. (1989), 'The Consolidation of 'Old Age' as a Phase of Life, 1945-1965', in Jeffreys (1989), 43-61.

Heller, P.S., Hemming, R., and Kohnert, P.W. (1986), *Ageing and Social Expenditure in the Major Industrial Countries, 1980-2025*, Washington D.C., International Monetary Fund Occasional Paper 47.

Jeffreys, M. (1989), *Growing Old in the Twentieth Century*, London, Routledge.

Jeffreys, M. (1990), 'The Demographic Shift: The Greying of the Population', in Bury and MacNicol (1990), 1-11.

Johnson, P., Conrad., and Thomson, D. (1989), *Workers versus Pensioners: Intergenerational Justice in an Ageing World*, Manchester, Manchester University Press.

Johnson, P., and Falkingham, J. (1988), 'Intergenerational Transfers and Public Expenditure on the Elderly in Modern Britain', *Ageing and Society*, VIII, 129-46.

Longman, P. 1987), *Born To Pay*, Boston, Houghton Mifflin.

MacDougal, D.J. (1988), 'The right to Participate: Ending Discrimination Against the Elderly' in Thornton and Winkler (1988).

MacNicol, J. (1990), 'Old Age and Structured Dependency', in Bury and MacNicol (1990), 30-52.

MacNicol, J. and Blaikie, A. (1989), 'The Politics of Retirement 1918-1948', in Jeffreys (1989), 21-42.

Midwinter, E. (1989), 'Workers versus Pensioners?', *Social Policy and Administration*, XXIII, 205-10.

OECD, (1988), *Ageing Populations: The Social Policy Implications*, Paris, Organisation for Economic Co-operation and Development.

Office of Population Censuses and Surveys (1987), *Population Projections 1985-2025*, London, HMSO.

Schmahl, W. (1989), 'Labour Force Retirement and Social Pension Systems' in Johnson et al. (1989).

Taylor-Gooby, P. (1985), *Public Opinion, Ideology and State Welfare*, London, Routledge.

Thomson, D. (1989), 'The Welfare State and Generation Conflict: Winners and Losers', in Johnson et al. (1989).

Thornton, J.E., and Winkler, E.R. (1988), *Ethics and Ageing*, Vancouver, University of British Columbia Press.

Verniere, L. (1990), 'Retraites: l'urgence d'une reforme'. *Economie et Statistique*, CCXXXIII, 29-38.

Note

1. This paper was written while the author was a visiting fellow at the Institute of Advanced Studies, Australian National University.

10 'Last time buyers'; markets and marketing in services for the elderly

ROD SHEAFF

Early in the 1990s there were signs that the British government was furtively abandoning the policy that the National Health Service (NHS) would guarantee free nursing care for elderly people.[1] Residential and nursing care for the elderly was increasingly being shifted from the NHS to the private sector, where the Social Security system would meet the costs only up to a specific limit (lower than many nursing homes' actual prices) and then on a means-tested basis. Any shortfall had to be met by the patient or her relatives. The first case of a patient having to sell her house to pay the shortfall was reported recently.[2] This cost-shifting was itself part of NHS hospitals' response to another government policy, that of recurrent NHS cost cuts ('efficiency targets'). After the Health Service Ombudsman ruled against the practice[3] new administrative guidelines to NHS hospitals were drafted recommending that it should become routine.[4] From 1st April 1993 responsibility for community care - of which elderly people are the bulk of recipients - transferred out of the NHS into local authority social services. These were already being reorganised in the form of an 'internal market'.

Defending the NHS over one *cause celebre*, a representative of the National Association of Health Authorities (since renamed the National Association of Health Authorities and Trusts) argued that provision of nursing home care for the elderly was not a proper function of the NHS. Implicitly he was arguing that the function of the NHS is to provide health care for elderly people, but not social care. By 1994 many local authorities were using this demarcation between health and non-health care to justify charging for domiciliary care of the elderly. In most local authorities an elderly person would have to pay for help with taking a bath if the bath was a 'social bath' provided by non-NHS staff but paid nothing if NHS staff helped her take a 'health bath'.[5] One nurse's attempt to differentiate the two kinds of bath proposed criteria which include: the client's own preference, her functional ability, her access to alternative willing and able helpers, 'and - most important of all - nurses' professional assessment of need'.[6] British national policy guidance, however, steers clear of stating specific criteria demarcating 'health' from 'non-health' care, leaving that awkward decision to Health Authorities, local authorities and general practitioners.

This demarcation dispute poses two questions. One is, whether these changes are justified in terms of what health care elderly people need? Defenders of the new policies implicitly hold that they are justified because the NHS would over-reach both its purpose and its resources in providing elderly people with non-health services that cannot coherently be classed as health care at all, and there would be other disadvantages too (see below). These non-health services should be provided by other means. Its defenders see a new, narrower definition of 'health care' as a reason, its critics as a pretext, for a policy of extending market and reducing public provision of services for the elderly. Either way, a second question arises: whether, or to what extent, or in what ways nursing homes, residential care and other 'welfare' services for the elderly ought to be marketed and provided through markets much as most other consumer goods are? Even if welfare services for elderly people remain a public sector activity, how far should policy-makers go in transforming that sector into a synthetic or surrogate market?

What considerations tell against the 'social care for the elderly is not health care' argument? Critics of the reforms might start by pointing out that the definitional question of what is to count as 'health care' and what is not is rather arbitrary at the linguistic level. Not only is our everyday use of the phrase 'health care' ill-defined and ambiguous, but one could simply stipulate either way how the phrase should be used in future. Definitions and linguistic practice should here be decided by theoretical and policy considerations, and in Britain the policy considerations, critics could say, point towards counting nursing and residential care for elderly people as health services.

Leaving aside strictly moral considerations, the critics could continue, nearly all of us have strong prudential reasons to guarantee access to nursing and residential services, because almost everyone comes to need them ('need' as a means to maintaining their activities of daily life). Except for the presumably negligible number of people who plan to commit suicide before then we all either intend to live into old age or have already done so; and an ever-increasing proportion of those who intend to live to old age actually do so. (Incidentally younger people with rapidly progressive diseases also need to guarantee access to nursing and residential care because, although they may not

162

live to be old in conventional chronological terms, their disease will bring them prematurely to the life-cycle events described as 'old age' above.) A peculiarity of services for the elderly (as opposed to services for, say, computer-users or people with speech impediments) is that everyone confronts a non-negligible, indeed empirically increasing, probability that they will come to need residential and nursing care in old age. All those who will not die suddenly will need some form of terminal nursing and residential care, irrespective of whether this be done in the elderly person's home or whether the alternatives be designated as 'hospital', 'hospice', 'nursing home' or 'residential care'. Wherever it is provided, that element of services for the elderly meets what Daniels would call a 'course-of-life need'.[7]

In Britain the NHS is the one provider of nursing and residential services which guarantees access on grounds of need to the services which it provides. For many elderly people and their families the practical, financial implications of withdrawing these services from the NHS will be to prevent elderly people from accessing them to the extent they will need, or at all. So, the critic can continue, in Britain the institutionally simplest (and cheapest) way to guarantee access to nursing and residential services for the elderly is to define these services as 'health care' and hence as an NHS responsibility.

In effect, this argument urges that NHS hospitals should adopt - or resume - a function which researchers in the 1960s observed; that of compensating for the lack of other arrangements for meeting (in this case, elderly) patients' physical needs and needs for social care once their medical condition has been stabilised at as high a level as current medical techniques allow.[8] To meet the point about the dangers of overstretching NHS resources, the critic can reply that NHS does not have to use acute hospital beds to meet this need (which continues to occur, as 'bed-blocking'). Instead it could use what other systems call 'social beds'; beds with lower levels of medical and nursing staffing and equipment, such as already exist in some NHS community hospitals, and are correspondingly cheaper than acute beds. The NHS could also set up its own nursing and residential homes. By taking this turn, however, the critic's argument comes close to conceding that what the occupants of these beds need is not really health care in the sense of acute treatment but ordinary domestic and relatively straightforward nursing care, with an element of health maintenance.

Valid though many of these points are, the critic, like the government, is actually proposing to redefine the responsibilities of the NHS under cover of a redefinition of 'health care'. It is more accurate and explicit to acknowledge that what is really at issue is not the connotation of the words 'health' and 'health care' but the scope of NHS and of non-NHS, including market, provision of nursing and residential services for elderly people. To define the latter as health care is stretching the definition of 'health care', and by implication the definition of 'health', too far.

Ageing is of course a normal part of our life-cycle, arising from a natural process and not inherently unhealthy until its terminal stage. It is not *a priori* a sign of medicalisable illness if, beyond a certain age, a person is no longer able to respond to an episode of treatment for illness by returning to the full level of function and painlessness sufficient for normal self-care in the social role she previously inhabited. This suggests that the term 'elderly' should be taken to refer not to a person's chronological age but to the life-cycle stage at which her physical and mental functioning have deteriorated so far as to be no longer sufficient for her to achieve the level of independent self-care which is normally necessary for a member of the society she inhabits. For it is only at this moment that a person starts to need (in the sense noted above) the complex of services we are considering - nursing care, social care, domiciliary services, higher levels of income support and so on. (For short we can collectively label services of this kind 'welfare services for the elderly'.) Classifying these deteriorations of function as occurrences of ill-health tempts us towards two practical mistakes.

One is, of pointlessly using health care resources which will have a negligible effect upon the functioning or pain of their elderly recipient. (Generally the effects of health care are slower and smaller in elderly people[9]). It might be argued that using health care resources in this way at least serves the symbolic purpose of reassuring people that everything possible will be done to restore their health after accidents or illness in old age. Against this is Shaw's warning about arousing false hopes that the physical effects of aging can be avoided in the end; 'Do not try to live for ever. You will not succeed'[10]. Indeed over-medicalisation of services for the elderly can be counterproductive. Physical iatrogenesis, to which elderly people are more vulnerable and slower to recover than younger people, is one risk. Another is the loss, through underuse, of capacities for the activities of daily life (continence, mobility etc.) through institutionalisation. The opportunity cost of ineffective health care is, familiarly, a foregone opportunity to treat someone else effectively (on the assumption that health care resources are scarce, irrespective of whether this scarcity unavoidable or, as seems more likely in the British case, a result of fiscal policy instead[11]). Even if healthcare resources were not scarce, it would still be wasting them.

Nevertheless elderly people who cannot be restored by health care to their previous level of independent functioning evidently do need nursing or residential care to substitute, as far as practicable, for the natural (physical and mental) capacities which they have partly lost. But what they do not necessarily need, once their level of functioning has been stabilised and their pain controlled as far as possible, is (medicalised) health care. What they do need are welfare services for the elderly; nursing care, residential care, assistance with transport or mobility, home helps, meals-on-wheels and the like. This is where Thatcherites and like-minded 'reformers' of the British welfare state, who are for the time being committed to maintaining the NHS in something like its present form, bring in the market. Partly they do so for fiscal and electoral reasons, as a means of shifting the costs of (*inter alia*) nursing and residential care for elderly people from the state and employers onto elderly people themselves, their relatives, other informal carers, charities and other voluntary bodies. However they also do so, in part, for ideological and theoretical reasons, which brings us to our second main question: how sound are these reasons?

There are two aspects of the arguments for and against market provision to consider here; many of the most influential arguments have been couched in rather general terms, covering but not restricted to services for the elderly. Even the general arguments, however, tend to apply more strongly to services for the elderly because elderly people commonly need larger amounts of health and social care, and the more complex forms.[12] Also there is a more specific aspect to these arguments: the extent to which these general considerations apply in a different way where welfare services for elderly people are concerned. (Space limits this discussion to the most influential objections to markets and marketing[13]).

Some standard objections to the marketisation of welfare services apply with particular force to services for the elderly. One such objection is that consumers in markets for 'welfare' services are usually ill-placed to choose services critically and to bargain hard, in the way that classic welfare-economics legitimations of markets assume.

In certain types of markets there is less scope for choice among competing goods than classic legitimations of markets assume. Some services, for instance therapies, usually cannot be tested or sampled by a consumer before she decides whether to buy.[14] Terminal care is the extreme example. In these cases, elderly users cannot learn from their own experience how to 'play the market'. They can learn, but only once it is too late, in respect of welfare services whose work, unlike many other 'normal' consumer goods, is irreversible.[15] This is a larger point than the truism that the consumption of goods services is temporally irreversible. Rather, the argument in the case of services for the elderly would be that social (and health care) is often iatrogenic and a change of social status (selling one's home, spending one's life savings) is often an irreversible, one-off event.

Many elderly people have small bargaining power in markets, being less well able to use markets for their own benefit than many defences of the market presume. Elderly people are often less assertive and critical than other clients[16] and likelier to accept disability and pain without seeking (eg.) medical help for 'trivial' conditions,[17] or other kinds of social care.

Some services for the elderly, such as the enforcement of building regulations on access for elderly people (especially when physically disabled) are, it is maintained, public goods: they are indivisible and non-excludable, and there is no rivalry in their consumption. Market provision would be impracticable, according to 'free rider' arguments, because once someone provided a public good everyone else can get away with using it without paying; so either no-one would provide public goods through a market or public goods' prices would bear no resemblance to their marginal utilities, which according to welfare economists is necessary for Pareto-optimal market allocations of goods. (Pareto optimality is defined as the economic outcome where no redistribution of goods and services will make one or more persons better off without making one or more persons worse off. It is a theorem of welfare economics that any general equilibrium outcome that a set of perfectly competitive markets will produce, is Pareto-optimal. How much - or rather, how little - that proves is however another matter.[18])

Nursing care, residential care and indeed many other social support services are also held to be much more 'basic' goods for elderly people than for others; 'basic', in being means to securing many more, or more important goods, than most other instrumental goods. The more important goods which these services secure for elderly people might, if one followed Daniels, be taken as preserving one's 'normal species functioning' as much and as long as possible. Capacity for normal species function is especially jeopardised by the process of aging. Daniels justifies preserving species-normal function because 'impairments of normal species functioning reduce the range of opportunity open to the individual in which he may construct his "plan of life" or "conception of the good"'[19], reducing the options otherwise available to her[20] or prejudicing equal opportunity (how that is further justified). Doyal and Gough, and Weale see similar connections between health care, capacity for independent action and other goods.[21]

Titmuss objected to markets in and marketing of blood products as threats to social solidarity, as well as a threat to the quality of the blood and blood products available to patients. Markets and marketing are, he argued, likely to subvert the relation of trust between health services and their users (see below). These characteristics could easily be attributed to welfare services for the elderly and Titmuss himself expressly argued that he did not consider his conclusions to be limited to the case of blood products alone.[22] One might, for instance, expect reassurance about social solidarity to be especially valuable to people who feel vulnerable because of their stage in the life-cycle and who for the same reason are liable to social isolation. An economist's variation of this argument is that interpersonal comparisons, including concern for others' welfare, provide even welfare economics with a theoretical argument for 'collective' ie. public, non-market provision;[23] when interpersonal comparisons affect individuals' utilities, it can no longer be demonstrated that all perfectly competitive general equilibria are Pareto-optimal. Concern for others and concern to sustain the relationship of trust explain why, even in market systems, professionals offer discriminatory pricing instead of the uniform prices which welfare economics sees as a condition of Pareto-optimal equilibria.[24]

Some hold that elderly people have a right to receive welfare services[25]; a right based on the cash contributions these earlier generations have made to social insurance or pension funds. This right may be seen as repaying a sort of debt or dividend that later generations owe to the elderly for their past collective contribution to economic development or (more crudely) to the survival of the social order and later generations through past wars.[26] More sophisticated arguments ground such rights in a general theory of justice or prudentially. For instance, if rising economic productivity allows the *per capita* volume of welfare services to each generation of the elderly to increase, each generation will receive back more goods and services when it becomes elderly than it now pays to sustain the generation who are now elderly. This makes it prudent for today's economically active generations to introduce and sustain welfare services for the elderly on this basis. The language of 'rights' gives the arrangement a durable legitimation. It is next assumed that guaranteeing welfare services to the elderly would be a corollary of recognising their right to these services, and that markets cannot provide this guarantee. Conversely, when unwilling elderly people need to receive services compulsorily, say to prevent them being (in the words of English law) 'a danger to themselves or others', markets fail because market transactions are voluntary. Similarly, if it is judged only prudent for oneself and to be in others' interests that everyone should be compelled to make financial provision for their old age, voluntary market transactions are useless.

Markets in general are also alleged to be inefficient, stimulating waste activities and production, and generating expensive but superfluous insurance companies and other financial bureaucracies ('transaction costs'). Supposing these activities are wasteful, markets in services for the elderly seem particularly prone to stimulate them. To counter their commercial unattractiveness to insurers (see above), elderly Americans often take multiple insurance, duplicating costs and administrative loading.[27] Insurance markets encourage people to take cheaper, short-term insurance whilst they are young although this will increase their insurance costs and cost them more in total than if they took out lifetime insurance whilst young.[28]

Marketers of services for elderly consumers also come in for further criticisms for promoting ageist, patronising and offensive stereotypes of elderly people. With reason; a relatively recent discussion of services for elderly people a marketing journal noted;

> the proliferation of sobriquets attached to the market. No longer OAPs, the target audience are Greys, Mature Individualists, Third Agers (the first age is for learning, the second for work and the third for living), Glams, Grampies ("Growing retired active monied people in an excellent state"), Frops ("Filthy rich old people"), Woopies ("Well-off older people"), and even, unkindly, Wrinklies.[29]

Above all there is the market access problem. There are certain goods and services, the very need for and lack of which prevents people from entering markets and conducting market transactions to get them (or to get the other goods and services they also want or need). Markets are inherently unable to provide this category of goods for the people who most acutely need and lack them. Healthcare for elderly people is a classic example of this 'adverse selection'. On US evidence elderly people are more likely than young and middle-aged people to be underinsured or uninsurable, and those that are insured face higher care costs.[30] Propertyless elderly people are likely to have low eligibility for the large, long-term credit required to buy healthcare or social care in a market system.[31] Insurers have an incentive to use 'moral hazard' arguments to discourage claims.[32] This can delay provision of care, making it unnecessarily harmful, risky and costly and, especially for elderly people where time is (so to speak) biologically against them, less likely to be effective. Worse, market mechanisms may deter claims and prevent care altogether. US evidence also suggests that hospital failures more often occur in hospitals tending poorer and marginal clienteles[33]; elderly people are one. Many non-healthcare services for elderly, such as nursing and residential care, fall exactly into this category of goods too. Of all the objections to the marketisation and marketing of welfare services for the elderly, the market access objection is the most damning and intractable.

Yet the arguments do not all point one way, especially if we suppose that the alternative to markets is provision by the state through 'command economy' forms of organisation similar to those used in the NHS and most British local government social services until the early 1990s.

Nearly all the aforementioned standard objections to markets and marketing in services for the elderly appeal to the belief that these services are in economic terms an exceptional 'special case'. With varying degrees of explicitness, nearly all the writers cited above tend to accept the tenets of standard welfare-economic theory that perfectly competitive markets are an efficient, normal and desirable way producing (Pareto-) 'optimal' allocations of goods and services, unless a case can be made to the contrary. Given that assumption, the way one makes the case to the contrary is by showing that the goods and services that one wishes to exempt from the market system (here, welfare services for the elderly) have certain peculiar characteristics.[34] These characteristics differ from those which welfare-economic attributes to 'normal' goods and services in such a way that where these special cases are concerned, transactions in perfectly competitive markets cannot be relied upon to produce Pareto-optimal general equilibria.

Some of these claims are often overstated in the case of services for the elderly. Take the argument that welfare services for the elderly are 'public goods'. In fact rather few services to the elderly really are 'public goods'. The triple criterion of indivisibility, non-excludability and non-rivalry is very restrictive. Most services to the elderly are both divisible and excludable: nursing and residential care, social work, home helps, GP and hospital medical care, sheltered housing, access to self help groups and advice centres, to name but some. But even if they were public goods, this is only a *prima facie* argument against market provision. Consider another public good, of much interest to many elderly Britons: the use of burglar alarms to deter and prevent burglaries. When they are fixed conspicuously on a house wall (as they often are) burglar alarms presumably create a deterrent uncertainty among intending burglars besides warning the householder when undeterred burglars do break in. Since my house cannot be excluded from the indivisible, non-excludable deterrent effect of making potential burglars think that many burglar alarms do work and lead to the burglar being discovered, my house sports a dummy burglar alarm. There is no rivalry between me and other householders so long as potential burglars cannot tell the difference between dummy and real alarms and do not know what the ratio of real to dummy alarms is. Neither are real alarms made less mechanically or psychologically reliable by my fake. Yet I do not know of any advocate of the mixed economy who recommends a National Burglar Alarm Service to replace the conventional market in burglar alarms.

On closer inspection it turns out that what applies to the 'public good' claim also applies to the other supposedly special characteristics of welfare services for the elderly. They are not so exceptional after all. For every one of these characteristics a counter-example can be found of a good or service which also has the special characteristic but which, according to 'our' intuitions or the consensus to which so many philosophers appeal, is normally and desirably left to the market economy. Table 1 lists the special characteristics with their corresponding counter-examples.

Table 1: Services for the elderly; 'Special Characteristics' and counterexamples

Special characteristics of welfare services for the elderly	Counter-examples where characteristic is found in what is subject to market provision
Compulsory use	Car insurance
Rights to services[35]	Compensation for car accident damage
Compulsory prudence	Buildings insurance for mortgage-holders (UK)
Users cannot judge technical quality[36]	Personal computers
No opportunity to experience[37]	Arrangements for one's own funeral and will
Irreversible effects of services[38]	Demolition, land clearance, haircuts
Deference to professionals	(UK) house-buyers building surveyor
Consumer choice self-negating	Brokerages or agencies, eg. funeral services
Uncertain, irregular or unpredictable demand	Repairs to clothes, car, house
Unpredictable outcome	Betting, stock-markets
Public goods	Burglar alarms (see text)
Basic good-many instrumental purposes	Food (symbolic, nutritive and ritual uses)[39]; oil; money (in market society)

171

Table 1 continued

Necessary for market entry	Workman's tools and raw materials; capital
Social solidarity[40]	Gifts for birthdays, Xmas etc
Equal opportunity	Newspapers carrying job adverts
Externalities[41]	Cars (effects of environmental toxins – if cumulative, elderly people more susceptible) marketing (imposes costs of competition on other firms who must respond in kind)
Relationships of trust	High-technology goods (cameras, over-the-counter pharmaceuticals); baby-sitters
Waste (1); excessive administrative overheads[42]	Accounting, financial services, agencies and brokerages
Waste (2); over-processing	Food
Compromising quality, safety, to reduce costs	Cars[43]

Gavin Mooney claims;

> while no single feature or characteristic is unique to health care, there are few if any goods which have all the characteristics of uncertainty, irrationality, unpredictability, large monopoly elements, paternalism and important externalities.[44]

It is true that few marketed commodities in the private part of the mixed economy have all these characteristics, although we shall shortly see that some come close; but equally few health services and services for the elderly have all these characteristics either. If one lumps all health services together, or lumps

172

together all welfare services for the elderly, then one can indeed assemble a conglomerate of commodities which, taken collectively, do have all the six characteristics Mooney mentions, for instance by grouping together enforcement of building regulations with social work services, counselling for emotional crises during terminal care and meals-on-wheels. Taken individually, however, none of these welfare services has all six characteristics (and, incidentally, few, if any, health services do). However one can equally assemble similar collections of commodities which taken together also have all six characteristics but, according to most advocates of the 'mixed economy', are properly provided through markets (eg. car purchase taken with car insurance, car repair services, legal advice on how to claim compensation after an accident and catalytic converters). Further, some commodities that should on the mixed economy view be left to the conventional markets do have all six characteristics that Mooney names. Consider computerised databases - for instance those selling data on individuals' or firms' credit-worthiness. If it be replied that this counterexample is rather exceptional or marginal even in modern economies, here is another: accountancy, a ubiquitous activity in developed capitalist economies.

It seems difficult to sustain a convincing argument that services for the elderly should be exempted from market provision because these services have ethically or theoretically significant characteristics (or sets of characteristics) which other goods normally supplied through conventional markets do not have.[45]

Neither can certain inadequacies of many services provided through publicly-owned, 'command economy' forms of organisation be denied. (In Britain the nineteenth century precursors of these organisations were deliberately designed to produce 'less eligible' care than any alternative.) Townsend, Martin and others have drawn attention to the poor quality of residents' lives in many residential and nursing-care services of this kind, to these institutions' unreceptiveness to innovative models of care, and to their failure to meet elderly persons' needs in an individualised way.[46] Elderly people are after all a very diverse group; their age range alone is some 30 years.[47] This last fact suggests that one objection to marketing may have less force in services for the elderly than in other markets. The main economic role of elderly people is precisely as consumers, and minor nuances of service amenity, design or presentation may matter to more to people whose consumption of these services figures large among their everyday activities. It has been in amenities and presentation (aspects of marketing, outside the command economy) that non-marketed welfare services for the elderly have compared least favourably with their marketed counterparts.

The strongest reply to the market access objection is that only non-market funding of (say) nursing and residential services, not non-market provision, is necessary for guaranteeing elderly people access to them; and sufficient to guarantee access. Instead of individual (here, elderly) consumers' buying services, services are bought for them by public bodies or (in Britain) GPs and care managers whose bargaining power and technical competence to judge service quality exceeds most users' (even if in practice political objectives, especially cost-containment, may compromise the way public buyers exercise judgements on quality of care). Once services are purchased in this way, the actual service providers may be publicly-owned welfare services (directly managed or quasi-commercial 'Trusts'), voluntary organisations or even commercial, for-profit providers. Which organisations may provide services, whether they compete with each other, whether they are allowed to market their services, and whether there is price or non-price competition or both, then become subordinate, technical arguments about organisational means and efficiency.[48] The most influential supporters of this sort of position tend to hold that stimulating competition will widen consumer choice whilst creating incentives for innovation and high service quality. All this can be done whilst keeping services free at the point of use, available on the basis of need without financial obstacle.[49]

Such 'social markets' are alleged by their supporters to resist the old criticisms of marketisation and marketing in welfare services[50], including services for the elderly. (Different designs of social market are also called 'internal markets'[51], 'quasi-markets', 'planned markets', 'managed competition', 'planned markets' or 'public competition', depending on the author, context and characterisation.) Social markets can, it is argued, guarantee access to welfare services for elderly people, whether as a sign of social solidarity or to realise a right. They escape the 'basic good' and equal opportunity objections to conventional markets, the market entry objection and the worst effects of private insurance systems and uncertain demand because there is no conventional market between providers and users. That insulates users who are ill-informed or in a weak bargaining position from pressures to buy low-quality or unsuitable care. (However these defences of internal markets are hardly compatible with the political rhetoric that internal markets strengthen user choice[52]). What is more, social market advocates add, public buying authorities can so manage these social markets as to prevent the distortions in the range of services offered, and the instabilities of prices and supply found in conventional markets.[53] A subsidiary rationale for UK policy-makers is that internal markets in services for the elderly will increase the scope for insurance-funded provision.[54]

This last point reveals that two types of standpoint towards social markets are possible. One is to regard social markets as a second-best policy solution to the problem of what to do about welfare: either as a politically necessary stopping-point on the road 'back' from a command-economy welfare state to conventional markets;[55] or as the nearest it is technically possible, alas, to come to a perfectly competitive conventional market in welfare services. In the British context this standpoint implicitly takes rebuilding the welfare state as a set of social markets not so much as a reform as a 'retro-form'; a partial relapse to pre-welfare state models. Certainly retro-form is a feasible (which is not to say desirable) project. The obvious way to pursue it would be to encourage wealthy individuals, insurers and employers to enter the social market for (say) nursing and residential care for the elderly as purchasers alongside the public purchasers, and to encourage commercial service providers compete for public as well as private contracts for services for the elderly. Much British policy guidance recommends exactly this.[56] However a more subtle and, in Britain a more politically defensible, way would be to compel publicly-owned providers in a social market to operate in the same way as commercial, for-profit providers. Three conditions are severally necessary and jointly sufficient for this:

1. providers compete for service contracts (and other sales of services or goods); and
2. ability to invest in service innovations gives providers a competitive advantage; and
3. providers have to generate this investment from their own profits (either by reinvesting profits or repaying borrowed capital out of future profits).

Condition 1 is inherent in most forms of social market (include those which are being created for nursing and residential care for the elderly in the UK). Where it applies, condition 2 is a technical requirement. Condition 3 has been created as a matter of policy in the UK, the stated reason being to place public and private service providers on an equal footing in terms of costing and pricing.[57] These conditions create an imperative to maximise profits irrespective of whether a service provider is publicly or privately owned.

However an alternative standpoint is possible, and not one that would commend itself to Mrs Thatcher. This is to regard social markets as unwitting experiments in developing new, hybrid forms of economic organisation. A radical extension of this project would extend the work of deliberately redesigning the former public provision of services for the elderly welfare sector, retaining some elements both of markets and of NHS-like organisations, but hybridising to produce a new form of welfare organisation (or forms? - many varieties of social market are conceivable[58]) that has more differences from than similarities to markets. The above discussion suggests that the critical feature to retain from the command economy welfare state is the abolition of market relations between consumer and provider, so as to guarantee access to services for the elderly, to ensure that policy-makers can manage this part of the welfare system as a whole, and to protect the interests of elderly consumers when they conflict with those of service providers. From the market might be retained openness to new providers and new models of care, and the marketing of services for the elderly in the sense of creating incentives for attention to the amenities and presentation of those services; but not the commercial incentives for profit-maximisation. Saltman and Von Otter's discussion of 'public competition' moves in this more radical direction,[59] although it concerns health services rather than welfare services for the elderly. The resulting forms of social market would be so different from conventional markets (as from command economy welfare systems) as to make the phrase 'social market' a misnomer.

We end up with a new set of conceptual problems. New concepts (even new vocabulary) are necessary, but barely available yet, with which to articulate this radical, post-market development of the social market project. These problems are of wide significance for two reasons. We will nearly all become elderly if we are not so already, and so nearly all of us have an interest in understanding more clearly how best to design the organisational arrangements for providing services for the elderly, and why. Nevertheless, services for the elderly are not such a unique case. By considering what the organisational solutions to the problems of markets and marketing for them are, we reach conclusions which apply to other economic sectors too.

Notes

1. Brindle, D., 'Tories mask NHS failure in care of old', *Guardian*, 15 November 1991.
2. *Guardian*, 22 January 1996, p.5.
3. Cp. NHS Management Executive, *El(94)6*, Leeds, 28 July 1994, Cases 3,8.
4. NHS Management Executive, *HSG(95)8/LAC(95)5. NHS Responsibilities for Meeting Continuing Health Care Needs*, NHS Management Executive *HSG(95)39/LAC(95)17. Discharge from NHS Inpatient Care of People with Continuing Health of Social Care Needs: Arrangement for Reviewing Decisions of Eligibility for NHS Continuing Inpatient Care*; Mihill, C 'Government "passes buck" on care of old', *Guardian*, 13 August 1994.
5. Brindle, D., 'Councils charging for home care', *Guardian*, 27 September 1994.
6. Evers, H., 'Who should do the housework?', *The Health Service Journal*, 11 July 1991.
7. Daniels, N., 'Health Care Needs and Distributive Justice', *Philosophy and Public Affairs*, (Spring 1981), vol. 10, no. 2, pp.152-3.
8. Forsyth, G., *Doctors and State Medicine*, London, 1966, p.101.
9. Battin, M.P., 'Age Rationing and the Just Distribution of Health Care: Is there a Duty to Die?', *Ethics*, (1986), vol. 97, no. 2, p.333..
10. Shaw, G.B., Preface to *The Doctor's Dilemma*.
11. Sheaff, R., *The Need for Healthcare*, London 1996, (Routledge), ch. 7 sec. 2.
12. Battin, M.P., 'Age Rationing and the Just Distribution of Health Care: Is there a Duty to Die?', p.333.
13. Not considered here for reasons of space and because they are less often cited are: Culyer's account, and Grossman's, of health as capital (Culyer, A.J., *Need and the National health Service. Economics and Social Choice*, London 1976 (Martin Robinson) p.24; Grossman, M., 'On the Concept of health capital and the demand for health', *Journal of Political Economy*, (1972), vol. 90,; Dickman, R., 'Operationalising Respect for Persons: A Qualitative aspect of the right to health care', in Bayer, R.: Caplan, A. & Daniels, N., (eds). *In Search of Equity; Health Needs and the Health Care System*, New York 1983 (Plenum)); arguments from the non-independence of supply and demand in healthcare; and Marxist objections to markets *per se* (eg. Marx, K., *Capital*, Harmondsworth 1976 (Penguin) and many other editions).
14. Arrow, K., 'Uncertainty and the Welfare Economics of Medical Care', *American Economic Review*, (1963), vol. 53, no. 5, p.949.
15. Culyer, A.J., *The Economics of Social Policy*, p.121; Plant, R.,' Gifts, Exchanges and the Political Economy of Health; How should health care be distributed?', *Journal of Medical Ethics*, (1978, vol. 4, no. 1, p.6.
16. Kilner, JF.., *Who Lives? Who Dies?*, New Haven, 1990 (Yale UP), p.80.
17. Cartwright, A., *Patients and their Doctors*, London 1967 (RKP) p.201.
18. Sheaff, R., *The Need for Healthcare*, ch.8§2.
19. Daniels, N., *Just Health Care*, Cambridge, 1985 (Cambridge UP), pp.27,57.
20. Daniels, N., *Just Health Care*, pp.34,57.

21.   Doyal, L. & Gough, I., 'A Theory of Human Needs', *Critical Social Policy* (1984), vol. 10, pp.10,16; Weale, A., (ed.) *Cost and Choice in Health Care,* London 1988 (Kings Fund) p.13.

22.   Titmuss, R., *The Gift Relationship. From Human Blood to Social Policy*, London 1970, (Allen & Unwin).

23.   Arrow, K., 'Uncertainty and the Welfare Economics of Medical Care', p.954.

24.   Arrow, K., 'Uncertainty and the Welfare Economics of Medical Care', p.953.

25.   Estes, C.C. & Binney, E.A., 'Towards a Transformation of Health and Ageing Policy', *International Journal of Health Services*, (1988), vol. 18, no. 1, p.76, Bodenheimer, T., 'Should we Abolish the Private Health Insurance Industry?', *International Journal of Health Services*, (1990), vol. 20, no. 2, p.200.

26.   Cf. Beveridge, W., *Social Insurance and Allied Services*, London 1942 (HMSO; cmnd.6404), p.171 (the Beveridge Report).

27.   Bodenheimer, T., 'Should We Abolish the Private Health Insurance Industry?', pp.213-4.

28.   Bodenheimer , T., 'Should We Abolish the Private Health Insurance Industry?', pp.216-7.

29.   Anon, 'The Greys are coming', *Marketing Business*, April 1990, p.20.

30.   Estes, C.C. & Binney, E.A., 'Towards a Transformation of Health and Aging Policy', pp.70,72,76.

31.   Kilner, J.F., *Who Lives? Who Dies?*, p.181.

32.   Bodenheimer, T., 'Should We Abolish the Private Health Insurance Industry?', pp.202,212.

33.   Whiteis, D. & Salmon, W.J., 'The Proprietarisation of Health Care and the Underdevelopment of the Public Sector', *International Journal of Health Services*, p.55.

34.   Arrow, K., 'Uncertainty and the Welfare Economics of Medical Care', p.953.

35.   Estes, C.C. & Binney, E.A., 'Towards a Transformation of Health and Ageing Policy', *International Journal of Health Services*, (1988), vol. 18, no. 1, p.76; Bodenheimer, T., 'Should we Abolish the Private Health Insurance Industry?', *International Journal of Health Services*, (1990), vol. 20, no.2, p.200.

36.   Culyer, A.J., *The Economics of Social Policy*, p.120.

37.   Arrow, K., 'Uncertainty and the Welfare Economics of Medical Care', p.949.

38.   Culyer, A.J., *The Economics of Social Policy*, p.121; Plant, R., 'Gifts, Exchanges and the Political Economy of Health; How should health care be distributed?', *Journal of Medical Ethics*, (1978), vol. 4, no. 1, p.6.

39.   As Daniels comes close to recognising; *Just Health Care*, p.32.

40.   Titmuss, R., *The Gift Relationship. From Human Blood to Social Policy*, London 1970, (Allen & Unwin).

41.   Culyer , A.J., *The Economics of Social Policy*, p.119; and in another way, World Health Organisation, *Health for All by the Year 2000*, Geneva 1985 (WHO).

42.   Hellander, I.; Himmelstein, D.U.; Woolhandler, S. & Wolfe, S., (1994), 'Health Care Paper Chase, 1993: The Cost to the Nation, the States and the District of Columbia', *International Journal of Health Services*, Vol. 24, no. 1, pp.1-9; Bodenheimer, 'Should We Abolish the Private Health Insurance Industry?', pp.202,212.

43.   Nader, R., *Unsafe at Any Speed*, New York 1966.

44. Mooney, G.H., *Economics, Medicine and Health Care*, Brighton 1986, (Wheatsheaf), p.31, original emphasis.

45. Cf. Mooney, G.H., *Economics, Medicine and Health Care*, p.27.

46. Townsend, P., *The Needs of the Elderly*, Exeter 1973, (Exeter UP): Martin, J.P., *Hospitals in Trouble*, Oxford 1983, (Blackwell).

47. Victor, C.R., *Old Age in Modern Society*, London 1987, (Croom Helm) pp.2,13.

48. Eg. Department of Health, *Working For Patients*, London 1989, (HMSO), p.24.

49. Department of Health, *Working For Patients*, Margaret Thatcher's foreword; Willetts, D., *Reforming the Health Service*, London 1989, (Conservative Political Centre); Enthoven, A.C., *Reflections on the Management of the National Health Service*, p.41. The second Griffiths report is much more equivocal; Griffiths, R., *Community Care: Agenda for Action*, London 1988, (HMSO) p.2.

50. David Willets, Alan Maynard and Alain Enthoven publicly reaffirmed this view in their presentations at the Institute of Health Services Management conference 'Internalising the Market; Quality, Information and Choice', London, 25th January 1991.

51. The main policy documents are: Department of Health, *Working For Patients*, London 1989, (HMSO); Department of Health,, *Caring For People*, London 1989, (HMSO): Enthoven, A.C., *Reflections on the Management of the National Health Service*, London 1985, (Nuffield Provincial Hospitals Trust).

52. Department of Health, *Working for Patients*, pp.4-5,45,54-5,67-9.

53. Eg. Enthoven, Maynard and Willets at the conference mentioned in note 49; Willets, D., *Reforming the Health Service*, pp.42-3.

54. Department of Health, *Working for Patients*, p.69.

55. Cf. Marx, K., *Capital*, Harmondsworth, 1976 (Penguin), vol. 1, pp.228f,949-951.

56. On 'market testing' see NHS Management Executive, *EL(93)37* of 20 April 1993 and *EL(93)55* of 24 June 1993.

57. See NHS Management Executive, *Costing and Pricing Contracts: Cost Allocation Principles*, under *EL(90)173* of October 1990, with amplifications and amendments in *FDL(92)53* of 11 June 1992, *EL(93)26* of 6 April 1993 and *HSG(93)85* of 4 August 1993: also the NHS National Steering Group on Costing *National Costing Manual*, Leeds 1993 (NHSME).

58. Sheaff, R., 'What kind of internal market? A cross-Europe view of the options', *International Journal of Healthcare Planning and Management*, (1994), vol. 9, no.1, pp.5-24.

59. Saltman, R. & Von Otter, C., *Planned Markets and Public Competition. Strategic Reform in Northern European Health Systems*, Buckingham 1992 (Open UP).

11 Justifying ageism
OLIVER LEAMAN

It is never easy to think of good ethical grounds for discriminating against one sort of person to the advantage of another sort; but age seems like a good candidate. That is, where one is in the invidious situation of having to choose between two individuals, or between two groups of people, if one person is a lot older than another person, it might be argued that she has already had a rich variety of life's experiences in comparison with the younger person, and so there are good grounds for discriminating against her if a choice has to be made. If one is doing a consequentialist calculation comparing life spans, the sums would work out quite neatly, in that a ten year old, for instance, might be expected to have available to her a lot more years than an eighty year old. In that case, it might seem desirable to choose to employ limited resources on the former rather than the latter. Naturally one would first of all see whether there was an alternative form of action which could preserve both individuals, but if this was not forthcoming and a decision had to be made, it might seem fairly obvious to save the younger person at the expense of the older person. Although, clearly this is to discriminate against the older person on grounds of age, and ageism is in principle just as pernicious a doctrine as racism or sexism, it would seem to be justifiable to take age into account here, since it has a direct bearing upon the quantity and generally the quality of life which one can generally expect to lie in front of the individual. Nevertheless, whether this is as reasonable as first appears needs some careful investigation.

Perhaps the strongest argument for such discrimination is what has been called the 'fair innings argument' by John Harris; and it is worth considering in some detail. Harris (who does not himself endorse the argument) suggests that 'a reasonable form of the fair innings argument might hold ... that people who had achieved old age or who were closely approaching it would not have their lives further prolonged when this could only be achieved at the cost of the lives of those who were not nearing old age' (Harris, 1985 pp.93-4). The criterion of old age is what reasonable people would say about what age constituted a fair innings, and would necessarily be imprecise. The basis of 'the fair innings argument points to the fact that the injustice done to someone who has not had a fair innings when they lose out to someone who has is significantly greater than in the reverse circumstances' (*ibid.*, p102). The strength of the argument is in its adjudication between two kinds of injustice. It would be just for everyone to be saved, where the resources are available to make this possible. Where the resources are limited, neither person merits death and so the death of either constitutes an injustice. But less injustice is done if a younger person is saved at the expense of an older person, because the older person has already experienced much of the sort of life which is available to human beings, something which the younger person has yet to achieve. It is a shame that she has to die, but it is fair (or less unfair) that she should step aside and make way for a younger person to enjoy a relatively long life span. The 'fair innings' label captures nicely the feeling that many cricketers have when watching a batsman ploughing on in a slow and methodical fashion instead of taking risks and making way for those lower down the list. Some players have the reputation of being selfish in this way, ensuring that they amass large scores but not working towards the success of their team. Observers might well comment that they have had a fair innings when they reach a certain score, and it is then up to them to increase their chances of getting out by playing more adventurously. It is fair to put the interests of the team ahead of their own interests in piling up runs for the sake of improving their batting average.

There are good reasons for thinking that the 'fair innings' approach is part and parcel of contemporary social attitudes towards old people. In Britain old people are predominantly poor, live in inferior housing and are generally treated with condescension or contempt. With the decline of the extended family has come a growing unwillingness to look after older members of the family, by contrast with younger members. It is quite socially acceptable to dispose of an elderly relative in an institution under circumstances when it would not be felt appropriate to do the same with a younger relative, such as a child. Old people are not on the whole treated seriously and come generally into the category of being a problem or being perceived as a problem. There are no doubt complex social explanations for this phenomenon which will not be explored here, but it is important to establish that in our society there are markedly different attitudes towards old and young people which work to the detriment of the former. While many people would feel guilty at admitting to racist or sexist attitudes, ageist attitudes do not tend to gain the same opprobrium. It just seems natural that old people, with their greater tendency towards illness, dependency and inconvenience to others, should be expected to make way for younger people when this is necessary.

It might also be argued that discriminating in favour of younger people is what Harris calls a non-vicious' choice. I shall not repeat my criticisms of this notion (see Leaman, 1986), but it must be said that there are good grounds for thinking that such discrimination provides a unique justification in this sort of case. What we seem to have here are two injustices, and we have to choose he less unjust, in this case preserving the younger person at the expense of the individual who has achieved his 'fair innings'. This is not the same as discriminating against a Black person or a woman when it comes to deciding whom to treat, since there are good consequentialist grounds for believing that the life span available to a younger person is to be valued more highly than that available to the attainer of the 'fair innings'. If we generalize in the case of discrimination against Black people, or women, we get a situation in which welfare has not increased, assuming that life spans in these groups are more or less the same as in White male groups, and moreover many people are very upset by the levels of racism and sexism which influence their ability to survive and live comfortable lives. Although older people might be rather put out at the idea that they have reached an appropriate ceiling in terms of age, it could always be argued that these feelings, added to the number of years they have left to them with treatment, are still outweighed by the feelings of joy over survival by younger people, added to the larger number of years of life they have in front of them. There is also the suggestion implicit in the 'fair innings' slogan that old people would be rather selfish if they expected to survive at the expense of the young. Indeed, it would not be difficult to discover that this attitude has become quite widely internalized by old people themselves. But would they be correct in having this view?

There are interesting consequences to the 'fair innings' argument. One is that it involves an extreme form of egalitarianism. The fact that someone lives longer than someone else is regarded as patently unfair, and it is just to seek to equalize as far as possible the life spans of different individuals. Now, there are few views of justice which do not closely identify it with equality. Indeed, it might seem not worth arguing for a view of justice which does not identify justice with equality, although this would mean jettisoning a whole variety of more conservative theories which do have something to be said for them. Perhaps it is easy to identify justice with equality when it comes to looking at wealth, since money and possessions are essentially quite easily divided up in various ways, and they do not bear an essential relationship to people's lives (although doubtless misers would object to this point!). But age is not the same sort of thing as wealth: it bears a much closer relationship to us than our possessions, and redistribution of life among different individuals is a much stronger policy than a redistribution of financial assets. One might even suggest that different theories of justice could apply to different aspects of ourselves, ie. more progressive theories to our possessions and more conservative theories to our lives. The sort of extreme egalitarianism involved in the 'fair innings' thesis implies treating the length of years which people have in front of them and behind them as some kind of possession that may be available for reallocation and redistribution in the interests of justice and equality. Even a determined egalitarian might be worried at the idea that lives should be subject to the same sort of redistribution as the property of the living citizens.

The sort of conservative theory of justice which one might have in mind here is well represented by John Lucas in his *On Justice*, where he claims that 'it is not inherently unfair if someone has more than anybody else, but only if others are done out of their due' (p.8). This nicely captures what is so difficult to accept in the 'fair innings' thesis; the idea that someone is done out of his due where someone older than him is given the chance to live at the younger person's expense. Yet it might be argued that if financial redistribution is justifiable, and a significant part of our taxation system is built upon the principle that it is, then why is there not a redistribution of lives themselves? After all, lives are even more important than money, and if the latter can be redistributed, why not the former? When it come to resource allocation, it is tempting to turn to 'maximizing principles', as delineated, for example, by Jonathan Glover (1977), which have as their object the preservation of as many lives as possible for as long as possible; and detailed calculations might be based on the number of lives at stake or on the total amount of life. We might then come to accept that it is fair for older people to give up their remaining years for younger people, in much the same way that we think it is fair for richer people to give up (some of) their money for the sake of poorer people; and all that remains is for discussion about the precise mechanism of transfer to be worked out in the optimal manner.

However, in many ways my life is mine in a way that my money is not. My life is not just a series of experiences which I possess, but a relationship between those experiences and me. Chance is important here; I may have been lucky or unfortunate, and these chance events are important aspects of me. For example, I may have decided to drink and smoke heavily as a young man, or to climb high mountains, or to explore dangerous regions of the world, and as a result be in a terminal physical state much earlier than would otherwise would probably be the case. Alternatively, I may have spent a lot of my time preserving my body through adopting a healthy regimen, or just through living prudently and carefully. It seems iniquitous if the prudent older person is to be obliged to give up her remaining years for the sake of someone younger solely because they are younger. It seems just as iniquitous if the older person has reached a considerable age in spite of, rather than because of, their past behaviour. Were such a reallocation of lives to become the norm, it would change our whole attitude to the ageing process. The nearer we got to the 'fair innings' level, the more nervous we would be about our future chances of surviving much longer, and not for the normal reasons connected with the reduced likelihood of remaining natural life. We should worry that we were entering the age where our lives become fair game for the redistributors, and it might be felt to be more prudent to live well and recklessly while younger, since the benefits of a healthy old age might not be enjoyed not by us but by someone younger than us.

However, this difficultly in identifying our lives with our financial resources might be regarded as an effect of ingrained habit rather than philosophical acuity. After all, conservatives tend to regard the reallocation of financial resources as somewhat dubious, given our assumed right to hold onto what we acquire or inherit. But it is not difficult to argue that the relationship we have with our money and possessions is very different from our relationship with our lives. For one thing, we can be deprived of our material possessions and yet continue to exist, perhaps to reconstitute our fortunes, Once our existence is redistributed there is nothing left to us; we are not just poorer but no longer around at all. Yet might it not appear unjust for someone to cling on to her few remaining years, judged in terms of probability, when these could be transferred to someone else and might be expected to realise a much longer span for a younger person? This involves being able to compare lives in much the same way as we compare other aspects of those lives, and this is a questionable procedure. The last few years, or months or even days, of an older person might be very significant in their lives. It might be that in the last stages of their natural lives they come to bring their affairs to an orderly end in such a way as to believe that they can now with some degree of satisfaction approach death. Those last few periods of time may have for them a significance which nothing that preceded it possessed. It may be that the way in which their lives come to an end gives meaning to everything which comes before. This is very much a part of what is meant by calling a life span 'natural', which is not the same as calling it long. Some people die far too early, statistically speaking, and tragically early deaths are just as natural as normal life spans. The fact that an apparently minor event, like a slate slipping off a roof or an illness proving difficult to overcome, may result in the untimely death of an individual is a basic metaphysical fact of contingent creatures in a world such as this. Two children may be crossing the road together, and one may be fatally struck by a car while the other may escape injury completely. Has the more fortunate child, by virtue of her survival, done down the dead child? Is it unfair that one should live while the other is killed? If it is unfair, then the source of the inequity is to be found in the arrangement of natural events, not in the arrangements which human beings might make.

Of course, it would be quite natural for the parents of the killed child to think it was unfair for their child to be harmed and the other to be spared, even though the latter had done nothing to contribute to the sad end of her friend. The parents might even blame the surviving child herself. But such feelings are irrational, and we all know that it is a feature of this sort of world that we hardly ever know when people are going to die. Although it is quite rare for young people to die in accidents, it does happen, and may affect anyone in the wrong place at the wrong time. We may blame the way of the world, but such an attitude does not really make sense unless we think there is some agent behind that world, and even then there are clever arguments to excuse such an agent for responsibility in these cases. Now, it might be thought that this common feature of our world, the transitory nature of life and the omnipresence of sudden death, provides a useful additional argument for the 'fair innings' thesis. We may accept that nature behaves in arbitrary and apparently unfair ways, but with the 'fair innings' strategy we can to a degree civilize nature by imposing our own organization on the question of who dies and who lives. We can ensure that relatively old people do not survive at the expense of young people, which is 'fairer' than the situation in our world where resources can be expended to preserve the lives of old people rather than for the sake of younger people with a greater span and superior quality of life before them. We cannot control young people dying in accidents or through sudden illness, but we can so reorganize the allocation of resources as to preserve the lives of the young at the expense of the lives of the old. In this way we shall be doing our best to make up for the arbitrariness with which nature disposes of people regardless of their proximity or not to the 'fair innings' level of years.

When I read this paper at the Manchester conference in 1992 it was suggested, to my mind plausibly, that most old people would see it as entirely reasonable for younger people to be saved at their expense. Another discussion on living wills and euthanasia showed how easy it would be to inveigle old people into not demanding the application of medical resources to preserve their lives once they started to become inconvenient to their carers and relatives. We

185

do live in a society which values health, wealth and youth, and once people possess none of these characteristics they may well seem, even to themselves, no longer to be worth preserving. It is very much the argument of this paper, though, that such a view is mistaken. From a consequentialist point of view it encourages people to devalue the latter part of a normal life span. It encourages them to regard themselves at a particular point as disposable. It gives them no control over their lives once they reach a particular age and no right to make decisions about their own lives. Such attitudes would lead to a wholesale decline in the quality of life for all people, even if only a small number of old people are sacrificed for the sake of younger people. It could well be argued in addition that the fact that many old people are already possessors of these very attitudes displays how far down the road we are in their progressive degradation and devaluation. It has often been pointed out that the strongest form of oppression occurs when the victims themselves internalize the attitudes which society has about them.

At this point adherents of the 'fair innings' thesis tend to get impatient and talk about particular cases. Suppose that I was the only medical practitioner in an emergency and I had the choice between saving an older critically injured person and a younger critically injured person, such that their age does not enter into the likely success or failure of the operation. Would I not, while decrying the lack of resources, obviously apply myself to the younger patient, since he has the most years (other things being equal) in front of him? The answer here has to be 'no', because we are dealing with something here, ie. life, which is indivisible. As Hobbes puts it in *Leviathan*; 'some things there be, that can neither be divided nor enjoyed in common. The Law of Nature, which prescribeth Equity, requireth, That the Entire Right ... be determined by Lot' (ch.15). No-one has the right to decide what is to be done by us and through us when something as significant as our very lives is the issue. Valuing our autonomy is not an exercise in selfishness but rather an assertion of belief in our own value as a person, and if we are to be used as a means of saving others, this requires our consent. We cannot be obliged to do it, although we may chose to as a supererogatory act. For such a choice to be a genuine choice, we must be free of false consciousness and capable of valuing ourselves despite our age and illness.

The beauty of the 'fair innings' thesis is that it provides us with some sort of decision procedure for dealing with difficult cases, and without it we just will not know what to say when we have to chose between two individuals. It has been the argument here that we should beware the attractions of coming to an

186

answer where it is far from clear that it is the better answer. If we are to make difficult moral choices, these should not be on the basis of the prejudices and resentments which we hold against sections of our society. Ageism is thus no less vicious a form of discrimination than racism or sexism, and there can be nothing 'fair' in its application to resource application.

Acknowledgement

I should like to thank Peter Edwards for his helpful comments on an earlier version of this paper.

References

Glover, Jonathan, *Causing death and saving lives*, Penguin, Harmondsworth, 1977.
Harris, John, *The value of life*, London, Routledge, 1985.
Hobbes, Thomas, *Leviathan*, London, Dent, 1943.
Leaman, Oliver, *Evil and Suffering in Jewish Philosophy*, Cambridge, CUP, 1995
Leaman, Oliver, *Death and Loss*, London, Cassell, 1996
Leaman, Oliver, 'Harris on non-vicious choice', *Analysis* 46, 2 (1986), 106-7.
Lucas, J.R. *On Justice*, Oxford, Clarendon Press, 1980.

12 The felicific calculus strikes back

ALAN CRIBB

Introduction

Medical advances, the costs of high technology care, the number of people living longer. We have become accustomed to the items on this list, or similar lists, being used to introduce a discussion about health care resource allocation. There is some irony, although there may also be some unhappy logic, in the fact that many proposed methods of resource allocation would have the effect of disadvantaging older people, so that though the existence of a National Health Service enables people to live longer, once they have reached old age they would have to recognise the claims of younger people taking precedence. Some people seem to find this intuitively acceptable. If someone in their mid-thirties, say, becomes seriously ill or dies this is often seen as inherently worse than the same thing happening to their mother or father. In turn this seems to have implications for the way medical resources should be divided between individuals. For example, some might argue that individuals who are no longer economically productive (a deceptively simple idea) and are somehow a 'less sensible investment' than others should accordingly be allotted fewer resources. This is one kind of economic rationale for resource allocation (and a particularly pernicious one) but it is not one I will be concerned with in this paper. However, there are other economic analyses, which are *prima facie* less value-laden, but which have comparable implications for the health care of older persons. The most clear-cut of these is the argument that resources should be allocated to forms of treatment, and to individual people, so as to maximise the overall number of life years gained by the expenditure. I want to look at a well known variant of this approach which aims to take into account quality as well as quantity of life. For the common sense objection to the pure 'life years gained' approach is that it fails to take into account the quality of life gained, and that a health care intervention that adds an average of four years to people's lives is not necessarily better than an intervention which adds an average of three years but at a much higher quality.

It seems sensible to say that we should spend health care resources in the way which does most good, but if this is taken to mean that we should spend them so as to 'buy' the population as many years of good quality life as possible it becomes controversial. Amongst other things this entails that it is generally better (more productive) to spend money on younger rather than older people. In what follows I consider the use of 'quality adjusted life years' (QALYs) as a means of resource allocation. The inherent ageism of this approach, along with its other shortcomings, has been well demonstrated elsewhere (eg. Harris, 1987,1988; Smith, 1987); yet despite this QALY talk continues to be influential. I believe it is important to analyze the continuing plausibility of the QALY rationale, and to ask which elements of this rationale are convincing, and which are misguided.

A common criticism of methods of resource allocation, including QALY analysis, is that insofar as they involve 'choosing' who lives and who dies then they are morally objectionable. A closely related proposal is to ask for an absolute priority to be attached to saving lives before any consideration of health care productivity. This may be seen, contingently, as protecting the interests of older members of the population. I will conclude by examining the force of this criticism and the related proposal.

The problem - incommensurability versus opportunity cost

If we were asked to choose between a society in which 2 per cent of people were blind and 1 per cent deaf and a society in which these figures were reversed how would we respond? One response would be to deny that such a choice is possible, or more accurately to deny that any objective comparison and judgement is possible. The values of sight and hearing, along with the other valued states of affairs associated with health, are incommensurable. There are qualitative differences between all health outcomes which make comparative evaluation impossible. Another response would be to insist that we can, do and indeed ought to make this sort of comparative judgement. This is the response of the health economists. The fact that we ought to, they say, follows from the fact that we can - otherwise we will be responsible for bringing about a world which contains more suffering than is necessary. The fact that we can, they might say, follows from the fact that we do. By the way we allocate health care,

189

and other, resources we bring about one set of outcomes rather than another. We do make these sorts of decisions and we feel, at least some of the time, that they are not arbitrary or irrational. To the extent that we do this we do not accept the incommensurability of different outcomes.

Both of these responses have an initial plausibility, but I am particularly interested in the plausibility of the health economists' argument. On the strength of this argument various economists have built a supposedly neutral model for informing resource allocation decisions; a new arithmetic of happiness or 'felicific calculus' (Bentham, 1962) which enables us to spend the health care budget in a way that maximises welfare. QALYs are the best known formulation of this approach. They are a way of operationalising and comparing the 'health output' of interventions according to the number of life years (adjusted for quality) added by each intervention. One leading proponent explains as follows:

Suppose .... the cost of a QALY for a range of activities was something like this:

Activity A	£15000	per	QALY gained
Activity B	£ 8000	per	QALY gained
Activity C	£ 3500	per	QALY gained
Activity D	£ 2000	per	QALY gained
Activity E	£ 1000	per	QALY gained
Activity F	£ 750	per	QALY gained
Activity G	£ 200	per	QALY gained

Does it then not seem natural to say that if we want to improve people's health as much as possible (ie. maximise the number of QALYs gained) we should first of all expand Activity G to the limit, then F, then E, and so on, and when we run out of resources, stop.

...There are, of course, some barely hidden complications in this simple minded view of the world. The first of these is that one QALY is assumed to be of equal value to everybody. This is obviously a convenient analytical assumption, but it has to be judged not in those terms, but whether you believe that to be the appropriate ethical position for a health service to adopt... More complex ethical positions will of course require more complex calculations, but that is a minor matter (Williams, 1987).

These comments represent two key dimensions of QALY analysis. Firstly they make a case for using QALYs as a means of maximising the 'output' of health services. Secondly they concede that this is a value-laden position and that others might prefer to make different 'calculations'. This is indicative of the way proponents of QALY analysis defend it against criticism (Rosser, 1989; Gudex, 1990). They accept that we need to improve the measurements of QALYs; furthermore, they accept that we may want to adjust their application (eg. by including weightings for age, or condition, or equity etc.) However we must, they maintain, accept the essence of the system. We need to operationalise opportunity cost - we make these choices implicitly and it is better (more efficient, more democratic) to make them explicitly. Some sort of measure, like QALYs, it is argued, must be utilised to inform these choices. None of the criticisms of the new felicific calculus will strike home unless they address the soundness of this underlying rationale.

Two systems of comparative evaluation

In order to resolve the apparent tension between incommensurability and opportunity cost, we need to distinguish between two pictures of comparison. According to the first picture every intervention has an 'intrinsic potency' and produces a definite output. This output can be identified and, within limits, measured. A combination of interventions which produces more output is to be preferred. This system also requires a common denominator so that different outputs can be compared and aggregated. According to the second picture, an intervention is valued according to the extent to which it can contribute towards producing the overall optimum outcome. In this case it may be difficult, or impossible, to single out the 'output' of a particular intervention, and the 'output' would in any case vary according to the context in which the intervention takes place. Hence comparison of the respective benefits of two different interventions will be relative to particular situations. It seems to me that the former is, roughly speaking, the picture assumed by QALY analysis; and that the latter is, roughly speaking, the true picture.

If we can put a frame around the situation of choice without eliminating important factors, eg. if we are comparing the benefit of two types of treatment for one patient, we can adopt the 'intrinsic potency' picture, provided we are conscious of the frame and the simplification entailed by it. The circumstances are those in which two or more interventions are directed at precisely the same objective, have the same kind of costs, and have negligible or negligibly different 'side' effects. Most of the choices of health care resource allocation, or of any other kind, do not arise in these circumstances.

Imagine a man who is making a choice between owning a big house or a big car, and imagine that he only has his own interests to consider. This is a choice between two different lifestyles, and if he is rational he would make it by considering the likelihood of the two options contributing to the satisfaction of his welfare requirements. Even this trivial example makes it clear that such choices are about trying to set and meet the criteria for a full or happy life. They are partly a matter of deciding what counts as welfare, and the idea of invoking a common denominator (which we could *call* welfare) is manifestly odd. Similarly the idea that owning a car has a determinate intrinsic potency of welfare units regardless of context is absurd.

It seems then that QALY analysis gains its plausibility by (1) insisting upon the importance of opportunity cost and hence the necessity of choice between incommensurables, (2) making the assumption that opportunity cost choices depend upon the existence of a common denominator (health output or QALYs), (3) using some examples in which 'intrinsic potency' and common denominator picture is relatively sensible and (4) implying that all examples are of this type, thereby obscuring the distinctions between very different kinds of choices.

Thus the view of the QALY rationale as in principle sound but is in practice difficult to apply is upside down. The rationale is *in principle* misguided, and we should only use this form of reasoning in the limited circumstances where it is most appropriate, and then only to provide indicators for decision making. This is, of course, the same objection that undermined the original (arguably more sophisticated) felicific calculus - there are qualitatively different kinds of benefits that cannot be meaningfully compared in terms of amounts or intensities of some other generalisable benefit. The fact that this way of thinking has gained currency again is perhaps partly explained by the technical-looking graphs and tables deployed by economists, and partly by the supposedly narrow focus on 'health' rather than welfare as a whole. The most widely cited measure of QALYs uses the reduction of physical disability and distress, as well as increased life expectancy, as the measure of health output (Kind, Rosser, Williams, 1982). Attaching priority to these factors as providing the basic conditions for most other human goods seems, at first sight, to be a credible stance. However on reflection this is, at best, one stance in a debate about narrow versus broad conceptions of quality of life; a debate which cannot be short-cut simply by the adoption of a narrow measure.

It seems, therefore, that the imperative of facing up to opportunity cost in health care resource allocations does not mean, and should not be confused with, the maximisation (or optimal distribution) of 'health output' - except in some metaphorical sense. QALYs only exist as artifacts of economists' measurement procedures, and in most cases there is no reason for us to make the assumption that one QALY is 'equal' to another. Indeed, this conclusion has been anticipated by some of the economists working on the application of QALYs who have pointed out the advantages of using 'programme-specific', and thus more sensitive, QALY measures, even though this involves acknowledging the possibility that 'certain groups in society are being discriminated against in health service resource allocation due to an insensitive across-programme measure outcome' (Donaldson, Atkinson, Bond, Wright, 1988, p. 239). The problem is that the adoption of programme-specific measures of outcome would undermine the possibility of this kind of analysis determining the relative productivity of different types of intervention, and hence its role in macro resource allocation.

The recognition that opportunity cost choices do not imply the existence of a common denominator dissolves the most common defence of QALYs. In principle they are open to improved systems of measurement and application, which might embody other moral positions in 'more complex calculations'. But in practice any actual application aimed at weighting different types of intervention for different populations will be contestable, and will rest upon unwarranted assumptions about the commensurability of the QALYs involved.

Health care in the good society

What then is the equivalent for a whole society of the 'big car versus big house' type of decision? Again, even assuming that we are considering the interests of only one society there is the problem of balancing expenditure on transport, housing, and health care etc. All of these forms of expenditure have an effect on the level and distribution of health. But even if we leave this aside, there are clearly very difficult decisions to be made about what range of health care interventions have an objectively discernible intrinsic potency and to transform these decisions into arithmetical calculations. By contrast I want to maintain that these decisions are essentially moral and political decisions about what kind of society we want to live in. To some people this will sound like a way of effectively dodging the issue, and it is partly by contrast with this that the superficially practical and open approach advocated by the economists gains its currency. However, the first thing to say is that alternative ways of allocating resources need not be arbitrary; we can, indeed ought to, bear a number of different kinds of good in mind. For example, all of the following seem relevant: (1) life saving, (2) reducing forms of suffering and disability, (3) variety of provision, (4) the importance of meeting 'demand', (5) the claims of equal consideration, and (6) the degree to which allocation decisions should be 'democratic'. Even taken together these criteria do not constitute a formula; rather they are in many ways in tension with one another. To list them, or any similar set, is no more than the beginning of a public policy debate. Furthermore there is a sense in which all formulas are bound to be inadequate because in one important respect these decisions are 'cognitively under-determined' ie. we can make more than one distribution compatible with our limited 'knowledge' about want and welfare satisfaction. It may even be that we could make a number of equally good (or bad) distributions, because even a 'perfectly' informed rationale debate may not completely eliminate the scope for choice. I want to look briefly at two aspects of this debate:- (a) the relationship between the ends and the means of health care delivery, and (b) the function of health care;- partly to illustrate further the deficiencies of the QALY rationale, and partly to make some tentative suggestions about alternative approaches.

In order to think clearly about effective health care provision it is necessary to consider the mechanisms as well as the principles of distribution. There is no point in conceiving of a supposedly ideal outcome without some picture of how this distribution can be achieved in practice. Under existing systems (market, non-market or quasi-market) demand is not equivalent to need, and systems are further distorted by variations in supply (which are not determined wholly by either demand or need). But we cannot afford to dismiss these mechanisms as irrelevant. There is some moral weight to be attached to responding to the demand for health care, because this is one way of respecting patient autonomy, and because it is one arbiter of need. The QALY approach is frequently presented as a rational and neutral alternative to the real world system of irrational traditions and vested interests. Unfortunately, if it is taken too seriously it is incompatible with any real world system, because resource allocation has to deliver the optimum distribution of resources compatible with a real world of professionals, patients, and institutions in which we could and would want to live, and not merely an optimum distribution in the abstract. At its most basic level this means we need to work at the level of institutional arrangements and not only on types of intervention in the abstract. It also means, and this is a more challenging point, that we have to take into account the arguments (well rehearsed in other social policy debates) about the cost of trying to *enforce* distributional ends. The arguments against centralised planning of services have been well rehearsed, and their relevance to this setting in which both consumer choice and clinical freedom are seen as key values should not be underestimated.

However, unless we assume that our health needs would be best met by a completely free market in health care, it is also important to ask questions of principle - about the functions of the health service and welfare policy - and to see how provision might be informed by such principles. There are a number of ways in which moral principles may help to set the parameters for the distributive mechanisms. For example we might attempt to rule out certain interventions for normal public provision as luxuries, on the grounds that they fail to meet real or significant needs. Or we might try to formulate a narrow conception of health as part of an account of basic entitlements to health care. It is not difficult to imagine arguments for and against these moves. The QALY approach is a parallel case; it sets parameters based on the idea of optimising something imaginary called 'health output'. So the questions we must start from is 'What contribution should health care provision make to our way of life?' This cannot be considered by simply looking at the contributions of types of intervention in isolation.

If someone running a lunch counter wanted to increase the overall level of satisfaction of their customers they might start by asking everyone to rank the items of food and drink on the menu according to how much each item would be missed. But if they then, taking into account cost, supplied only those few things that would be missed most, this would be bizarre. Not only is this outcome unfortunate for the minority interest groups; it is madness for the majority. It is to assume that every portion of carrots is of equal worth regardless of what you eat it with, or how often you eat carrots. This is an illegitimate way of using the original preferences by abstracting them from the context in which they were expressed. It is clear, at least in this instance, that it would be better to begin by asking the customers about the range of foods they would choose. If the menu is to be changed at all it is likely that the preferences will change as a result. However this effect can to some extent be reduced by concentrating on *the range of provision* rather than by pretending that particular foods can be treated as if they have an independent value.

It seems to me that the thought-experiments built into the QALY approach fall into the same 'lunch counter' trap by attempting to set values for each intervention separately. However in reality each of these valuations is made according to assumptions about the contexts of intervention. If a QALY analysis was used to bring about a very different pattern of services this would amount to an unreasonable application of the original weightings away from the context in which they made sense. I would argue that a more useful thought-experiment would be to ask individuals to divide up their share of the health care budget between a range of services. Faced with this challenge each individual would have to balance together the costs and benefits of different types of intervention in 'packages' rather than as discrete items. It would be necessary to 'hedge one's bets', for example, by splitting resources between being kept alive and being kept active and comfortable.

This too could be translated into a series of psychometric tests, but these would suffer from all the same methodological and conceptual difficulties as the QALY tests (not least the problem of how to combine different people's scores). In addition such decisions which depend upon statistical and epidemiological analysis would be complex and technical. For these reasons it is sensible to see this suggestion only as a thought-experiment. It might be presented in a fashion like that used by Rawls (1971). Imagine a group of individuals who have to set up a social system in which they do not know what position they will occupy - eg. whether they will be male or female, Black or White, young or old. They are given epidemiological literature on the causes and risks of death, depression, dependency and so on, plus the available research on the specific costs and benefits of various types of intervention, and are asked to decide broadly how to split resources between different types of intervention, eg. preventative medicine, and acute care. It is then agreed that the distribution of resources a rational self-interested person would opt for under these conditions must be a just distribution, since there is no reason to favour any particular group as such. This method is clearly supposed to engender a disinterested rationality; it is an attempt to transcend conflict between social groups with different priorities and needs. However this has been subject to many criticisms (eg. Lukes, 1977). Indeed, any pattern that emerged from such a forum (or that we imagine emerging) would still be informed by a conception of the good life, including not only an attitude to death and disease, but also an attitude towards risk-taking, and towards such things as the relative importance of equity and efficiency in health policy, and therefore could not be genuinely neutral. None of the profound moral and political decisions about resource allocation are avoided by taking this route; it could not be used as an alternative form of 'neutral' decision making.

Nor should it be thought that such a thought-experiment could lend some kind of democratic legitimation to its conclusion. It is important to distinguish between considering people's perspectives for epistemological reasons and consulting people as a democratic mechanism. The former is clearly an essential means of ensuring politics are rational and grounded in fact. The latter may or may not protect people's interests. The proponents of QALYs often place great emphasis on people's perceptions and preferences (Williams, 1988) but fail to clarify the kind of role these should be given in decision-making.

Nonetheless it seems to me that this sort of thought experiment is useful precisely because it forces into the open the debate about the functions of health policy and of health services. The debate cannot be reduced to the application of mathematical formulae, but it is necessary to use empirical evidence about risks and benefits, and to do so within a framework in which the opportunity cost of types of intervention is made explicit. I would suggest that the rationale behind this thought experiment forms a necessary part of health care resource allocation. We have to make allocations with a picture of the whole provision in mind, as it might exist through the lifetime of an abstract individual; and we can only make these allocations reasonably by entering into a conversation about the elements of a valuable life, and about the other social goods which ought to be protected or promoted through health policy. I cannot see how these broad choices about the parameters of provision can be resolved (theoretically or practically) except through moral and political debate. It is in this area that QALY analysis is least useful unless we are prepared to grant sense to comparisons of the utility, for example, of terminal care and preventative dentistry through some common denominator.

Part of the moral debate is to point out that potential applications of QALYs are unfair. They do not begin to address any aspect of equity, as opposed to efficiency. My concern is that in some ways such criticisms pay too much respect to the idea of QALYs. In most decision contexts the application of QALY analysis is not so much unfair as incoherent. For this reason we should be equally cautious about the idea that QALYs only constitute a servant and not a master. Either this sort of analysis is appropriate to the type of decision under consideration or it is not.

Choosing who will live

Finally I want to consider an important objection to any attempt to fix the parameters of resource allocation. Do they not entail that we will be choosing who lives and who dies? Furthermore may they not mean that some people's deaths will be 'traded off' for improvements in other people's quality of life?

It seems unlikely that a pattern of services coming out of a public policy debate would give absolute priority to life saving. Yet it could be argued that just such absolute priority is what is morally required, that no person's death can be allowed to come about in order that someone else's welfare be improved, however dramatically.

The first response (to this objection) is to point out that it is not clear what giving priority to life-saving procedures means. As well as dramatic cases of life saving surgery, and other high profile interventions such as the supply of kidney machines, there are routine preventative interventions which are aimed at life saving. Indeed the treatment of most medical conditions arguably affects longevity and therefore contributes to 'life saving'. It doesn't make sense to try to force a rigid conceptual split between interventions which affect quantity and interventions which affect quality of life. Secondly, giving priority to keeping people alive can be taken to more and more extreme lengths. We know people do not want to be kept alive under any and every set of circumstances.

It is useful to make comparisons with other aspects of public policy. We build and operate road systems and there is a cost in lives. Although a lot of resources are devoted to safety there is a cut-off point in such expenditure. Talk of the cost-benefit ratio as a means of justifying this seems out of place because the benefit (which many may contest) is essentially a way of life. In fact, it is worth asking in what sense, if any, are these deaths 'chosen'? Choices are made which result in deaths but it is far from clear what the alternative could be, and what its social and human costs would be.

The health service is apparently different because it is sometimes expressly concerned with life saving, and it seems odd to say that life protection is a side constraint of health policy as it is for transport policy. But it is worth pursuing the parallel. A system that devotes all its resources to saving those lives immediately at risk is not necessarily the system that saves the most lives. (This is the thrust of the demand from advocates of preventative medicine to 'move upstream' ie. focus on the prevention of disease and death - in this sense the whole of health care can be seen as partly preventative). In addition it is impossible to envisage the social and human costs of the kind, and extent, of social engineering which would be needed to ensure that all resources were used in the 'approved' life-saving way. This is one application of the earlier reminder about the costs of enforcing distributional ends in social policy.

Yet this might be thought to amount to the argument that we must still give an absolute priority to life saving but that we must do so intelligently, and that working out the implications of this policy is a challenging process. I don't think this restatement of the objection meets the responses outline above. The general point is that human beings value other things apart from being kept alive, and they fashion forms of organisation and practices in the light of a number of competing goods. This is the reason that we do not give an absolute priority to life saving, and 'worlds' in which more people die later are not necessarily thereby better or more desirable worlds. It is important to see that idea of contrasting essential goods (eg. life) and non-essential goods (eg. comfort), if pushed too hard becomes seriously misleading. Even life itself is only worth something as part of a package.

It is inevitable that choices we make now about the parameters of health care provision will have an impact on how and when individuals will die in the future. This is a necessary consequence of providing any one pattern of care rather than another. Because of the indeterminacy of the future, and the notorious difficulties of achieving predictive validity in the human sciences, it is extraordinarily difficult to trace the connections between today's policy decisions and tomorrow's mortality patterns. So these decisions only amount to 'choosing who will live' indirectly. This is different from deliberately ending the lives of specific individuals on resource grounds. However the fact that this is 'action at a distance' does not dissolve moral responsibility. In some cases there are clear forms of discrimination built into certain health plans. In these circumstances we can see that the life chances of certain groups (such as older persons) are, in effect, being deliberately sacrificed for the advantage of others. This will certainly happen if we take the new felicific calculus seriously.

Acknowledgements

I would like to thank Harry Lesser for his helpful comments on an earlier draft of this paper.

References

Bentham, J., (1962) *Introduction to the Principles of Morals and Legislation*, (ed.) M. Warnock, Collins, Glasgow.

Donaldson, C,; Atkinson, A.; Bond, J.; Wright, K., (1988), 'Should Qalys Be Programme-Specific?', *Journal of Health Economics*, vol. 7.

Gudex, C., (1990), 'The Qaly. How Can It Be Used?' in *Quality of Life, Perspectives and Policies*, (eds.) Baldwin, S.; Godfrey, C; and Propper, C., Routledge, London.

Harris, J., (1987), 'QALYfying the Value of Life', *Journal of Medical Ethics*, 13, no. 3.

Harris, J., (1988), 'More and Better Justice', in *Philosophy and Medical Welfare*, (eds.) Bell, J.M. and Mendus, S., Cambridge University Press, Cambridge.

Kind, P.; Rosser, R.; Williams, A., (1982), 'Valuation of quality of life: Some Psychometric Evidence', in *The Value of Life and Safety*, (ed.) Jones-Lee, M.W., North-Hollard, Geneva.

Lukes, S., (1977), *Essays in Social Theory*, Macmillan, London.

Rawls, J., (1971), *A Theory of Justice*, Harvard U.P., Cambridge, Mass.

Rosser, R., (1990), 'From health indicators to quality adjusted life years: technical and ethical issues' in *Measuring the Outcomes of Medical Care*, (eds.) Hopkins, A., Costain, D., Royal College of Physicians, London.

Smith, A., (1987), 'Qualms about QALYs', *Lancet*, vol. 1.

Williams, A., (1987), 'Health Economics: The Cheerful Face of the Dismal Science?' in *Health and Economics*, (ed.) Williams, A., Macmillan, London.

13 Justice and the principle of triage

HARRY LESSER

Although the principle of triage has often been used in practice in order to decide how to distribute medical resources under conditions of scarcity or emergency, it has so far had fairly little theoretical consideration. I think, however, that such theoretical consideration is needed, not simply for its own sake, but because with the increasing pressure on resources has come pressure to use the principle over a wider area. One factor in deciding whether this is or is not desirable must be working out exactly what kind of principle it is, and what it implies. In particular, we need to see whether it is a utilitarian principle or a principle of justice, and what the ethical consequences are in each case; and it is this that I want to consider in this chapter, with particular reference to the ethical consequences for treatment of the elderly.

Triage was first used by surgeons on the battlefield to decide whom to operate on when a shortage of doctors, equipment and time made it impossible to treat all the wounded men before they died. The principle requires the doctor to make a rapid assessment of those needing treatment, and to assign each of them to one of three groups - those who will probably die, even if treated; those who will probably recover, even if untreated; and those who, again probably, will live if treated and die if not treated. The first two groups are then 'put on one side' while everything possible is done to save as many members of the third group as one can - this being the best use of limited resources.

It is clear that in some ways this 'sorting' is rough and ready. First of all, it can be based only on probabilities - no one can be quite certain who will die and who will live. Secondly, some arbitrary decisions have to be made: how soon must a person be likely to die to put in group one, and how long must another person be likely to live to be put in group two? Moreover, if a person can survive untreated, but only in permanent pain and/or seriously maimed, they should probably be put in the third group, which would thus include not only those whom treatment can save from death but also those it can save from a terrible life. Conversely, it should presumably not include those who can be

201

saved from death only to face a terrible existence. These considerations would apply also, presumably, if the doctor happened to know that a person who could be saved was suffering from some other condition that meant they were in any case very shortly doomed to death or an unbearable life. And once again, an arbitrary decision has to be made as to what kinds of life are as bad as, or worse than, death.

So the use of triage requires that the doctor works from probabilities and makes arbitrary, but not irrational, decisions about when death is imminent and when life is intolerable, having regard not only to the present emergency but to other things they may know about a person's state of health - and all this at very great speed: it could not be rational to use time that could be spent actually saving people for deciding whom to save! There is one other consideration, and that is the amount of time, human effort and resources needed to save a person. The practical use of triage requires that those who could be saved, but only by diverting resources from many other people, have to be put in the same category as those who cannot be saved; and on the other hand that those for whom a very small amount of resources would guarantee that they were saved ought to be given those resources, even if it is probably (but not certainly) unnecessary. The principle, thus involves, like all practical activity, the use of predictions based on probabilities and of classifications that involve 'grey areas' where decisions have to be arbitrary. These modifications of the principle to include intolerable life as well as death, and consideration of the amount of resources needed to save a person as well as whether it is possible to save them, would probably be seen by a doctor operating triage as simple commonsense: but they may turn out to be important once one is considering the ethical basis of the principle, its implications, and what happens when it is extended beyond emergency situations.

So what justifies the principle of triage? First of all, it seems to many people - perhaps most - intuitively right. There is some evidence that this is even more true in the practical situation, and that doctors faced with an emergency feel even more strongly that it is right to act in this way. But it is worth noting that the intuitions of both doctors and layman are different once the situation is not an emergency, and also that is always right to ask on what one's intuitions are based, and to see whether they are rationally defensible - to distinguish genuine moral intuition from the prejudices of particular social groups is notoriously far from easy.

It is commonly supposed that the moral justification for this particular 'intuition' is utilitarian, that using triage will result in doctors doing the maximum amount of good with the resources at their disposal, subject only to the problem that, as always, predictions cannot be a hundred percent perfect. Certainly, given that the top priority in medicine is to save life, or at any rate the lives of those who can be restored to a worthwhile life, triage provides the most efficient use of scarce medical resources. But to maximise efficiency towards a given end is not the same as to maximise happiness, or welfare, or the satisfaction of desires or needs in general, as utilitarian moral theories require.

For the principle of triage aims simply at saving lives, or at any rate lives that reach some minimum standard of 'being worthwhile'. But there could be people who fall into the group of 'probable' survivors, and therefore do not absolutely need treatment, but whose lives are of such value to society that the right course of action for a strict utilitarian would be to make absolutely certain they survive, even at the expense of some people for whom treatment is a life-or-death matter. There could also be people who will 'probably die', but who similarly are so valuable that utilitarian would have to hold that resources should be diverted to at least doing everything possible to save them. On the other hand there could be people who could be saved, but who are so unlikely to be of any use to themselves or others if they do survive that, although treatment should be provided for them if possible, the application of utilitarianism would require that they go to the back of the queue, whereas the application of triage requires that they form part of the priority group. Even if such facts were not known or knowable, strict utilitarianism would probably require that the young and healthy among the 'probable survivors' took precedence over the aged and infirm among those in the 'life or death' group.

It might be possible to argue that utilitarianism, 'the greatest good of the greatest number', does not have these consequences. But even the fact that it might shows two things about triage. One is that triage does not necessarily produce the same moral results as utilitarianism, which shows that it cannot simply be an application of the utilitarianism principle. The other is that to apply utilitarianism rather than triage, if it would lead to consequences of the sort suggested above, seems distinctly unjust. And this brings out a crucial point, but one that has, I think, often been overlooked: we are disposed to agree with the principle not only or primarily because it leads to the most efficient use of resources (though it does), but even more because it squares with our notions of what is just - those who are in the greatest need of treatment, ie. those for whom it will probably make the difference between life and death, have a right to go to the head of the queue, and those who can probably manage without it, or whom it probably will not help, should be dealt with, if resources permit, after them. So the vital feature of triage is not so much that it leads to an efficient distribution as that it leads to a just distribution of medical resources.

At this point it might be objected that distribution according to need is only one interpretation of justice, and not one which is universally accepted. But what I am claiming here is not that distribution of all goods should be according to need, but that distribution of medical resources should. It does seem fairly clear that questions of worth or desert are not relevant here, and that if preference were to be given, say, to someone whose survival was vitally important to the nation, this is not a matter of justice, but of justice in this instance being subordinated to the public interest.

It may well not be possible to prove that the just distribution of medical care and resources should be according to need. But one can show that this is in line with some very strong moral intuitions. Consider two patients, one whose life is in danger, and one who needs treatment but not urgently. It seems clearly unjust to treat the second patient rather than the first, or even before treating the first, on the ground that they are able or willing to pay more for the treatment, or on the ground that they deserve it more: the relevant consideration, as regards justice, is simply need.

This does not apply only to life and death situations. The same would apply to two patients, one in intense pain and one in appreciable but bearable pain, with regard to the administering of a pain-killer. It would apply, other things being equal (which they are not always), to help with conceiving a child, as between say, a woman near the end of her fertile years with no children and a woman much younger with a child already. It could even apply, in psychiatric medicine, as between a psychotic and a neurotic patient.

It is important to stress that this applies only in conditions where the difference in need is clearly marked and time and resources are limited. Very often, differences in need are not immediately knowable, or not that significant anyway: there are simply a number of people who need help. Sometimes the differences do not really matter, even if they are significant, because everyone can be treated within a reasonable period of time ('reasonable' though, sometimes has to mean 'very short'). Often, too, the time required to sort out patients according to need can be better spent by getting straight on with the treatment; and too much concern with justice would result in a situation that was neither just or sensible. But in principle, need is the supreme criterion: the G.P., for example, who normally sees patients in the order of their appointments and concentrates on each in turn, will think it right, in a real emergency, such as a life-or-death matter, to give preference to the person who cannot wait and whose need is vital.

Three further points need to be made. The first is that need is a function not only of the seriousness of one's condition but also of how much help the treatment is likely to be: this is why in the use of triage those almost certain to die even if treated are regarded in the same way as those who can manage without treatment. If the treatment, for whatever reason, will not in fact help, then the patient, however desperate their condition, does not need it. One should also note that there can be many reasons why a treatment cannot help - because the disease is too far advanced, because the patient cannot tolerate the treatment physically or psychologically, because it has to be self-administered and the patient cannot learn how to administer it, etc. Finally, this applies relatively as well as absolutely - not only as between one patient who needs the treatment and one who does not, but also when one patient needs it markedly and obviously more than another, the greater need being the product of two factors - how serious their condition is and how likely the treatment is to help them. Because there are two factors, assessment of need - which can be problematic at the best of times - becomes even more uncertain. But it is not impossible: it can sometimes be clear that at least one factor is very low, and therefore the need slight or non-existent, whether because the condition is not serious or because the likelihood of the treatment being beneficial is small; and it can be clear, at other times, that the condition is serious, the likelihood of the cure if the treatment is applied is very great, and hence that the need is about as great as it could be. But assessment of need cannot *always* be made, even approximately: the importance of this will emerge later.

Up to this point I have argued that under conditions of scarcity or emergency it is just to allocate a particular health care resource according to need, and that if the scarcity or emergency is serious enough this requires using the principle of triage. Two objections could be made here. The first is that the definition of health care, as apposed to social care, is unclear: this point is raised, in a different context, in Rod Sheaff's paper in this volume. To this one can reply that, while this is true, the same moral considerations apply to both, if they are in short supply - certainly to the kinds of social care that border on health care. It is worth noting also, in case there is any feeling that social care is less important than health care, that both can be required, on occasion, to fulfil desperate needs: one person, may for example, need regular visits in order to be saved from a suicidal depression as much as another person may need a life-saving operation. So for these purposes nothing hangs on the precise definition of what is a health care resource.

Secondly, it has, particularly recently, sometimes been argued that, while overall 'worth' or 'merit' is not relevant to the distribution of health care resources, one particular kind of merit is relevant. This is the 'merit' of those who are ill or injured through no fault of their own, as apposed to those who have to some degree brought their condition upon themselves by, eg., overindulgence or taking unnecessary risks. The question is whether in justice people in the second group should receive less of scarce resources than those in the first group, or should come lower in the queue for such resources.

The question is complicated; but for our purposes it may be enough to point out the empirical difficulties of putting this into practice, even supposing it to be just. First, there is the difficulty of deciding when a person has been self-indulgent and when in contrast they have run necessary or praiseworthy risks - even smoking may for some people be the only way of 'steadying their nerves' sufficiently to enable them to do their job and/or look after their family. Secondly, except with very clear cases, such as self-mutilation, it is usually hard to tell to what extent the present illness or injury is the result of stupidity or self-indulgence. Thirdly, it has been pointed out that the fact that someone has developed an illness which they could have avoided does not mean that they are overall costing society more than if they had not developed that illness: thus the smoking-related diseases, such as lung cancer, often strike a person after their working life (or most of it) is over and before they have become a drain on resources because of the ill-health of old age, so that, whatever harm smokers do to themselves or those near to them, their smoking is not a 'social cost' overall. Given all this, establishing merit or demerit in entitlement to health resources seems to be a hopeless task.

It is also worth noting that, although in the abstract many people feel this would be just in principle, there is no enthusiasm for it in practice. For example, though it is common for nurses to feel a deep anger against people who mutilate themselves, and much resentment that time they can ill spare has to be given over to treating and caring for people who need never have required treatment, no one has actually suggested that they should not be cared for. In this connection, we should note that the reports, still sometimes repeated, that smokers have sometimes been denied heart operations, are incorrect. What has happened on occasion is that undertaking to give up smoking has been made a condition of being allowed the operation, on the ground that otherwise the operation will not succeed in prolonging life and will be a waste of time, effort and resources. But this is an entirely appropriate application of the principle of triage itself: a person has no claim to treatment which will do no good, least of all when it will be their own voluntary behaviour that will prevent it from doing any good.

We may conclude from this that, as well as providing a just way of allocating resources in an emergency, triage also can provide a just ground for withholding resources, even when there is no emergency, if providing those resources will do no good. This can be either because their use is unnecessary and will not improve or hasten recovery, or because it will have no effect: there is of course a question as to exactly how small the chance of doing good has to be before one brings triage into operation, but eventually it must become appropriate. The question now is, whether the principle can and should be much further extended. For, it might be argued, we are always in an emergency situation, since there are always more demands on a health service than there are resources to meet them: hence, if it has been shown that triage is just in a clear emergency, it follows that the right and just way to distribute resources is always according to triage, so that priority should always be given to saving life, as the greatest need, followed by treatment of the most painful and/or crippling conditions, with preference always also being given to those for whom the treatment has the best chance of success. If it is right in the one case, it must be generally right. Therefore, it might be argued, triage should be used as a systematic principle for allocating health care resources to the people for whom they will do the most good.

But there are two objections to this. The first is the apparent impossibility of finding any reasonable way of deciding, when dealing with the system as a whole, which needs are greatest. In the standard uses of triage, one is dealing either with one overriding criterion for treatment - whether it is likely to make the difference between life and death - or with one particular type of treatment, so that the criteria for need are relatively well defined. Even here, assessments are rough and ready, and subject to error. But in dealing with the whole health service there are at least three further complications.

First, one would have to deal with types of patient, rather than individuals, to make a general judgement about which conditions are the most life-threatening and the most serving of priority. This inevitably would not totally correlate with individual needs, but would favour some patients and disadvantage others, ie. those for whom a particular condition is abnormally serious. Secondly, health needs are of at least three types - the need for life, the need for adequate physical and mental functioning, and the need to be free from pain. Often, these go together: very often, indeed, to provide medical treatment is to meet all three of these needs. But this is not always the case - some of the hardest dilemmas in medical ethics precisely involve decisions whether, eg. prolonging life or relieving suffering is more important. This suggests that the proposal above, of giving preference to saving life, and then to dealing with what causes the most suffering or incapacity, is too simplistic, that there is no straightforward way of ordering needs across the board, even when one confines oneself to the most serious needs. It can indeed by plausibly argued that in this situation, unlike the emergency situation, there is no right answer to the question who should be given priority - it is not merely a matter of being liable to error, but of asking an inappropriate question.

Finally, there is the further problem of comparing very different types of illness and injury. As long as one is dealing only with threats to life, this may not matter: one can try to assess the relative gravity of various threats - how likely they are to kill, and how soon - even if they are very different in kind. But with incapacity and suffering there are great difficulties - how, for example, does one compare physical and mental suffering, or pain with indignity? Is it more urgent to relieve pain or to try to prevent adult incontinence? Is a psychiatric illness more or less disabling than a physical one?

To all this the advocate of triage might make two replies. First, they could argue that these problems can be overridden, if, as is the case in a developed society, we have sufficient resources to meet all serious and major needs, so that we need to be concerned only with very substantial and obvious differences in need - all serious needs could be in priority categories and only what is genuinely unnecessary would be dispensed with. Secondly, it could be argued that, however crude and imperfect such a process proved to be in practice, it would nevertheless be a more just way of allocating resources than any other - treatment would more often, though not always, go to those most entitled to it.

The first of these points is by no means certain, given how costly in time and resources some life-saving treatments have to be: also, it is not clear that there is any objective agreement as to which 'needs' are the really essential ones. But the crucial one is the second, which balances the second objection to triage as an overall principle. It may be that, as regards the practical issue, triage could be operated in no more crude and arbitrary a way than any other principle - though, as we have seen, this is very questionable. But the big question is whether, given that the use of triage is just in an emergency, it is also just whenever needs outstrip resources.

It is, I think, fairly clear that it is not, for the following reason. In an emergency, what is most important totally overrides what is less important: in a 'normal' situation one has to try to meet all claims, not only the most important. For example, suppose that the person - metaphorically or literally - at the head of the queue has a painful but non-dangerous skin complaint. It is right and just that an emergency case should overtake him, especially if it is a matter of life and death. But it is not right and just that everyone with a more serious illness or injury should overtake him, so that, probably, he is never treated at all, but, so to speak, has to watch while he is constantly passed by new, but supposedly more pressing, cases. In short, what has exclusive priority in an emergency has only greater priority under normal circumstances, even though resources are limited, So, a just health service has to provide, or to try to provide, resources for all levels and types of health needs, as its basic goal, and to introduce 'prioritization' only as it becomes necessary and in particular contexts. These are probably all too frequent; but there is a big difference between making priorities within the system and eliminating some types of care from the system altogether.

That the first option is more just can also, I think, be seen by applying a version of Rawls' 'veil of ignorance' test (see *A Theory of Justice*, Harvard, 1971). Consider a person who has no means of knowing what demands they are likely to make on health resources in the course of their life: this is in fact the situation of many of us. Such a person would presumably prefer a service that tried to meet all types of health needs over one that tried to guarantee meeting the most crucial needs but ignored various others. Now, people in this position are people with no personal axe to grind, people able to evaluate neutrally competing claims, since they have no knowledge of which claims they themselves will make, Hence, their preferences can be seen as being requirements for a fair system - the fairest system is the one that people would opt for if they had no idea whether it would or would not benefit them personally, ie. the one that as far as possible would benefit everybody, while giving more to those is greater need. (I have argued earlier for the relevance of need for a just distribution of health resources)

We may, I think, therefore conclude that the principle of triage has two proper applications. It provides a rough and ready way of identifying, in an emergency, the people with the strongest claim to treatment. It also provides a valid reason, whether or not the situation is an emergency, for withholding treatment - namely, that the treatment will do no good, either because the patient will die in any case or because they cannot respond to the treatment; but it is not a fair principle on which to base an overall system of medical care, because this would inevitably lead to ignoring claims to care which are not the most vital but which are still legitimate.

What implications does this have for the distribution of medical resources to the elderly? Essentially, it shows that the triage principle gives no ground of any kind for discriminating against them. It is true that, if the principle is followed, treatment will be more often withheld from those in the higher age-groups. But this is so because there are more people in these groups who are either going to die very shortly whatever happens, or unable to benefit from treatment. Their age as such is never relevant: what is relevant is their physical condition.

This means that to assume, on the grounds of triage, that treatment should be withheld from patients above a certain age cannot be right. There can be good grounds for not resuscitating certain patients, if their death is imminent anyway or if they would be resuscitated to an intolerable existence. But there is no age, however high, above which this is always the case. Hence a blanket policy of not resuscitating patients over a certain age - as, it is alleged, has been sometimes adopted - cannot be right; and the same would apply to any other treatment. Still less could there be any ground for regarding the medical needs of the old as less important simply because they are old and supposedly going to die soon - this would be doubly wrong, since it would also, as has been argued above, be applying the principle to the health service as a whole, which is in itself illegitimate. Triage requires only question only to be asked, under normal conditions, namely 'Can the patient benefit from treatment?' Under emergency conditions it requires the asking of a second question, 'Who needs treatment most urgently?' The effects of ageing, which are different for different people, are sometimes relevant to this question: the chronological age is not.

There may be one exception to this. It is possible that there are some conditions which invariably arise after a certain age, so that everyone above that age may be legitimately assumed to have them. These conditions might be physical or mental: for example, since the ability to learn new skills decreases with age, there may be some complex methods of self-medication that cannot be taught to people of a certain age. This is possible, and if the evidence is good enough, it could be legitimate to assume without investigation of every individual case that everyone over the appropriate age is in this physical or mental condition. But great care is needed in the use of evidence, to ensure that the assumption really is an appropriate one to make. Moreover, even if there are some treatments that are only suitable for younger people, and one cannot find even the occasional old people who can benefit from them, it is still the physical or mental condition, and not the age itself, that is the relevant consideration. We should also note that the question of benefit is not to be answered in an overall utilitarian way but simply with regard to whether the treatment will appreciably prolong life or remove something detrimental to the quality of life. If it is not at all likely to do one of these, it should not be given; but this applies to the young as much as to the old.

I have thus argued (1) that triage is a principle of justice; (2) that it is the appropriate principle to use in an emergency; (3) that it would not be just to extend its use to all decisions about the distribution of medical resources; (4) that it should be generally used as a ground for withholding treatment from those for whom the treatment is extremely unlikely to do any good; and (5) that although more elderly people than young people come into this category, age in itself is never a valid ground for concluding that the treatment cannot be beneficial or for withholding the treatment.

In short, we should be tough-minded and unsentimental, and resist the temptation to do what will almost certainly do no good, simply because we feel we must do something. But we should not pretend that easing or extending a person's final years, or months, or even days, is 'doing no good'!

Reference

Rawls, J. (1971), *A Theory of Justice*, Harvard UP, Cambridge, Mass.

14 Health care access, population ageing, and intergenerational justice

CLARK WOLF

Population ageing, intergenerational conflict, and the role of normative theory

As time passes, we all age. But the ageing of individuals may or may not be accompanied by the ageing of the society in which they participate. Demographic shifts in the patterns of birth and death can lead to a greater or lesser proportion of older to younger members, and such changes imply corresponding changes in the pattern of individual human needs. When the pattern of needs changes, it may often be necessary to reform the social institutions that are intended to respond to them. Recent demographic changes in the United States have generated political pressure for just such reforms as the proportion of elderly to young Americans has swiftly grown: the number of Americans sixty-five years of age and older has more than doubled since 1950, while the number over age eighty-five has more than quadrupled. In the same period, fertility rates fell until 1976, and are still relatively low. The overall effect is that there are many more elderly retirees for every younger worker. Since US institutions provide for those who are currently elderly by taxing pre-retired workers, this has led to severe strains on the social institutions designed to serve the needs of the elderly, and has created an ever-increasing burden for the young. These problems have been most keenly felt within institutions that provide health care and income support for the elderly.

As Norman Daniels notes;

> employed workers - young and middle aged adults - pay the overwhelming share of all health-care costs. On the average, their annual health-care insurance premiums - partly in the form of employer benefits, partly in the form of their own payments, partly in the form of payroll taxes - far exceeds their actual health-care costs. There is a transfer of health-care resources to children, and even more dramatically to the old.[1]

This distribution of burdens for the young and benefits for the elderly has led, in the United States, to charges of intergenerational inequity. In the popular press, there have been charges that current institutions, operating at the behest of 'Greedy Geezers'[2] are 'Consuming our Children.'[3] The American Association of Retired Persons (AARP) has come to be regarded by many as a political menace, and is widely perceived to be supporting programmes that unfairly burden the relatively poor, younger workers in order to provide benefits for wealthy older retirees. This view of the AARP is not altogether fair, but it is increasingly widespread. There is a general sense that the young and old are in competition for a limited set of resources, and lobbyists have been active on behalf of both groups.[4]

It has been widely recognized by those who have written on this subject that the notion of 'intergenerational equity' is subject to facile misunderstandings. One kind of inequality exists in a society when one age-group is better off than another. For example, if children tend to be poorer than middle aged workers, who in turn tend to be worse off than the elderly, this constitutes a kind of inequality. But we might judge that such inequalities are unproblematic from the standpoint of fairness or justice if we were to find that life prospects for members of these three groups were more or less equal. A more disturbing kind of inequality exists when children's lifetime prospects are systematically worse than those of their parents. If our concern is for intergenerational fairness, we need to make comparisons across birth-cohorts rather than simply comparing the wealth of the elderly with the relative poverty of the young.

Reflection on these different types of intergenerational comparisons opens the way for a series of questions: What conception of intergenerational equity, if any, should we use to evaluate the justice or fairness of our institutions? Under what circumstances is it unjust to require the young to bear the costs of care for members of the previous generation? Under what circumstances, if any, could it be just to deny or to fail to provide care to the needy elderly or to needy children? What social institutions will best protect the interests of old and young alike? And finally, how can such institutions be put into place in a democratic society? There is no broad agreement in the US on answers to these questions, or even on their meaning. In popular discussions of justice between generations, participants often seem to be talking past one another. In such a context, there are two distinct roles for normative philosophical discussions of the problem of intergenerational justice. First, such discussion may serve to clarify the problem, and to help focus attention in the right place, avoiding the red-herrings set down by interest groups and pundits. Second, a well worked out philosophical account of justice between young and old should provide guidance for policy makers in their efforts to improve and reform social institutions so that they may more adequately respond to demographic changes and changing social needs.

Some philosophers have sought to accomplish this by providing an 'ideal theory', an account of the normative principles that would govern the functioning of institutions under circumstances of perfect justice. Such a theory, it is hoped, may provide us with insight into the ways in which our actual and imperfectly just institutions might be improved and reformed. With a clear understanding of our final goals for our institutions, we may be able better to understand what we now need to do to make our institutions more just. But we may have reservations about such ideal theories of justice: the old saying that 'The best is the enemy of the good' teaches us that we may sometimes do worse if we strive for perfect justice than we would have done if we had instead worked toward more modest, but still achievable goals. A full normative theory should not merely provide a description of an ideal; it should also provide us with guidance as we make policy decisions under conditions of restricted information, and under realistic political and financial constraints. Where perfect justice is not a realistic, achievable goal, we still need criteria for evaluating those outcomes that are achievable, so that we can effectively work toward the improvement of our institutions and social policies.

In this paper, I will examine the practical and philosophical problem of distributive justice between young and older members of society. I begin with a discussion of what is clearly the best current theory of intergenerational distributive justice: Norman Daniels' Prudential Lifespan Account (PLA), articulated in his recent book *Am I My Parent's Keeper?* (Daniels (1988) henceforth PK) After a critical examination of Daniels' account, I will evaluate it by making pairwise comparisons between the PLA and two alternatives: (i) a modified utilitarian alternative that minimizes expected lifetime costs due to illness or deprivation for each representative member of society, and (ii) a 'sufficiency' alternative that includes a universal right to a basic minimum of health care but leaves needs for resources beyond this basic minimum to the distributive mechanism of the market. While each of these theories has, I will argue, some advantages over Daniels' prudential lifespan account, I will argue that the latter view represents an alternate ideal that is more realistically achievable, and which would still be a dramatic improvement on current institutions in the US and elsewhere.

Daniels' Prudential Lifespan Account

The account of age-justice developed by Daniels in his 1988 work is in many ways a continuation of the theory developed in his earlier book, *Just Health Care* (1985), but represents a significant development and extension of this earlier view. These two works have set the agenda for discussions of justice in the distribution of health care in much the way that Rawls' *A Theory of Justice* has continued to set the agenda for political philosophy: whether one agrees with Daniels or not, his work is the place to start. While my discussion of Daniels' view will be mostly critical, and while I will defend an alternative to that view, it is important to recognize the degree to which my discussion is indebted to his work. Daniels has clearly brought discussion of the problem of justice between neighbouring generations to a new level. In what follows, I will first present what I hope is a sympathetic reading of the main elements of Daniels' view.

Daniels begins by reframing the problem of justice between young and old. The conflict between these groups, he argues, is in some ways illusory. Since we all age, the current young will eventually be old, and will stand to benefit later in life from institutions that may seem to burden them now. We should therefore replace questions about the apparent conflict between young and old with questions about the way in which our institutions respond to the changing needs of different birth-cohorts as they pass through the stages of their lives from childhood to old age. If we are concerned about fair treatment of persons, we should be less concerned about differences in treatment of young and old, and more concerned about differences in treatment and lifetime expectations between cohorts. Institutions that impose burdens on the current young may not treat persons unequally, provided that those who currently bear the costs will have the opportunity to reap compensatory benefits when they are older. Daniels is right to point out that some aspects of intergenerational conflict disappear when we compare cohorts instead of age groups.

But this reframing of the problem is not sufficient to generate a full theory of justice between generations. In addition, it is necessary to provide an account of the way in which institutions should respond to people's changing needs over time. In this interest, Daniels recommends that we should consider what would be chosen from behind a Rawlsian 'veil of ignorance' by prudent agents searching for principles to govern the structure of health care institutions under which they will live complete lives, from birth to death. As in Rawls' (1971) theory, the veil of ignorance extends first-person prudential concern so that

215

rational individuals will take into account the interests of each member of society. It accomplishes this by imposing a constraint on those who are charged with the task of choosing principles for the distribution of health care resources: while these prudent choosers know general facts about society, about patterns of disease and demographic changes in the society's age-profile, they do not know their own identities, nor do they know to which sub-groups of society they belong. They must choose principles that will determine the structure of distributive institutions without knowing precisely how these institutions will affect their special interests. So they must consider the way in which their choice will influence the life of each person in society. On Daniels' view, the specific question these choosers are to address might be stated as follows: 'What normative principles should regulate the basic institutions that govern the distribution of health care resources among younger and older members of society, and how should these institutions operate to distribute each person's fair share of these opportunities or resources over the course of a complete life?' This choice is framed, Daniels insists, within the assumption that other problems of distributive justice have already been solved, and that the overall budget that prudent deliberators must allocate over each person's lifespan has been defined by the solution to this prior problem:

> In our restricted or framed problem, the problem of justice between age groups, we are to suppose that hypothetical deliberators already know what inequalities in lifetime expectations are acceptable. That is, they already know what counts as a fair share, and they must decide a further question: How should that lifetime expectation of enjoying a certain level of primary social goods be distributed over each stage of life so that lifetime well-being is maximized? (PK 61-2)

By considering what prudent agents would choose if they did not know their race or gender or religious affiliation, Rawls (1971) ensures that the principles of justice chosen from behind the veil of ignorance will not be tailored unfairly to serve the interests of any particular subgroup in society at cost to other groups. Daniels extends this Rawlsian argument to cover distribution over time within a life, but this requires the imposition of a different kind of constraint: those who choose principles from behind the veil of ignorance must not know their present age. Because of this restriction, they will be unable to tailor institutions to serve the interests of their particular age group. This makes the problem of justice between age-groups analogous to the problem of budgeting resources to be used over the course of a complete life. Daniels writes 'The age-group problem is equivalent to a problem of budgeting within a life only if we assume institutions operate over the whole lifespan. The prudent consumers designing it must plan accordingly, that is, without reference to - or knowledge of - their actual age. Only by denying individuals information about how old they are can we retain the frame within which the appeal to prudence may be justified.' (PK 51)

The conditions on the choice situation Daniels describes can be summarized in four broad requirements:

3. The choice is one in which prudent deliberators are to settle on principles that will govern the design of institutions that distribute resources over a lifespan.
4. Their choice is made from behind a 'veil of ignorance', which insures that their choice will not be inappropriately partial, and that the principles they choose will not unfairly be tailored to serve their special interests. In addition, they do not know what conception of the good they will adopt at different stages in their lives, but must instead gauge their prospective well-being by reference to a Rawlsian list of primary goods.
5. They are assumed to know that a more general theory of justice already adequately addresses the more traditional problem of distributive justice between persons. The problem that remains is only the problem of distribution over time within a life, across various stages of life.
6. Finally, Daniels' prudent choosers must assume that they will live through each stage of life under institutions governed by the principles they choose.[5]

How would prudent agents reason in such circumstances? Has Daniels given a sufficiently rich description of the circumstances in which this choice is to be made that we can predict how they would reason, and what they would choose? Daniels claims that such agents might prudently reason as follows:

In thinking about my well-being over my lifetime, prudence demands that I abstract from the perspective of my current plan of life, including my knowledge of my stage of life. One way to do this is to imagine that I know I shall have a conception of what is good in life, but that I do not know exactly which one it is. I may think of myself as free to form and revise my plan of life over time, and my lifetime well-being will depend on my having available to me at least a fair share of the all-purpose means for pursuing my ends, whatever they may turn out to be. (PK, 61)

As we age, our conception of what is valuable in life is likely also to change. It will be important to insure that these changes in our evaluative conception can be made under circumstances that allow us to be epistemically justified in the evaluative conception (or 'conception of the good')[6] on which we settle. As prudent agents decide how each person's fair share of health care resources should be distributed over the course of a complete life, they will be centrally concerned to protect these abilities. In consequence, argues Daniels, they will choose principles of fair equality of opportunity that will provide people with basic primary goods, and with opportunities to form, and to rationally revise and pursue, a conception of the good. In applying the principle of fair equality of opportunity over the lifespan, argues Daniels, prudent agents will find it important to protect their age-relative normal opportunity range.

The normal opportunity range for a given society is 'the array of life plans reasonable persons in it are likely to construct for themselves.' (PK 69) Since the normal opportunities available to a person will be different in different societies, Daniels relativizes this notion to particular societies. Since the normal opportunities available to a person will be different at different stages of life, the notion of an age-relative normal opportunity range identifies the kinds of opportunities available to individuals at different stages over the course of a complete life. Daniels claims that prudent choosers will accept the following principle:

> Principle of Age-Relative Fair Equality of Opportunity: Social resources should be allocated so as to insure that everyone can attain the normal age-relative opportunity range for his or her society. (PK 73-82)

He regards this principle as an application of a more general principle of fair equality of opportunity which, as he has argued, will be a crucial component of any acceptable theory of justice. In addition to the Age Relative Equality of Opportunity Principle, Daniels claims that agents will choose the following 'Income Preservation Principle:'

> Income Preservation Principle: Each individual should have available at each stage of life, an adequate income to pursue whatever plan of life he may have at that stage of life. (PK 121)

As the 'Principle of Age-Relative Fair Equality of Opportunity' governs the distribution of health care resources, the 'Income Preservation Principle' should govern institutions involved in income support over the course of a complete life (PK 124-5). Daniels argues that prudent agents will choose this principle, since, as he claims, prudence requires individuals to have equal concern for their well-being at all stages of their lives. Combined with the view that we should focus on inequalities in lifetime prospects, these two principles constitute the central features of the Prudential Lifespan Account of justice between age groups.

There are two general questions we may ask in considering whether Daniels has provided an adequate theory of distributive justice between young and old, and over the different stages of a complete life. First, we may ask whether Daniels has described the choice from behind the veil of ignorance in a way that is normatively adequate. According to Daniels, the choice situation connects prudence with justice. He writes 'Whatever is prudent from this perspective constitutes what is just' (PK 92). But this can be true only if Daniels' account of prudence is defensible, and only if the restrictions on individual choice that he describes are appropriately connected with a defensible conception of justice. Second, we may ask whether prudent agents faced with the choice Daniels has described would in fact choose the principles Daniels recommends. In what follows, I will consider each of these questions. First, in section III, I will consider Daniels' account of prudence, and the argument in support of the Income Preservation Principle, which depends on an assumption that individuals should be equally concerned with well-being at every stage of their lives. I will argue that this 'requirement of equal concern' is not a requirement of prudence, and will suggest a more modest alternative. Then in section IV I will consider Daniels' argument for the Principle of Age-Relative Equal Opportunity. Again, I will argue that problems in his account of the requirements of prudence undermine this argument. It follows that Daniels' argument from prudence underdetermines the principles that constitute the PLA. This opens the way for alternative prudential accounts of intergenerational justice.

Constraints on self-interest, and problems with prudence

From behind Daniels' veil of ignorance, agents do not know their age, and are to assume that they will live a complete life under the institutions they choose. One might think that it follows from such considerations that the very young are in a better position than the old when it comes to such budgeting decisions: their current interests give them reason to weigh the prospective benefits of eldercare against the costs they will bear, while the interests of the elderly are served when

219

costs, which are born by younger workers, are ignored. But Daniels insists that the perspective from which the choice should be made is not the perspective of the young:

> If we set fully informed consumers the task of budgeting their fair share of health care over their lifetime, we would have to restrict them to choices made at an early point in life. Otherwise, jumping from plan to plan would lead them to exceeding their fair share. But then we seem to bias plans in favour of what the young take to be prudent and ignore the prudence of the old (PK 63-4).

Young people already have a conception of what is valuable in life, and this conception may be quite different from the evaluative conception they will later have when they are older. One reason for this is that people's values change over time, but another reason is that the old and the young have different interests, since institutional change will affect their lives in different ways. Since older people are, for the most part, beneficiaries of health care institutions which they are presumed to have supported when they were young, their current interests would be served by changes to institutions that provide increased benefits to them in their remaining years. While the young stand to benefit from such institutions when they are older, they will also bear the increased costs that such changes would imply, and therefore have an incentive to balance prospective benefits against current costs. By imposing a veil of ignorance to constrain the choice of principles, Daniels reduces the influence of such differences in perspective and interest.

But if there is a difference between (i) the perspective of the young, who have a current conception of the good, but who also have an interest in protecting their interests in youth as well as in old age, and (ii) the dissociated perspective Daniels imagines his prudent agents adopting behind the veil of ignorance, it is not clear what difference this will make for the choice of principles. The young might make impetuous and imprudent choices from behind the veil, but this cannot be the difference, for Daniels stipulates that the choice will be prudently made. If this is a distinction without a difference, then we might do better to imagine the parties to the choice behind the veil to be young persons who anticipate that they will bear the costs as well as incurring the benefits.

Daniels considers his argument for the veil of ignorance to be substantively different from that of Rawls. Rather than stressing the impartiality of the choice to be made, he instead offers prudential reasons for accepting this constraint. He writes, 'To demonstrate an equal concern for all parts of their lives, the prudent deliberators should not base their choices on the details of the plan of life they happen to hold at the time of choice' (PK 120). There are two separate components of this 'non-Rawlsian' argument for the veil of ignorance. The first is Daniels' Requirement of Equal Concern, which stipulates that 'A rational person should be equally concerned about all the parts of his future' (PK 159). The second component is the claim that rationality requires that we maintain circumstances in which it is possible for us to form and to rationally revise and pursue our changing conception of the good.[7]

We may question whether either of these components should be included as a requirement of rational prudence. In arguing for the Requirement of Equal Concern, Daniels considers a series of common arguments that have been raised against the practice of discounting the future. Jeremy Bentham (1984/1789) claimed that it was appropriate for rational persons to care more about their proximate futures than about their more distant futures, but Bentham's claim has been rejected by subsequent philosophers and by many economists as well. One of the most persuasive arguments Daniels' offers is an argument that discounting implies a discontinuous and disjointed conception of individual well-being over time, since the value of well-being at any stage in life will be different, depending on the perspective from which it is evaluated:

> When we look at the graph of a continuous function through a magnifying glass, the segment in focus seems discontinuous with the rest of the line. It is on a new scale. We can move the glass along the line, and the effect is not a new, continuous function, but relocation of the discontinuity. A Discounter looks at his well-being through such a magnifying glass. As he ages, the utility he cares about, discounted utility, will lead to different assessments of his well-being for the same point in his life. At E, his discounted utility for point L will be a different value from what his discounted utility for L will be at L (PK 167).

Daniels is not the only philosopher to argue that discounting can be intertemporally inconsistent in this way. John Broome (1992) and Peter Hammond (1988) have offered more formalized versions of a similar objection. But if Daniels' aim is to support the Requirement of Equal Concern, it is not sufficient to argue against discounting of this sort. There are ways in which an individual might distribute concern for different portions of her life unequally without being intertemporally inconsistent in the way that Daniels describes: one might persistently place different values on well being at different points in one's life. Consider, for example, a college student deciding whether to spend the years of her youth travelling and seeing the world instead of finishing an advanced degree. She might decide that travelling while she is young is likely to have costs, and may result in her being worse off in old age. Still, she might rationally decide that travelling-while-young is something she simply wants to do, and wants to-have-done when she is old. She might decide that the overall shape of her life will be better if she chooses to travel in spite of the fact that this may diminish opportunities in later life, so that she will be worse off then than she might otherwise have been. Such a plan might be part of a well thought-out understanding of the shape she wants her life to take overall. Absence of regret is sometimes considered a guide to prudence: but even if, in later years, she were worse off as a result of this early decision, since some plans of life might be unavailable to her as a result, she might not regard it as having been imprudent, and she might not regret having made it. It is difficult to see why we should convict such a person of irrationality. If not, we must abandon Daniels' Requirement of Equal Concern.

There is a further problem in Daniels' argument for the Requirement of Equal Concern. Daniels fails to notice that this requirement applies equally, whether one discounts future misery in pursuit of present delights, or endures (discounts) present misery in the hope that one may be compensated by future well-being. Consider the choice faced by a student who decides to endure years of gruelling school work, in the hope that he will be compensated later in life, after graduation. Such a choice reflects a willingness to make trade-offs between present and future well-being, and may represent a self-conscious decision to distribute well-being unequally, such that he will be worse off while younger. But such choices need not involve intertemporal inconsistency, and are not typically considered to be irrational or imprudent - indeed, such foresight is often taken as a paradigm case of prudence. Daniels' argument gives us no reason to regard either of the choices I have described as imprudent. He has therefore failed to provide adequate support for the Requirement of Equal Concern.

The Requirement of Equal Concern is the first component of Daniels' 'non-Rawlsian' argument for the veil of ignorance. Without this requirement, it is difficult to see how Daniels could support the Income Preservation Principle, which is one of the main components of his theory. If prudence does not require equal concern for all portions of one's life, then it might not be irrational for prudent agents to choose health care institutions that distribute well-being or income unequally over the lifespan, although prudence might still require agents to make sure that they will not lack a basic minimum of income and health care at any stage in life. As I will argue, this suggests an account of intergenerational justice quite different from the one Daniels articulates.

Revisability and rational choice

The second component of Daniels' argument for the veil of ignorance is developed from his claim that prudent agents will be concerned to protect their ability to revise their conception of what is valuable in life, and their ability to pursue the evaluative conception they come to accept. Clearly, people's understanding of what is valuable in life changes over time. According to Daniels, recognition that one's values and one's conception of the good will change in this way will give prudent agents reason to insure that they will not, at any of the various stages of their lives, lack the resources and opportunities necessary for the adoption, and the rational revision and pursuit, of their evolving conception of the good. Along with the Requirement of Equal Concern, this argument from revisability and rational choice provides crucial support for Daniels' claim that prudent agents will choose a Principle of Age-Relative Equality of Opportunity - the second key element of his prudential lifespan account.

As Daniels acknowledges, this argument has recent roots in a well known paper by Allen Buchanan (1975), but Buchanan himself traces its deeper historical roots back to Kant. The argument points out that rational persons must take into account and plan for the fact that their understanding of what is valuable in life will change over time. Buchanan argues that if one accepts that valuation is, at least to some extent, a rational enterprise, one will also recognize that one's current values are conditional on many current beliefs. Recognizing that we are not infallible, we should recognize that our values may change as we gain information and revise our current beliefs. As Buchanan writes, 'One will realize that one's life plan or conception of the good may eventually require serious modification, perhaps even abandonment, in the face of a successor conception. No matter how unlikely one thinks it to be that one's (current) conception of the good will turn out to be mistaken, one must at least remain open to the possibility that one's present conception is mistaken,'[8] and that new information or reflection may cause one to call current commitments into question. Buchanan recommends that we adopt the following Revisability Principle:

R: One ought, ceteris paribus, to maintain an attitude of critical revisability toward one's own conception of the good (or life plan) and of open-mindedness toward competing conceptions.

Buchanan argues that the revisability principle is a principle of practical rationality for any agent. Daniels apparently accepts Buchanan's argument, holding that R, or something like it, must be a principle of prudence, for he ascribes to his prudent agents a line of reasoning quite similar to the reasoning Buchanan uses in his support of principle R. In particular, Daniels uses this argument to provide the essential support for his own principle of Age-Relative Equality of Opportunity.

Is R a principle of prudence? It may well be rational for most of us to insure that we will possess the necessary resources and opportunities to revise and rationally pursue a conception of the good that will change over time. But while most of us have good reasons to accept Buchanan's revisability principle, it is not obvious that this principle is a basic requirement either of rationality or prudence. If prudence required that we do what we can to maintain circumstances in which rational revisability is possible, then it would be impossible for a prudent agent knowingly to choose to limit future opportunities for such revision and rational pursuit. But under some circumstances, it might well be prudent to limit one's ability to revise one's conception of the good, or to impede one's future ability to pursue the conception of the good one expects eventually to adopt. Consider, for example, the case of a person who reflectively endorses her present conception of the good, but recognizes in herself the capacity for backsliding on her present commitments. It might be prudent for such a person to endeavour to limit later opportunities to relinquish the values she now holds dear, or even to take steps to limit her later opportunities to pursue different values which she now reflectively regards as inferior. If it can be prudent to restrict one's ability to change one's values, or to restrict one's future ability to pursue the evaluative conception one will in the future come to accept, then the revisability principle cannot be a requirement of prudence.

From my claim that the revisability principle is not a requirement of prudence, it does not follow that most prudent agents will not or should not accept this principle, nor does it follow that prudent agents would not choose Daniels' principle of Age-Relative Equality of Opportunity from behind an appropriately restricted veil of ignorance. It does follow that their choice of this principle is underdetermined by Daniels' account of prudent choice from behind a veil of ignorance, opening the possibility that they might choose an alternative principle. Since I will be considering alternatives to Daniels' account without rejecting the central features of his evaluative framework, this is a crucial component of my argument.

Separating general justice from age-justice: two objections

As a methodological assumption, Daniels argues that the question of age-justice should be addressed separately from other considerations in the general theory of justice. We are to consider the problem of distribution through the lifespan on the assumption that other more general questions of distributive justice have already been answered. These prior questions settle the size of the 'fair share' that is available for distribution over each person's lifespan, thus framing the age-group problem in a way that makes it more manageable. He claims that the attempt to solve the age-group problem without framing it within a settled theory of distributive justice would be like 'trying to budget health care over the lifespan without knowing how much we have to budget' (PK 48).

While this methodological assumption simplifies the problem he hopes to address, it also implies a range of more questionable assumptions which Daniels leaves more or less unexamined. Two of these assumptions deserve serious reconsideration: First, Daniels' methodology implies a presumption that what a general theory of justice entitles people to, as individuals, is a finite budget of health care resources and primary goods, to be distributed over the lifespan. This is different from the assumption that total social health care expenditures will be finite, and that the overall budget should be used in a way that will minimize each person's expectation of suffering and harm due to illness or disability,[9] for the former implies that each person must get a fair share, while the latter might allow distribution according to need. On need-based distribution principles, those who are not in need might get no share at all of public resources. In fact, Daniels' methodological assumption seems to cut off the possibility that this plausible alternative could even be considered. I discuss this first objection in more detail in sections VI and VII below. Second, framing the problem of age-justice within what we suppose to be a finished general theory of justice implies unidirectional influence of the account of age-justice by the general theory of justice. It rules out the possibility that our understanding of age-justice might lead us to revise our understanding of the general theory. Daniels provides no argument for his implicit claim that we should not make revisions of this sort. This second objection will be discussed in sections VIII and IX.

First Objection: Should we understand age-justice in terms of health care resource distribution within individual lives, or health care access over a population?

The first assumption, that what justice entitles people to is a finite budget of resources, to be distributed to individuals over the lifespan, is a convenient assumption, since it encourages us to believe that the problem of justice in distribution over the lifespan can be addressed in much the same way as other problems of distributive justice where there is a finite pie to be divided. It might seem that this assumption is supported by the reflection that the total health care budget really is finite, and needs to be distributed in some way or other over the population. But different people have quite different needs, since different lives are different. When people's needs are different, it may be quite appropriate to distribute resources unequally. Daniels's assumption incorporates questionable substantive moral commitments that deserve further examination.

To uncover these implicit substantive moral commitments, we might compare his account of choice from behind the veil of ignorance to a contractually based utilitarian alternative.[10] This alternative accepts Daniels' contractarian assumption that principles of justice should be chosen from behind a veil of ignorance, and also accepts his account of just what information this veil screens out. In this sense, this alternate view is a form of contractualism, and not a straightforward utilitarian view. But instead of considering how each person's share of a finite stock of resources should be distributed over a lifespan, this utilitarian alternative sets the prudent agents the task of choosing how to allocate the sum total of social resources (as opposed to individual resources) devoted to health care for persons at various stages in life. From behind Daniels' veil of ignorance, it might seem natural to suppose that prudent agents who assume that they will live complete lives under the institutions they choose would at least seriously consider the following proposal: Social institutions should be arranged and social resources should be used in such a way that for each individual, his or her expectation of suffering due to ill health or deprivation is minimized.

As an alternative to Daniels PLA, I have in mind the following procedure, which might be followed by prudent agents faced with the choice Daniels envisages: From behind the veil of ignorance, agents might first decide what portion of public expenditures should go toward health care needs. This initial choice will reflect the relative importance of these needs in comparison to alternate legitimate uses for public funds. Once this choice has been made, they still need to decide how to allocate those resources that have been reserved for health care. At this stage of the process, why would they choose Daniels' PLA rather than a negative utilitarian principle that recommends that these resources should be used in such a way that they minimize, for each individual, the expectation that she will suffer from ill health or deprivation? Since this proposal incorporates Daniels contractarian assumptions (choice from behind the veil of ignorance) but recommends a negative utilitarian principle in place of the prudential lifespan principles, we may call it Contractual Negative Utilitarianism (CNU).

While CNU reflects utilitarian assumptions, it is quite different from other typical utilitarian proposals. A standard utilitarian recommendation for the distribution of health care resources recommends that resources should be distributed in such a way that we maximize quality adjusted life-years (QALYs) saved. This proposal is often rejected as unfair, since it would recommend shifting resources away from those who need them most, whenever those who need them less would more efficiently transform them into QALYs. Rather than maximizing well being or QALYs, the proposal under consideration here is that we should minimize suffering and deprivation (Dis-QALYs?). Negative utilitarianism focusses on those who are badly off, and more or less ignores those who are adequately well off (neither suffering nor deprived). Consequently, CNU is not vulnerable to many of the objections that people raise against classical utilitarianism. For example, unlike classical utilitarianism, negative utilitarianism forbids purchasing bliss for those who are well off at the price of even slightly deeper misery or unmet needs for the few. For the negative utilitarian, it is impermissible to promote happiness or bliss whenever doing so would also increase misery. How does CNU fare in pairwise comparison with Daniels' PLA? I will suggest that CNU has two key advantages, and that prudent agents would do well to choose it instead of Daniels' alternative. First, CNU is more efficient and effective in response to health care needs. Second, CNU incorporates a more adequate conception of fairness than the PLA.

Daniels argues that each person's fair share of health care resources should be distributed over the lifespan in such a way as to insure that each person will attain the normal age-relative opportunity range for his or her society (PK 73-82). Since this requires satisfaction of basic health-care needs, the PLA is responsive to people's needs. But the PLA takes age as a primary category for the distribution of health care benefits, while CNU takes need as the primary, indeed the only relevant criterion for receipt of benefits. For example, under CNU, those who are fortunate enough to be quite healthy throughout their lives, and who consequently don't need the same resources that some others will need, will not be allocated the same 'fair share' of resources, for over the course of their lifespan, they may not need their fair share. Instead, the resources they might have used will be spent on someone else who will benefit more. Why does Daniels reject such an approach? Under a utilitarian approach like CNU, each individual may not receive her fair share of resources - for example when these resources could be transferred to others who need them more, and who will benefit more from receiving them. In an interesting passage, Daniels explains that utilitarian approaches inappropriately treat transfers between different people in a way that is only appropriate for transfers within an individual life:

> The utilitarian who emphasizes 'quality adjusted life years saved' is interested in showing that a policy maximizes overall utility. In contrast, the prudential argument says that age-rationing would be acceptable when it does better for each of us to budget resources over the lifespan in a certain way. The prudential argument thus explains the intuition that the British system can be defended on the grounds that it 'does more good:' It does so for each of us. Although the utilitarian account of doing more good in the aggregate allows us to take from some people to give to others, the prudential account avoids crossing the boundaries between persons in that objectionable way (PK 95).

The general point is a familiar one, and it is one emphasized by Daniels in other parts of the book: simple utilitarian views ignore the boundaries between persons in a way that many of us find counterintuitive and morally objectionable. One context in which this observation is important is that of compensation: 'Someone's burdens cannot be compensated by benefits to someone else.'[11] But this kind of objection does not apply to CNU, which does not aim to maximize aggregate utility, but to minimize each person's expectation for disadvantage due to disease or destitution. This cannot sanction 'crossing the boundaries between persons' in the objectionable way that Daniels describes.

Daniels claims that his account will be better for each, even though he claims that the QALY based account would be better for all. This indicates that he means to compare his view with a simple utilitarian view that seeks to maximize overall well being, instead of maximizing individual well-being from behind a veil of ignorance as I have suggested above. A simple utilitarian view might offer benefits to those who are best off, as long as they were more efficient at transforming resources into QALYs. This would indeed be an example of inappropriately ignoring the boundaries between persons. But CNU is different from the simple utilitarian view Daniels criticizes. Its emphasis on the minimization of misery and deprivation rather than on the maximization of well-being means that it will not sanction transfers to those who are already quite well off when resources could be used to improve or lengthen the lives of those who are badly off. And since expected disutility is minimized from behind a veil of ignorance like the one incorporated by Daniels, the CNU will not allow inappropriate interpersonal trade-offs.

But is CNU fair? One might argue that it is not, since those people who are fortunate enough not to need their fair share of medical resources will not recieve their share. However, it is arguable that this does not imply that they are treated unfairly. For CNU inherits a conception of procedural fairness in two different respects: first, inasmuch as the idea of choice from behind a veil of ignorance incorporates a conception of fairness, CNU will be fair in this sense. In addition, while each person may not receive a fair share of resources, each can reasonably regard the system by which these resources are distributed as a procedurally fair system, since the system provides each with the same benefit (a low expectation of suffering from disease or deprivation).

CNU does allow some kinds of tradeoffs to be made between persons: those whose needs can be met by available procedures, and who would benefit more if the available funds were spent on them will receive care in preference to others whose needs are less easily met, or who would benefit less. But this is not the kind of interpersonal tradeoff that makes some utilitarian views objectionable. After all, from behind the veil of ignorance, one might just as easily be the fortunate person who would benefit less from care and who therefore needs it less, as be the unfortunate person who needs care more and who would benefit more from it. From behind the veil of ignorance, where we are denied knowledge of the particularities of our own circumstances, CNU leaves each of us better off. Once the veil has been lifted, we may find that the principles we have chosen imply that we will be allocated a relatively small share of the total resources available (for example, if we were fortunate enough to be quite healthy throughout our lives), but we could not claim at that point

229

that these principles are unfair or unjust. Like Daniels' view, the utilitarian view under consideration avoids crossing the boundaries between persons in objectionable ways.

However, CNU will allow trade-offs among the competing needs of different claimants, and these trade-offs may well be made in ways that resemble the standard utilitarian QALY-maximization approach. For example, CNU may well recommend, under constrained circumstances, that certain procedures should be rationed. But it is often argued that it would be inappropriate to include rationing schemes in health care distribution to the needy or the poor, since (so it is argued) it would be unfair to impose rationing on those who are poor while not imposing rationing on those who are better off. The point is one that is frequently misunderstood, and which commonly arises in discussions of health-care rationing. This objection interprets health care rationing as a cost to individuals, and claims that such costs should be equalized across persons. But rationing is not a cost of this kind. Those whose health care access is determined by a QALY-based rationing scheme are individually better off than they would have been under any alternative institution provided with the same budget. Appropriately managed QALY-based rationing would minimize each representative individuals' expectation that her life will be blighted or cut short by disease or deprivation. It follows that alternative distribution schemes offer each individual a worse expectation in terms of the quality and length of life. To the extent that Daniels' scheme is different from CNU, its implementation would involve an increase, for each person, in the expectation that she will suffer from ill health or deprivation. How will this lower expectation be justified to those who must endure it? And why would prudent agents, situated behind a veil of ignorance, choose Daniels' account over CNU?[12] Since Daniels justifies the principle of Age-Relative Equality of Opportunity on the ground that it would be better for each person, his own justificatory criteria favour CNU over the Prudential Lifespan view he defends.

Second Objection: Local v. Global Approaches to the Allocation Problem

There is a second problem with Daniels suggestion that the problem of age-justice should be framed within the assumption that a more general theory of justice already answers the more general distributive questions. As noted in section V above, this implies unidirectional influence of the account of age-justice by the general theory of justice. It rules out the possibility that our understanding of age justice might lead us to revise our understanding of the general theory of distributive justice. In an important way, this limitation is arbitrary, and it is especially surprising that Norman Daniels would have incorporated it, since he has, in other works for which he is quite famous, argued for a theory of moral reasoning that is far more flexible than the one he employs here.[13] The assumption that we can appropriately address the question of age-justice separately from other more general problems of distributive justice implies that there is no need to compare age-relative needs with other kinds of social needs that would be addressed by a general theory of justice. In consequence, it is impossible to weigh the importance of these needs against one another, or to balance and make trade-offs among them. Daniels' account should be rejected by Rawlsians, since it makes it impossible to apply the 'difference principle', which insists that social and economic inequalities should be arranged so that they provide maximal benefits for the worst off members of society: if Daniels' framing assumption were abandoned, we might find that judgments concerning the size of the budget to be allocated for lifetime health care needs might depend on a further judgment that this amount of total allocation would provide more benefits for the worst off than any alternative. Different ways of allocating this total might serve this end differently, so the total health care budget available to address the problem of age-justice might partly depend on the nature of the allocative scheme we choose. Such arguments are inappropriately shut off by Daniels' framing assumption.

Framing the problem of age-justice as Daniels does would make it impossible for health care distribution to focus on human need as a primary criterion for distribution, since it assumes that individuals will all have a valid claim to some share (a 'fair' one) of social resources. While it is true that people have different kinds of needs at different stages of life, those who are wealthy or fortunate may have resources of their own that will allow them adequately to respond to their changing needs. What share of social resources should be used to provide health care and income support for those who are already quite well off, and able to care for their own needs? We might want at least to consider the possibility that this question should be answered as follows: Social resources should be used to respond to the needs of those whose needs would otherwise go unmet. Those who are well enough off that they can care for themselves have no claim at all on social resources when those resources could otherwise be used to help others who are worse off, since their needs are unmet.

It is standard to compare views like Daniels' to a libertarian alternative that would leave all claims to be arbitrated by the market. It is clear that Daniels sees this strong libertarian view as an important alternative, since he offers powerful arguments against it (PK 37-39, 48-49, 68-69, 135-138). In general, many people find extreme libertarian views to be unacceptable, because of the very real risk that the claims of the truly needy would simply go unmet under a libertarian regime. The implications of libertarian policies are especially harsh for poor children, who cannot reasonably be held responsible for their plight, and who may be denied the opportunities and resources necessary to improve their situation, since a libertarian regime would take no steps to provide such positive benefits. If it is appropriate for a political regime to protect citizens against arbitrary and undeserved suffering and deprivation, then the strong libertarian view must be rejected, as Daniels and others have effectively argued. In pairwise comparison with Daniels' view, this strong libertarian view fares badly.

But there is an alternative that lies midway between strong libertarianism and Daniels' Prudential Lifespan Account: it is a view that includes a welfare safety net to insure that no one will fall below a sufficient minimal (SM) level of well-being and opportunity, but beyond this safety net, leaves individuals to care for themselves. Call this view SM. Such a view has been advocated by such liberal philosophers as Allen Buchanan (1984, 1987), Alex Rosenberg (1995), and Jeremy Waldron(1986), as well as by more libertarian-leaning scholars as Loren Lomasky (1995), John Gray (1993), and Friedrich Hayek (1960). This view has historical roots in the work of John Locke (1993/1697, 1963/1690), who argues that the truly needy must be provided with such goods as are necessary to make it possible to take care of themselves. Beyond the safeguards for the truly needy implicit in this basic safety net, SM would protect negative liberties, and would leave claims to the distributive mechanism of the market.

Like Daniels' account, a view like SM would need to take into account the different needs that people have at different points in life: children have special needs for education and play, while adults have special need for employment opportunities, and the elderly for social support and health benefits. Critics of views like SM have pointed out that health care needs are not like other needs, nor are they mere 'wants' or 'preferences'. Health care needs have a special urgency, and are associated with our ability to take effective advantage of opportunities that present themselves to us. But to this extent, SM may also be concerned with health care needs, since in its most plausible incarnation, SM insists that people must possess adequate substantive opportunities, not merely formal opportunities. It is not sufficient, on this view, merely to argue that people can take care of themselves as long as they have opportunities to participate in a fair economic market. If the background conditions are not in place that make it possible for people to take advantage of the opportunities that should, on this view, be provided, then their opportunities are not really adequate at all. When people's opportunities are inadequate, or fall below the minimal accepted level, then they merit aid and compensation. Daniels assumes that a broader theory of justice will include a principle of fair equality of opportunity. Only conceptions of justice that include such a principle will also include the Principle of Age-Relative Fair Equality of Opportunity he defends. But SM is not concerned with equalizing opportunities, but instead strives to insure that no one lacks adequate substantive opportunities. If we could insure that every person had adequate opportunities to pursue a reasonable conception of the good, there would be no need to curb the opportunities of those who were blessed with more than adequate opportunities of this sort. Once people are in a position to determine for themselves the shape their lives will take, and to rationally revise and pursue their goals as they see fit, it is permissible, on this conception of justice, to leave them alone. Once all are adequately provided for, there is no need to attempt to transfer opportunities or goods from those who are better off to those who are merely well-off. Over the lifespan, SM would guarantee that individuals have opportunities to provide for their old age, and will insure that the fundamental needs of the elderly do not go unmet. But beyond this, SM leaves people to care for themselves and to plan for their own futures.

How does such an alternative compare to Daniels' Prudential Lifespan Account? In many respects, the two views are quite similar: Daniels' PLA also includes a safety net to respond to the needs of those who are badly off. Recall the two principles that constitute the core of the Prudential Lifespan Account:

Income Preservation Principle: Each individual should have available at each stage of life, an adequate income to pursue whatever plan of life he may have at that stage of life (PK 121).

Principle of Age-Relative Fair Equality of Opportunity: Social resources should be allocated so as to insure that everyone can attain the normal age-relative opportunity range for his or her society (PK 73-82).

In place of these principles, the sufficiency alternative includes principles that guarantee a basic minimum:

> Minimal Income Preservation Principle: Each individual should have available, at each stage of life, an adequate income to meet basic needs and to pursue a minimal but adequate range of reasonable life plans. Principle of Age-Relative Adequacy of Opportunity: Social resources should be allocated so as to insure that everyone has adequate age-relative opportunities, throughout the lifespan.

But how are opportunity levels measured, and what level is adequate? It has sometimes been argued that such threshold levels must be arbitrary. Harry Frankfurt (1988), who in fact advocates a view quite similar to the one under discussion, concedes that 'Calculating the size of an equal share is plainly much easier than determining how much a person needs in order to have enough.'[14] But Rosenberg (1995) points out that the difficulty of identifying equal shares may be just as formidable as that of identifying a basic sufficiency level, and others, including Nussbaum (1992, 1995) and Sen (1985, 1990) have provided well-developed accounts of the way in which a non-arbitrary sufficiency level might be articulated. It is far from clear that all such indices will be arbitrary.[15]

In general, SM imposes lighter burdens on people as they pass through their working years. But it also provides smaller social compensatory benefits than Daniels' alternative, since the minimal safety net will most likely be less generous than Daniels' Income Preservation Principle (and perhaps less generous than CNU). However, to this extent, SM gives people greater freedom to choose how their income should be distributed over their lifespan. It allows those who are risk averse to put off present welfare in planning for the future, and it allows others to enact their preference for benefits received earlier in life. Daniels' account of prudence, which regards as irrational all choices that would result in unequal distribution of well-being or opportunity over the lifespan, would protect people against the risks involved in such choices by refusing to allow such risks to be taken. To effect such protection, individuals would presumably be taxed at a higher rate during their working years, and would receive greater compensatory benefits later in life. While the safety net ensures that no one will be left with fundamental needs unmet, SM gives people more autonomy to determine the shape of their own lives, without putting people at increased risk that their basic needs will be unmet.[16]

It should be noted once again that SM differs from the libertarian alternative in at least two important respects: First, SM includes positive rights to a basic minimum income and adequate opportunity, while standard libertarian views include no positive rights at all. Second, SM endeavours to insure that no one shall lack an adequate range of appropriate substantive opportunities at the different life stages. It is not sufficient that people have a formally adequate opportunity range, they must also possess the social and material resources necessary for them to make effective use of the resources available to them.

One important category of opportunity, in this regard, is the opportunity to make plans for one's own old age. Compared with Daniels' PLA, SM leaves people greater autonomous control over the resources they command. Therefore SM allocates a greater degree of responsibility to individuals, providing them with a greater incentive to plan for their own old age. Recognizing that the state will at most provide minimally adequate support, people will recognize that they need to use their substantive opportunities wisely if they would like to live better, in their later years, than that minimum would allow. The SM welfare net provides only for the truly needy. In fact, SM does not include 'age' as a relevant criterion for distribution except inasmuch as age exerts a qualifying effect on needs, which (as in Daniels' view) are relativized to age groups. According to SM, the primary category to be considered, from the perspective of distributive justice, is that of need.

In practical terms, how different are SM and PLA? Like SM, Daniels' PLA also includes limits on the extent of benefits one might receive under the principles he recommends. In articulating his Income Support Principle, he points out that possessing and 'adequate income to pursue whatever plan of life one has' is relative to one's lifetime fair income share (PK 121). The same limitation is imposed on the Age-Relative Equality of Opportunity Principle. The level of benefit supported by this principle would depend on the 'normal age-relative opportunity range' for one's society. If these limitations are interpreted as strict limitations, set at the level of the 'basic minimum' guaranteed by SM, then the two views might not differ much at all in their implications. But the way Daniels has articulated these principles, they leave open the possibility that one might be entitled to far more than SM would allow.

In sections III and IV above, I argued that the principles that constitute the PLA are poorly supported by Daniels' argument, since he employs a flawed account of prudence. If we substitute a more adequate theory of prudence, and imagine the choice from behind Daniels' veil of ignorance, what reason is there to believe that prudent agents would choose the PLA rather than the alternative I have outlined here? Daniels' view would guarantee equal opportunities over the lifespan, while SM would permit greater lifetime inequalities. Since, as I have argued previously, there are circumstances in which it would be rational for a person to choose to distribute well-being and opportunity unequally over the lifespan, this consideration favours SM over PLA. would provide individuals with less incentive to plan for their own futures, while SM leaves open the possibility that some people will be less well-off in old age than they would have been under PLA. Both views guarantee that basic health care needs will be met. It can be argued that SM achieves the most morally significant aims of PLA (protecting the needs of the vulnerable) while providing individuals with an additional motive for private saving. Once again, these considerations favour SM over PLA.

I cannot prove that SM would be chosen in place of PLA by prudent agents behind Daniels' veil of ignorance. My claim, at this point in the argument, is thus less bold than that of Daniels: I contend that nothing in Daniels' account shows that such agents would choose his Prudential Lifespan Account over the sufficient safety net I have described. If, as Daniels claims, 'Whatever is prudent (from behind the veil of ignorance) constitutes what is just' (PK 92), it follows that if SM could be chosen from this perspective, then SM is not unjust. If either PLA or SM could be chosen from behind the veil of ignorance, then it would follow that PLA and SM are joint members of the set of permissible conceptions of age-justice.

In comparison to CNU, SM is somewhat less flexible: in particular, SM can be applied only when there are sufficient social resources to provide each person with an adequate minimum, and gives no guidance when resources are too meagre for even this. When resources are adequate, as (I would argue) they are in most industrialized nations, CNU and SM both imply that we should provide each person with an adequate minimum. But in extremely wealthy societies, CNU might sanction more generous benefits than the basic adequate minimum recommended by SM. From behind the veil of ignorance, the choice of SM over CNU will imply a higher risk that one will suffer due to ill health or material deprivation. In fact, many of the same reasons that favour CNU over PLA from behind the veil of ignorance are also good reasons for preferring CNU over SM.

But we are not behind the veil of ignorance, and when we move from description of a philosophical ideal to the context of practical political argument and policy choice, there are good reasons to favour SM over either PLA or CNU. Because it places strict limitations on public expenditure, SM will be favoured by those who might be wary of utilitarian solutions like CNU. As a target for political reform of current institutions, SM is much better off than PLA, because it represents a more practical and achievable political ideal.

236

Practical politics, basic minimums, and the needs of children and the elderly poor

In the United States, recent policy changes have generally protected benefits for the elderly. Both Medicare and social security are considered to be political hot-potatoes, too risky to touch. Social Security benefits are often quite generous, typically yielding far more to older beneficiaries than they could have gained had they shrewdly invested their social security payments in the stock market rather than paying into the Social Security fund. Programmes for needy children, on the other hand, have suffered serious cuts, and many members of the new majority, and several contemporary presidential hopefuls, speak of rolling back welfare benefits for poor children and poor families altogether. In the current political climate, programmes that focus more closely on need as a primary criterion for eligibility seem more likely to be cut than programmes that focus on age: Suggestions that Social Security or Medicare might be reformed by instituting more need-based eligibility criteria have been met with strong political resistance. Consequently, the needs of the elderly poor are given little priority over those of the elderly rich. The poor elderly are a growing group in the United States, and institutions have not changed to keep pace with changing needs. In general, it is the poor, as a group, rather than the elderly, as a group, whose needs are inadequately addressed by current institutions.

Given the sources of political power, public choice economists would tell us not to be surprised by these inequities: we should predict the behaviour of our representatives by assuming that they are rational vote-maximizers; so they are likely to be responsive to the interests of those who vote, and unresponsive to the interests of those who don't. Children don't vote. The poor typically don't vote. The impoverished elderly are not, of themselves, a powerful interest group, even though the AARP is a strong political voice, promoting the interests of the elderly as a class. The result is that the redistributive institutions in the US are more responsive to the needs of the elderly as a broad undifferentiated group, and are frequently inadequate in their response to the needs of the elderly poor. And these institutions are woefully inadequate in their response to the needs of poor families in general, and poor children in particular. This is one of the most disturbing effects of poverty: poverty deprives people of substantive opportunities even when formal opportunities remain. To point out that the poor have the same voting rights as everyone else is to ignore the fact that people can be effectively disenfranchised by poverty and need.

The US Social Security system has also come under criticism. As it is currently run, social security benefits are paid directly from the payments of younger workers. As long as the number of workers is relatively large, and the number of retirees is relatively low, this system will work well. But as the Baby-Boomers retire, the proportion of workers to retirees is expected to diminish rapidly. If the burden on workers increases, as some economists expect, the system will eventually become insolvent, so that income support will no longer be available to support later retirees, who will have spent large portions of their earnings to support the retirement of wealthier retirees who received their benefits earlier. If this prediction comes true, it will be uncontroversially unfair to those whose burdens will have out weighed their benefits, and whose urgent retirement needs may go unmet. Since they will have been taxed for the benefit of the better off cohorts that preceded them, they may be expected to resent this: in many cases, those who receive Social Security benefits are much better off, both in terms of current wealth, and in terms of lifetime prospects, than the workers who pay their benefits.

Such regressive transfers could never be sanctioned by a conception of justice that holds human needs and lifetime prospects to be the primary criteria for distribution of benefits. In the US, the more important current social division is between those who have access to resources and adequate opportunities and those who do not, not the division between young and old. It is more important to get access for the poor and disempowered than it is to get equal access for the elderly as an undifferentiated group, regardless of their prudent use of their own past opportunities and regardless of their current means and current needs.

These considerations support the claim that need is more important than age as a criterion for distributive justice. This highlights a distinct advantage that both CNU and SM have over Daniels Prudential Lifespan Approach: both of these theories incorporate need as the centrally important criterion for receipt of social benefits. If needs are a primary consideration, then questions of age-justice cannot be separated from issues in the general theory of justice as Daniels claims. It is clear from Daniels' discussion of age-justice that the cases to which he imagines his theory applying are cases for which tradeoffs must be made between old and young, sometimes between the wealthy old and the needy young. If Daniels assumes that such situations might remain after general justice has been achieved, then he is assuming without argument that a theory of general justice cannot take need as a primary criterion for distributive justice, for such a general theory would not make a sharp separation between the question of justice between age-groups and the general theory of justice. Since

238

both CNU and SM take needs to be primary, it follows that Daniels assumptions prevent him from even considering these views.

I have argued that Daniels' theory focuses on age in the wrong way, and have claimed that US institutions designed to serve the elderly are likewise responsive to age in the wrong way. Current institutions often benefit the well-off at the expense of others who are less well-off, and no theory of age justice, including that defended by Daniels, can justify such transfers. Does it follow from these considerations that the US would do well to dismantle the institutions that have been set in place to protect the interests of the elderly? Here is Daniels' sensible response:

> Our concern about increased poverty among children and our legitimate worries about the stability of the transfer systems that will soon encounter the baby boom cohort should not tempt us to undermine what is valuable in our collective solution to the age-group problem. At the same time, we must devote adequate resources to meeting the needs of poor children - indeed, of the poor at any age. I am sceptical that dismantling the protection we have afforded the elderly poor will really be followed by more adequate transfers to the remaining poor (PK 138).

Our current institutions would more nearly achieve what justice requires if they were more effective in their response to human needs, and especially to the urgent needs of poor children and the impoverished elderly. If budgets are tight, and social resources are inadequate to meet the needs of both poor children and the poor elderly, we might in principle have good reason to favour the interests of children over the elderly. But from the practical perspective and in the context of current political disputes, we would do well to promote policies that aim to provide a basic minimum to everyone, as SM recommends.

Conclusion: Ideal theory and the constraints of practical politics

The most commonly expressed objection to the philosophical use of 'Ideal Theory' is that such theory is unacceptably utopian. Rawls (1971, 1993) has been criticized on the ground that his theory is so abstract, so distant from the imperfections of political reality, that it can provide no guidance for real people or for the structure of real institutions. In some circumstances, there is an effective response to such critics: Rawls argues that the ideal he articulates provides us with an account of the broader aims that should guide us in reforming our institutions. A clear account of the ideal can sometimes provide us with a better understanding of the ways in which our institutions fall short, and how they might be improved. In other cases, the objection has greater force: if a theory is so removed from reality that it fails to take into account the fragility of democratic decision making and the limits of political possibility, then it is utopian in a more pernicious sense, and may provide little guidance for policy makers. A complete theory should help us to make policy decisions even when ideal justice is unachievable.

There is reason to believe that an ideal egalitarian account of justice between age groups may be unachievable in democratic countries, for there is a serious tension between the requirements of justice and the likely outcome of democratic processes. The fact that the young, and future generations, do not vote means that their interests are under-represented in democratic procedures. And while an ideal theory of intergenerational fairness might consider the age problem by comparing the lifetime prospects of different birth cohorts, in practical political contexts the interests of the young and the interests of the old do conflict. For it is in the interest of those who are currently old to institute policies that increase benefits to the elderly regardless of the burden such institutions would place on younger workers. It is in the interest of younger workers to insure that burdensome policies to benefit the elderly should not be put in place, even if they are just, until these younger workers are themselves at the point of becoming elderly beneficiaries. The only group whose interests would be served if just institutions were set in place immediately is the very young, and even their interests would be better served if such institutions could be set in place much later, just before their retirement. Time moves in one direction, and as people get older, the interests of their group do change. If we assume that people will vote for policies that are in their interest, then we should predict that the policies that would get the broadest democratic support would be those that sacrifice the interests of the very young in favour of the interests of the moderately old, and especially in favour of those who are elderly. What is to be done if just policies are unlikely to be the object of democratic choice?

Daniels addresses this question with respect to the problem of health care rationing:

> Suppose that the only way for an age-rationing scheme to remain stable is for the grounds for the rationing to be disguised, and yet there are good prudential reasons for implementing such a scheme. Is the scheme just? In general, I think that principles of justice and the reasoning for them must be public, and that the conditions of publicity are rather stringent. (...) This does not mean, of course,

that the whole public must agree with or accept the scheme. Nor does it mean that a proposed policy is not a just one if it cannot be made acceptable to a particular society: It may be that what is ideally just is not feasible under some conditions, that is, if the publicity constraints are adhered to. We then need an account of what is permissible when what ought to be justifiable is politically infeasible. Here philosophers have generally fallen silent, and I shall too (PK 97).

Can philosophers afford to remain silent on such issues? What are we to think of an ideal conception justice that requires democracy and publicity, but also requires institutions that could not be the object of democratic choice if their structure were publicly known? Under such circumstances, we might either conclude that the conception of justice is flawed, or that the human condition is unfortunate. In either case, it would be appropriate to look toward a broader normative theory in search of steps we might take to improve our institutions, even if we cannot entirely mend them. Working to insure that basic needs are met, and to guarantee universal access to a basic minimum of care might not achieve the highest social ideal, but it would be a dramatic and badly needed improvement on the status quo. For those of us who are young, or who care about the prospects of our children as they grow into adults and on to old age, such changes would be prudent as well.

References

Bentham, J. (1984/1789), *Principles of Morals and Legislation*, New York, Hafner Press.

Brock, D. (1993), *Life and Death*, Cambridge, Cambridge University Press.

Broome, J. (1992), *Counting the Cost of Global Warming*, Cambridge, White Horse Press.

Broome, J. (1994b), 'Discounting the Future', *Philosophy and Public Affairs*, vol. 23, pp.128-156.

Buchanan, A. (1975) 'Revisability and Rational Choice', *Canadian Journal of Philosophy* vol. 3, pp.395-408.

Buchanan, A. (1984), 'The Right to a "Decent Minimum" of Health Care', *Philosophy and Public Affairs*, vol. 12, no. 1.

Buchanan, A. (1987), 'Justice and Charity', *Ethics*, vol. 97, no. 3, pp.558-575.

Callahan, D., *Setting Limits: Medical Goals in an Ageing Society*, New York, Simon & Schuster.

Chen, M. (1995), 'A Matter of Survival: Women's Right to Employment in India and Bangladesh', in Martha Nussbaum and Jonathan Glover, (eds.) *Women, Culture, and Development*, New York, Oxford University Press.

Cohen, G.A. (1989), 'On the Currency of Egalitarian Justice', *Ethics*, vol. 99.

Cohen, L.M. (ed.) (1993), *Justice Across Generations: What Does It Mean?*, Washington DC, American Association of Retired Persons.

Cohen, L.M. (1993), 'Majority Vote and a Just Age for Greed', in Lee Cohen (ed.) *Justice Across Generations: What Does It Mean?*, Washington DC, American Association of Retired Persons.

'Consuming our Children' *Forbes*, 14 November 1988, 222.

Cowen, T. and Parfit, D. (1992), 'Against the Social Discount Rate', in Peter Laslett and James Fishkin (eds.) *Justice Between Age Groups and Generations*, New Haven, Yale University Press.

Cowen, T. (1993), 'Comment on Daniels and McKerlie', in Lee Cohen (ed.) *Justice Across Generations: What Does It Mean?* Washington DC, American Association of Retired Persons.

Crocker, D. (1992), 'Functioning and Capability', *Political Theory*, vol. 20, pp.548-612.

Daniels, N. (1979), 'Wide Reflective Equilibrium and Theory Acceptance in Ethics', *Journal of Philosophy*, vol. 76, no. 5, pp.256-82.

Daniels, N. (1980), 'Reflective Equilibrium and Archimedian Points', *Canadian Journal of Philosophy*, vol. 10, no. 1 pp.83-103.

Daniels, N. (1985a), *Just Health Care*, Cambridge, Cambridge University Press.

Daniels, N. (1985b) 'Fair Equality of Opportunity and Decent Minimums: A Reply to Buchanan', *Philosophy and Public Affairs*, vol. 14(Winter), pp.106-110.

Daniels, N. (1988), *Am I My Parents' Keeper? An Essay on Justice Between the Young and the Old*, New York, Oxford University Press.

Daniels, N. (1989a), 'Justice and Transfers Between Generations', in Paul Johnson, Chistoph Conrad, and David Thomson, (eds.) *Workers Versus Pensioners: Intergenerational Justice in an Ageing World*, Manchester, Manchester University Press.

Daniels, N (1989b), 'The Biomedical Model and Just Health Care: A Reply to Jecker.', *Journal of Medicine and Philosophy* vol. 14, no. 6, pp. 677-80.

Daniels, N. (1990), 'Human Rights, Population Ageing, and Intergenerational Justice', in *Meaning and Method: Essays in Honor of Hilary Putnam*, George Boolos (ed.), New York, Cambridge University Press.

Daniels, N. (1993), 'The Prudential Lifespan Account of Justice Between Generations', in Lee Cohen (ed.) *Justice Across Generations: What Does It Mean?*, Washington DC, American Association of Retired Persons.

Fairlie, H. (1988), 'Greedy Geezers: Talkin 'Bout My Generation', *New Republic*, 28 March, 1988, pp.19.

Frankfurt, H. (1988), 'Equality as a Moral Ideal', in *The Importance of What We Care About*, Cambridge, Cambridge University Press.

Gray, J. (1993), *Beyond the New Right: Markets, Government, and the Common Environment*, New York, Routledge.

Hammond, P.J. (1988), 'Consequentialist Demographic Norms and Parenting Rights', *Social Choice and Welfare*,vol. 5, pp.127-45.

Hanson, M.J. (1994), 'How We Treat the Elderly', *Hastings Center Report*, September-October, 1994:4-6.

Harrod, R.F. (1948), *Toward a Dynamic Economy*, London, MacMillan.

Harsanyi, J. (1982), 'Morality and the Theory of Rational Behavior', in Amartya Sen and Bernard Williams (eds.) *Utilitarianism and Beyond*, Cambridge, Cambridge University Press.

Haydock, A. (1992), 'QALYs-- A Threat to our Quality of Life?' *Journal for Applied Philosophy*, vol. 9, no. 2, pp.183-188.

Hayek, F. (1960), *The Constitution of Liberty*, Chicago, University of Chicago Press.

International Research Group of the Institute for Bioethics (1994), 'What Do We Owe the Elderly?' *Hastings Center Report*: Special Supplement, March-April 1994, S5-S12.

Jecker, N.S. (1989), 'Towards a Theory of Age-Group Justice', *The Journal of Medicine and Philosophy*, vol. 14, pp.655-676.

Locke, J. (1993/1697), 'Draft of a Representation Containing a Scheme of Methods for the Employment of the Poor', in David Wootton (ed.), *Political Writings of John Locke*, New York, Penguin Books Ltd.

Locke, J. (1963/1690), *Two Treatises of Government*, Peter Laslett (ed.), New York, Cambridge University Press.

Lomasky, L. (1995), 'Justice to Charity', *Social Philosophy and Policy*, vol. 12(2), pp.32-53.

McDonnell, S. (1994), 'In Defense of QALYs', *Journal of Applied Philosophy*, vol. 11(1), pp. 89-97.

Menzel, P.T. (1990), *Strong Medicine: The Ethical Rationing of Health Care*, New York, Oxford University Press.

McKerlie, D. (1989), 'Equality and Time', *Ethics*, vol. 99, pp.475-491.

McKerlie, D. (1992), 'Equality Between Age Groups', *Philosophy and Public Affairs*, vol. 21, no. 3, pp.275-295.

McKerlie, D. (1993), 'Justice Between Neighboring Generations', in Lee Cohen (ed.) *Justice Across Generations: What Does It Mean?*, Washington DC, American Association of Retired Persons.

Nussbaum, M. and Sen, A. (eds.), (1993) *The Quality of Life*, New York, Clarendon Press.

Nussbaum, M. and Glover, J. (eds.), (1995), *Women, Culture, and Development*, New York, Clarendon Press.

Nussbaum, M. (1992), 'Human Functioning and Social Justice: In Defense of Aristotelian Essentialism', *Political Theory*, vol. 20, pp.202-246.

Nussbaum, M. (1995), 'Human Capabilities, Female Human Beings', in Martha Nussbaum and Jonathan Glover (eds.) *Women, Culture, and Development*, New York, Oxford University Press.

Parfit, D. (1984), *Reasons and Persons*, Oxford, Clarendon Press.

Pifer, A. and Bronte, L.D. (1986), 'Squaring the Pyramid', *Daedalus* vol. 115, pp.1-12.

Ramsey, F.P. (1928), 'A Mathematical Theory of Savings', *Economic Journal*, vol. 38, pp.543-59.

Rawls, J. (1971), *A Theory of Justice*, Cambridge, Harvard University Press.

Rawls, J. (1989), *Justice as Fairness: A Briefer Restatement*, ms.

Rawls, J. (1993), *Political Liberalism*, New York, Columbia University Press.

Rosenberg, A. (1995), 'Equality, Sufficiency, and Opportunity in the Just Society', *Social Philosophy and Policy*, vol. 12, no. 2, pp.54-71.

Sen, A. (1985), *Commodities and Capabilities*, Amsterdam, North Holland.

Sen, A. (1990), 'Justice: Means versus Freedoms', *Philosophy and Public Affairs*, vol. 19, pp.111-21.

Sidgwick, H. (1982/1884), *Methods of Ethics*, Cambridge, Hackett Publishing Company.

Sreenivasan, G. (1995), *The Limits of Lockean Rights in Property*, New York, Oxford.

Thomson, D. (1989), 'The Welfare State and Generation Conflict: Winners and Losers', in

Paul Johnson, Chistoph Conrad, and David Thomson (eds.), *Workers Versus Pensioners: Intergenerational Justice in an Ageing World*, Manchester:, Manchester University Press.

Waldron, J. (1986), 'John Rawls and the Social Minimum', *Journal of Applied Philosophy*, vol. 3, pp.21-33.

Wolf, C. (1996), 'Social Choice and Normative Population Theory: A Person-Affecting Solution to Parfit's Mere Addition Paradox', *Philosophical Studies*, vol. 81(2-3), pp.263-282.

Notes

1. Daniels (1988) p. 44.
2. Fairlie (1988).
3. 'Consuming Our Children', Forbes, 14 Nov. 1988.
4. Norman Daniels writes: 'The ageing of society forces major changes in the institutions responsible for social well-being. As the 'age profile' of a society-- the proportion of the population in each age group - changes, social needs change. As society ages, proportionally fewer children need education, fewer young adults need job training, but more elderly need employment, income support, and health-care, including long term care. Changing needs find political expression. Strong voices press for reforms of the institutions that meet these needs. At the same time, advocates for existing institutions and their beneficiaries resist change. The result is a heightened sense that the old and the young are in conflict, competing for a critical but scarce resource, public funds that meet basic human needs' (Daniels, (1990) p. 325).
5. See Daniels (1988), pp. 40-51, and also Jecker (1989), pp. 657-8. Daniels does not claim that prudent agents would use maximin reasoning from behind the veil of ignorance, as Rawls (1971) argued earlier. See Daniels (1988), pp. 88-89.
6. A 'conception of the good' may be understood as 'an ordered family of final ends and aims which specifies a person's conception of what is of value in human life, or alternatively, of what is regarded as a fully worthwhile life' Rawls (1989) p. 14.
7. See Buchanan (1975) for a similar argument. Buchanan argues that concern for one's changing interests over time constitutes a non-Rawlsian justification for the veil of ignorance.
8. Buchanan (1975), 398-9.
9. Daniels' methodology also rules out the more standard utilitarian view that social resources should be used in such a way that they maximize each person's expected benefit. Unlike Daniels's account, this classical utilitarian alternative might also permit distribution on the basis of need.
10. Several utilitarians have argued that it would be rational, from behind the veil of ignorance, to simply maximize utility (For example, Harsanyi (1982)). The view discussed here differs from Harsanyi, since I will recommend a negative utilitarian view that aims to minimize misery rather than maximizing well-being.
11. See Parfit (1984) p. 337, and PK p. 170.
12. A 'Pareto improvement' is a change of circumstance that is better for at least one person, and worse for no one. A strong Pareto improvement is a change of circumstance that is better for literally everyone involved. Daniels ((1988) p. 95, fn.

5) claims that his view represents a strong Pareto improvement over the current US system. But CNU would seem to represent a strong Pareto improvement over PLA, since it decreases each person's expectation of suffering and deprivation.

13. See Daniels (1979, 1980).

14. Frankfurt (1988) p. 134-36, quoted in Rosenberg, (1995) p. 66.

15. See Nussbaum and Glover (1995), and Nussbaum and Sen (1993) for arguments that such an account represents an improvement over standard utilitarian, egalitarian, and Rawlsian alternatives. In fact there are a variety of plausible alternative ways to articulate a threshold minimal level: one might set the minimum (i) at the level at which individuals are capable of being autonomous (Rawls (1971)), (ii) the level at which all basic needs have been met (Crocker, (1992) discusses such a view), (iii) at universal possession of basic resources (Dworkin, (1981)), or (iv) of opportunities (Cohen, (1989)), or (v) of the ability to exercise certain basic human capabilities (Sen, (1985, 1990)) or (vi) to function in basic, essential human ways (Nussbaum, (1992, 1995)). There is no time to sort out these alternatives here, but I will record my own preference for an opportunity-qualified version of Sen and Nussbaum's 'capability view'. At one level, this view is relativised to societies, like Daniels' Principle of Age-Relative Equality of Opportunity, but is not subject to the problems of circularity that face Daniels' view. See Buchanan (1984), Daniels (1985b) response, and note 11 above. See also Wolf (1996) for some further discussion of the minimum level, as related to negative utilitarian views.

16. This view is also consistent with a safety net defined in terms of fundamental human capacities (Nussbaum (1992)), or functional capabilities (Sen (1985, 1990)). In fact, I prefer a version of SM that is put in such terms. For now, I will use 'needs' to stand in for the broader conception of human well-being that Nussbaum and Sen incorporate in their 'Capability view'. See also Crocker (1992).